Virtue and Theological Ethics

Virtue and Theological Ethics

Toward a Renewed Ethical Method

Todd A. Salzman
and
Michael G. Lawler

ORBIS BOOKS
Maryknoll, New York 10545

ORBIS BOOKS
Maryknoll, New York 10545

Fathers and Brothers MARYKNOLL

Founded in 1970, Orbis Books endeavors to publish works that enlighten the mind, nourish the spirit, and challenge the conscience. The publishing arm of the Maryknoll Fathers and Brothers, Orbis seeks to explore the global dimensions of the Christian faith and mission, to invite dialogue with diverse cultures and religious traditions, and to serve the cause of reconciliation and peace. The books published reflect the views of their authors and do not represent the official position of the Maryknoll Society. To learn more about Maryknoll and Orbis Books, please visit our website at www.maryknollsociety.org.

Published by Orbis Books, Box 302, Maryknoll, NY 10545-0302.

Manufactured in the United States of America

Library of Congress Cataloging-in-Publication Data

Names: Salzman, Todd A., author. | Lawler, Michael G., author.
Title: Virtue and theological ethics : toward a renewed ethical method / by Todd A. Salzman and Michael G. Lawler.
Description: Maryknoll, NY : Orbis Books, [2018] | Includes bibliographical references and index.
Identifiers: LCCN 2018011889 (print) | LCCN 2018022966 (ebook) | ISBN 9781608337545 (e-book) | ISBN 9781626983045 (pbk) | ISBN 9781608337545 (ebook)
Subjects: LCSH: Christian ethics—Catholic authors. | Ethics—Methodology. | Virtue. | Virtues. | Christian sociology—Catholic Church. | Catholic Church—Doctrines.
Classification: LCC BJ1249 (ebook) | LCC BJ1249 .S3288 2018 (print) | DDC 241/.042—dc23
LC record available at https://lccn.loc.gov/2018011889

In memoriam Bruce J. Malina
Scholar, Teacher, Friend Extraordinaire

Contents

Abbreviations

AAS — *Acta Apostolicae Sedis: Commentarium Officiale* (Rome: Typis Polyglottis Vaticanis)
AL — *Amoris Laetitia*, Pope Francis, *The Joy of Love* (2016)
CCC — *Catechism of the Catholic Church*
CCE — Congregation for Catholic Education
CDF — Congregation for the Doctrine of the Faith
CRP — CDF, *Considerations Regarding Proposals to Give Legal Recognition to Unions between Homosexual Persons*, *AAS* 95 (2003): 41–57
DH — *Dignitatis Humanae*, Vatican Council II, *Declaration on Religious Freedom* (1965)
DV — *Dei Verbum*, Vatican Council II, *Dogmatic Constitution on Divine Revelation* (1965)
EG — *Evangelii Gaudium*, Pope Francis, *The Joy of the Gospel* (2013)
EV — *Evangelium Vitae*, John Paul II, *The Gospel of Life*, *AAS* 87 (1995): 401–522
FC — *Familiaris Consortio*, John Paul II, *Exhortation on the Role of the Christian Family*, *AAS* 74 (1982): 81–191
GS — *Gaudium et Spes*, Vatican Council II, *Pastoral Constitution on the Church in the Modern World* (1965)
HV — *Humanae Vitae*, Paul VI, *On Human Life*, *AAS* 60 (1968): 481–503
LG — *Lumen Gentium*, Vatican Council II, *Dogmatic Constitution on the Church* (1964)
LS — *Laudato Si'*, Pope Francis, *On Care for Our Common Home* (2015)
NE — *Nichomachean Ethics*, Aristotle, trans. David Ross (Oxford: Oxford University, 2009).
NFP — Natural Family Planning
OT — *Optatum Totius*, Vatican Council II, *Decree on Priestly Formation* (1965)
PG — *Patrologiae Cursus Completus: Series Graeca*, ed. J. P. Migne
PH — *Persona Humana*, CDF, *Declaration on Certain Questions Concerning Sexual Ethics*, *AAS* 68 (1976), 77–96

PL	*Patrologiae Cursus Completus: Series Latina*, ed. J. P. Migne
SRS	*Sollicitudo Rei Socialis*, John Paul II, *The Social Concern of the Church*, *AAS* 80 (1988): 513–86
ST	*Summa Theologiae Sancti Thomae de Aquino*
USCCB	United States Conference of Catholic Bishops
UUS	*Ut Unum Sint*, Pope John Paul II, *That They May Be One* (1995)
VS	*Veritatis Splendor*, John Paul II, *The Splendor of Truth*, *AAS* 85 (1993): 1133–1228

All abbreviations are listed in the footnotes. All translations from languages other than English are the authors'.

Introduction

This book is ultimately about four theological realities: ethical method, virtue ethics, human and sexual dignity, and their interrelatedness. All four of these realities will recur constantly throughout the book, sometimes explicitly, sometimes implicitly, but we introduce all of them here for two reasons: first, to underscore their importance for our analysis and arguments throughout the book and, second, to clarify and focus on each of them from the outset to ensure that they will not get obscured by and lost in the book's multiple arguments.

THEOLOGICAL ETHICAL METHOD

In this section we propose to describe, illustrate, and validate the method Catholic theological ethicists like us employ as they go about their theological task. It behooves us, therefore, to explain precisely from the outset what meaning we assign to the concept and word *method*. With Bernard Lonergan, we understand, intend, and will seek to exemplify throughout that a method is "a normative pattern of related [human] operations yielding cumulative and progressive results."[1] The human operations occur on four levels and are themselves fourfold: on the empirical level we experience, on the intellectual level we understand, on the rational level we judge, and on the responsible level we decide to act on our judgment.

On the empirical level, for instance, we read what Lot says to the men of Sodom in Genesis 19:8: "Do nothing to these men *for they have come under the shelter of my roof*." On the intellectual level, we understand that Lot is talking, not about the perverted homosexual intentions of the men of Sodom, all of whom were presumed to be heterosexual, but about the obligations of the Hebrew law of hospitality that binds both him and the men of Sodom: "When a stranger sojourns with you in your land, you shall do him no wrong. . . . You shall love him as yourself" (Lv 19:33). The Catholic Church continues to interpret the Sodom text without ever advert-

[1]Bernard J. F. Lonergan, *Method in Theology* (Toronto: University of Toronto Press, 2003), 4.

ing to the historical fact that every human being at the time was presumed to be heterosexual.[2] On the rational level, we judge that the story of Lot and the men of Sodom is not about the homosexual intentions of the men of Sodom but about the Leviticus demand for hospitality to strangers. On the responsible level, we decide to act on the interpretation that the story about the men of Sodom is a story about their inhospitality and not, as the Catholic Church continues to insist, about any prohibition of homosexual acts as we understand them today.[3] As the method is repeatedly employed, and not only for scriptural passages as we shall see, it yields cumulative results leading to the progressive clarification of Catholic theological ethics. Central to every Catholic ethical method is natural law, which both indicates what it means to be human and provides guidelines for attaining the fullest possible humanity. We deal in detail with natural law in Chapter 1. Here we need to add a further piece about method.

By common ecumenical, theological agreement, the data to which Christian ethicists attend, on which they reflect, which they seek to understand, on the basis of which they make moral judgments and decide to act on them, is mined from what is referred to as the Wesleyan Quadrilateral, four established sources of ethical knowledge in the Christian perspective, namely, scripture, tradition, science and secular disciplines of knowledge,[4] and human experience. The Second Vatican Council called for the renewal of Catholic theological ethics. We use the Wesleyan Quadrilateral to respond to this call and to propose a Catholic ethical methodological schema for the twenty-first century. We will expound our reasons for employing the Quadrilateral in Chapter 3—for now, it will suffice to note that use of these four sources may encourage ecumenical, methodological considerations that should inform Catholic ethics and aid in the formation of a well-formed conscience.[5]

The authority and inviolability of individual conscience is a long-standing teaching in the Catholic moral tradition and is, indeed, fundamental to it. That teaching became even stronger and more theologically based through

[2]There is no word for *homosexual* in either the Old or New Testament. The appearance of the word in any modern translation is the result of an erroneous translation by a translator. The word *homosexual* did not appear until 1869 from the Hungarian physician Karoly Benkert. It did not come into common use in the United States until the 1880s. In biblical times, homosexuality as we understand it today was unknown, since every human being was presumed to be heterosexual.

[3]For our full exegesis of the Sodom text and our analysis of what it means for Catholic sexual ethics, see Todd A. Salzman and Michael G. Lawler, *The Sexual Person: Toward a Renewed Catholic Anthropology* (Washington, DC: Georgetown University Press, 2008), 217–26.

[4]We understand by the term *secular discipline* any discipline distinct from, and not dependent upon, revelation. See Margaret Farley, *Just Love: A Framework for Christian Sexual Ethics* (New York: Continuum, 2006), 188–89.

[5]See James Gustafson, "Charles Curran: Ecumenical Moral Theologian Par Excellence," in *A Call to Fidelity*, ed. James J. Walter et al. (Washington, DC: Georgetown University Press), 211–34.

the careful and sustained work of the Fathers of the Vatican Council, particularly in their document on the Church in the Modern World, *Gaudium et Spes*, which speaks of conscience three times. First, it is "the most secret core and sanctuary of man . . . [where] he is alone with God whose voice echoes in his depth. In a wonderful manner conscience reveals that law which is fulfilled by love of God and neighbor" (no. 16). Second, among the things necessary for "leading a life truly human" is the right to action "in accord with the upright norm of one's own conscience" (no. 26). Third, the gospel of Christ "has a sacred reverence for the dignity of conscience and its freedom of choice" (no. 41). *Dignitatis Humanae,* the Council's Decree on Religious Freedom, went further and prescribed the authority and inviolability of conscience. "In all his activity a man is bound to follow his conscience faithfully, in order that he may come to God, for whom he was created. It follows that he is not to be forced to act in a manner contrary to his conscience. Nor, on the other hand, is he to be restrained from acting in accordance with his conscience, especially in matters religious" (no. 3). In the 1960s, these were unheard of words in Catholic magisterial circles and liberating words in educated Catholic lay circles, but the incontestable reality is that they express a teaching that is long-standing in the Catholic moral tradition and is fundamental to it.

Several points emerge from the above conciliar quotes on the nature and authority of conscience. First, conscience is sacred; it is among the gifts of the Creator-God to humans. Second, it is an intrinsic, essential part of the human person and, therefore, intimately related to human dignity. Third, following one's conscience on moral and religious matters facilitates human dignity; violating one's conscience on moral and religious matters frustrates human dignity. Fourth, one must never be forced to act against one's conscience; to be so forced is a fundamental violation not only of conscience but also of essential human dignity. Fifth, the authority granted to conscience presumes that one's conscience is well formed. Commenting on *Gaudium et Spes* before he became Pope Benedict XVI, Joseph Ratzinger wrote that "Over the Pope as the expression of the binding claim of ecclesiastical authority there still stands one's own conscience, which must be obeyed before all else, if necessary even against the requirement of ecclesiastical authority. Conscience confronts [the individual] with a supreme and ultimate tribunal, and one which in the last resort is beyond the claim of external social groups, even of the official church."[6]

To make a well-formed judgment of conscience involves two separate judgments: first, a grasp and a judgment of the first principles of practical

[6]Joseph Ratzinger, "The Dignity of the Human Person," in *Commentary on the Documents of Vatican II*, vol. 5, ed. Herbert Vorgrimler (New York: Herder,1969), 134.

judgment, which Aquinas calls *synderesis*,[7] and second, a gathering of as much evidence as possible related to the issue at hand, an honest and rational weighing and understanding of the evidence and its implications, and finally as honest a judgment as possible that this action is moral and to be chosen and that action is immoral and not to be chosen. A well-formed judgment of conscience, then, is a practical judgment that comes at the end of a rational process of collecting, weighing, and deliberating all the evidence available about an issue. It is an *individual* judgment, but it is far from an *individualistic* judgment. The Latin word *con-scientia* literally means knowledge together, but perhaps is better rendered as to know together. The communal character of conscience has been part of the Christian tradition since Paul, who clearly believed in the authority and inviolability of conscience (1 Cor 10:25–27; 2 Cor 1:12, 4:2; 1 Ti 1:5) and who wrote to his beloved Corinthians that the "stronger" consciences in the community should be sensitive to and careful of the "weaker" consciences that might easily be "defiled" by even the stronger's most conscientious actions (1 Cor 8:7–13). We characterize this communal conscience as the conscience of the People of God, and we suggest that, when individual consciences differ over whether they should embrace a change in any Catholic teaching, for the unity of the People-Church those consciences should be questioned in the same "dialogue of charity" and "spirit of collegiality and synodality" that Pope Francis found and praised in the 2014 and 2015 Synods on the Family.

OUR THEOLOGICAL VIRTUE ETHICAL METHOD

For the sake of conceptual clarity in the ethical argumentations that follow in our book, we set forth clearly at the outset our ethical method. We are well aware that our ethical method and our approach to normative theological ethics might appear different from the traditional Catholic method and approach, but we assert that they are not different *tout court*. Our method is historically conscious, open to the Catholic theological ethical tradition, follows natural law reinterpreted, is based on and seeks to facilitate human and sexual dignity, is rooted primarily in the human person rather than on his/her acts, is articulated from a Christian perspective, accepts the four ethical sources articulated in the Wesleyan Quadrilateral, is inductive rather than deductive, is virtue ethical, and accepts the authority and inviolability of a properly informed conscience. We briefly explain those ten elements of our ethical method.

First, our method is historically conscious, openly acknowledging that

[7]Thomas Aquinas, *Summa Theologiae* I, 79, 13 (hereafter *ST*).

humans, their communities, and the meanings and values they espouse are always in a process of gradual growth and change. Second, our method, therefore, looks to the Catholic ethical tradition that comes to us from the past, not as ethical facts to be uncritically accepted as diachronically true but as ethical data for conscientious discernment of their possible applications to a different, contemporary, contextual situation. This approach ensures that the tradition can be handed on to future generations stronger and more attuned to developing and contemporary human experience and human dignity. We stipulate that every contextual situation involves human beings and their culpability-diminishing weaknesses,[8] keeping consciously in mind Thomas Aquinas's, Pope Francis's, and universal human experience's valid principle: "the principle will be found to fail according as we descend further into detail."[9] Third, our method accepts natural law as an objectivist, universalist metaethical theory, but we argue in Chapter 1 to a rational/personal understanding of natural law rather than to the traditional natural/biological understanding. In light of that different understanding, we argue to the formulation of a very different normative ethic. Fourth, we define moral or right or good in principle as that which facilitates human dignity and human well-being/doing,[10] but we argue to a different, expanded understanding of sexual human dignity in the concrete from that of the Magisterium. Fifth, we argue from that expanded understanding of the dignity of the human person, rejecting the narrow, legalist, act-centered approach of the magisterial tradition and insist on the dignity of the rational human person, reintegrating theological ethics and spiritual theology.

Sixth, our method is thoroughly perspectival, as we will explain in Chapter 1, and the perspective that controls it is the Christian perspective that acknowledges Jesus Christ as the revelation of God. Seventh, our method accepts four sources of ethical knowledge for developing a normative method—scripture, tradition, science, and human experience—the Wesleyan Quadrilateral that we will explain in Chapter 3. On occasion, depending on the contextual situation that is central to our method, again we may select from the four sources, interpret them, prioritize them, and integrate them differently from the Magisterium.[11] Eighth, our method is thoroughly inductive. It begins not with a prescribed ethical norm from which it deduces the required ethical action in the contextual situation but

---

[8]See *Amoris Laetitia*, nos. 291, 294, 312 (hereafter *AL*); and *Catechism of the Catholic Church*, nos. 1735 and 2352.

[9]*ST*, I-II, 94, 4; *AL*, no. 304.

[10]We use this term *well-being/doing* throughout this book as our concretization of the more commonly used but vague term *fulfillment*.

[11]See Todd A. Salzman, *What Are They Saying about Catholic Ethical Method?* (Mahwah, NJ: Paulist Press, 2003).

with the contextual situation itself, always including the persons involved with their culpability-diminishing weakness, and inductively discerns a conscientious choice of the required ethical action in the situation. Ninth, our method is a virtue ethical method. It focuses primarily not on the acts a person must do to be ethical and virtuous but on the person and his/her character and only secondarily on the acts he/she must do to be virtuous. Tenth, our method accepts the long-established Catholic tradition on the authority of the well-formed individual conscience in general and the authority of the well-formed theological ethicist's conscience in particular. As Catholic ethicists, in communion with the People of God, we seek to develop a methodology and anthropology and to formulate and justify moral principles and norms that facilitate the attainment of human dignity.

Some of our theologian colleagues will no doubt dispute, indeed have disputed, that the Catholic ethical tradition and specifically the sexual ethical tradition is changeable, even suggesting that it is instead infallible.[12] We suggest that this is the result of a lack of historical consciousness. The historical fact is that, as has been amply demonstrated by historians of theology,[13] the living church has changed its teachings often in the past, and we are sure that it will continue to change them in the future as it seeks to "interpret the many voices of our age and to judge them in the light of the divine word. In this way, revealed truth can always be more deeply penetrated, better understood, and set forth to greater advantage."[14] No change has had more far-reaching theological implications, perhaps, than the shift in the basis of ethical theory suggested by *Gaudium et Spes*. Prior to the Second Vatican Council, ethical methodology and the approach to ethical questions were primarily deductive: they started with agreed-upon abstract ethical principles and norms and then applied them downward to particular concrete situations and acts. *Gaudium et Spes* directed the church to another method and approach, an inductive approach that starts with human persons and their experience and works upward to specific concrete ethical norms and general ethical principles. It emphasized two things. First, "there are a number of particularly urgent needs characterizing the present age. . . . To a consideration of these *in the light of the Gospel and of human experience,* the Council would now direct the attention of all."[15] Second, "[t]hanks to the *experience* of past ages, the progress of the *sciences*, and the treasures

[12]Germain Grisez and John Ford claim that the Magisterium's teaching against artificial contraception is infallible in their "Contraception and the Infallibility of the Ordinary Magisterium," *Theological Studies* 39 (1978): 258–312. See also Germain Grisez, "*Quaestio Disputata*: The Ordinary Magisterium's Infallibility: A Reply to Some New Arguments," *Theological Studies* 55 (1994): 720–32, 737–38.

[13]See, for instance, John T. Noonan, *A Church That Can and Cannot Change: The Development of Catholic Moral Teaching* (Notre Dame, IN: University of Notre Dame Press, 2005).

[14]*Gaudium et Spes*, no. 44 (hereafter *GS*).

[15]Ibid., no. 46, emphasis added.

hidden in the various forms of *human culture*, the nature of man himself is revealed and *new roads to truth are opened*."[16] This trilogy, human culture, experience, and science, is paradigmatic for our inductive approach.

VIRTUE

Since the notion of *virtue* is central to this entire book, we need to be clear what we mean by *virtue*. We need a virtue theory. We introduce our virtue theory now, and we will show in Chapter 2 how it is practical in our virtue ethics. We begin with Aristotle. He defines virtue as "a state of character concerned with choice, lying in a mean."[17] Thomas Aquinas has a more specific definition. A virtue, he argues, is a habit or a disposition[18] ordered to an act.[19] We offer a definition that has its ancestry in both Aristotle and Aquinas and that will control our future discussions of virtue. A virtue is a stable character state, habit, or disposition that moves us to feel, understand, judge, and act in a way that is an act of the virtue. Justice, for instance, is a character habit or disposition that urges us to do just acts; chastity is a character habit or disposition that urges us to do chaste acts; and so on for all the virtues. Virtue, as we have already suggested, is involved in both the emotional and the rational parts of the self.

As character state, habit, or disposition, virtue not only explains why a person acts this way in this particular situation but also why the person can be relied on to act this way in all similar situations or, given well-known human weakness,[20] at least most of the time. We can isolate three dimensions of a virtue: it is a character state, habit, or disposition; it involves a judgment of truth and a choice of action; and it lies on a continuum between excess and defect. These three dimensions of virtue are agreed by most proponents of virtue and virtue ethics as essential to its definition. "Each of the virtues involves getting things right, for each involves *phronesis*, or practical wisdom, which is the ability to reason correctly about practical matters."[21] Without *phronesis*, no right judgment, action, and therefore virtue, is possible.

Common to all theories of virtue is the essential notion that virtues are not only preconditions for human well-being/doing but also constituents of that

[16]Ibid., no. 44, emphasis added.

[17]Aristotle, *Nicomachean Ethics*, trans. David Ross (Oxford: Oxford University, 2009), II, 6, 1106b, 36. See Rosalind Hursthouse, *On Virtue Ethics* (Oxford: Oxford University, 1999), 11.

[18]*ST* I-II, 49, 1.

[19]*ST* I-II, 49, 3.

[20]See *AL*, no. 291.

[21]Hursthouse, *On Virtue Ethics*, 12.

well-being/doing. "A virtue," writes virtue ethicist Rosalind Hursthouse, "is a character trait that human beings, given their physical and psychological nature, need to flourish (or to do and fare well)."[22] The person who has the virtues of justice and love will be a person who will act justly and lovingly. This direction was mapped out by Aristotle, who names the ultimate human good *eudaimonia*,[23] happiness or fulfillment. It was Christianized by Aquinas, who describes the ultimate human good as union with God achieved through the virtue of *caritas*,[24] charity or self-sacrificing love. Given their different ends, happiness in the case of Aristotelian virtue ethics and union with God in Christian virtue ethics, we would expect the two ethics to be different, and we will argue in Chapter 2 that they are different.

A central element of Aristotle's definition of virtue is that it is the result of deliberation and choice; it is rational as man is rational (and for Aristotle it is always *a man* who is rational, never a woman, a gender inequity that contemporary ethicists rightly do not accept). Deliberation is of possible choices and actions, and choice is of one action in preference to others. Choice involves reason, thought,[25] and *phronesis* or practical judgment. It selects one action over others along the continuum that is appropriate and proportionate for this particular person, in this situation, and for this right reason. Aristotle's virtuous mean is not an arithmetic mean but a mean relative to both an individual and the circumstances in which she finds herself. The arithmetic mean between ten and two pounds of food is six pounds, but six pounds would be "too little for Milo" (a famous wrestler of Aristotle's day) and too much for "the beginner in athletic exercises." The mean to be chosen, then, lies "not in the object but relatively to us."[26] Virtuous action is a fluid mean, a mean that lies not so much midway between two extremes as on a continuum between them. The virtue of bravery, for instance, does not always lie midway between foolhardiness and cowardice but may lie in different locations on the continuum between them for different characters and even for the same character in different situations. Aristotle's virtue ethics is thoroughly teleological. The final end for humans is happiness or well-being/doing, and this end is not to be deliberated and judged; it is a given. Humans are to deliberate only means to that end. We deliberate only about what lies in our power to do or not to do;[27] actions we are forced to

---

[22]Rosalind Hursthouse, "Applying Virtue Ethics," in *Virtues and Reason: Philippa Foot and Moral Theory*, ed. Rosalind Hursthouse et al. (Oxford: Clarendon, 1995), 57–75, at 68. See also Hursthouse, *On Virtue Ethics*, 13; Brad Hooker, "Does Moral Virtue Constitute a Benefit to the Agent?" in *How Should One Live?: Essays on the Virtues*, ed. Roger Crisp (Oxford: Clarendon, 1998), 141–55.

[23]*NE*, I, 4, 1095a, 17–20.

[24]*ST*, I, 23, 6.

[25]*NE*, III, 2, 1112a, 17.

[26]Ibid., II, 6, 1106b, 3–8.

[27]Ibid., III, 3, 1112a, 31.

do are not freely chosen and, therefore, cannot be either virtuous or vicious, ethical or unethical. It is because we are rational that we can know, first, that action is called for and, second, that we can choose this virtuous or this vicious action.

HUMAN DIGNITY

We shall analyze human dignity in detail in Chapter 6, but here we initially clarify how we understand it. The word *dignity* denotes worth or worthiness, and human dignity denotes the worth or worthiness of every human being: black, brown, yellow, white, bisexual, heterosexual, homosexual, transsexual. *Gaudium et Spes* suggests an approach to the definition of human dignity. In its section on marriage and the family, it notes that "the moral aspect of any procedure [to harmonize conjugal love with the responsible transmission of life] . . . must be determined by objective standards. These [are] based on the nature of the human person and his acts."[28] The official commentary on *Gaudium et Spes* explains that this principle is applicable not only to marriage and sexuality, about which it is articulated, but also to the entire realm of human activity and is formulated as a general principle: "human activity must be judged insofar as it refers to the human person integrally and adequately considered."[29] Drawing on *Gaudium et Spes*'s personalist principle, Louis Janssens advances a theological anthropology that embraces six dimensions of the human person and his/her dignity. The human person is a subject; in corporeality; in relationship to the material world, to others, and, we add, to self and to God; created in the image and likeness of God; a historical being; and fundamentally unique but equal to all other persons.[30] Edward Schillebeeckx argues that these human characteristics present us with constitutive conditions, "which must always be presupposed in any human action, if man, his culture, and his society are not to be vitiated and made unlivable."[31] We consider each characteristic in turn.

First, the human person is a free and inviolable subject and should never be treated as an object or means to an end. Every subject is, at least potentially, a rational, knowing, judging, and freely deciding human being. This dimension of the human person founds that most important dimension of human dignity, namely, personal conscience, which we shall initially consider in the next section and consider in detail in Chapter 6. Recall that

[28]*GS*, no. 51.

[29]*Schema constitutionis pastoralis de ecclesia in mundo huius temporis: Textus recognitus et relationes, pars 11* (Vatican City: Vatican Press, 1965), 9.

[30]Louis Janssens, "Artificial Insemination: Ethical Considerations," *Louvain Studies* 8 (1980): 3–29.

[31]Edward Schillebeeckx, *Christ: The Experience of Jesus as Lord* (New York: Seabury, 1980), 733.

Dignitatis Humanae, the Second Vatican Council's Decree on Religious Freedom, insists on the freedom and inviolability of conscience and decrees that a man "is not to be forced to act in a manner contrary to his conscience. Nor, on the other hand, is he to be restrained from acting in accordance with his conscience, especially in matters religious."[32] Freedom of the rightly informed conscience is an irrefutable dimension of free human subjects and of their intrinsic dignity.

Second, the human person is also essentially corporeal; he/she is essentially an *embodied* person. A long-standing and well-known, but not so well-understood, Catholic teaching has been that the human is essentially composed of body and soul. That teaching poorly understood led to the negative presumption that men and women were dualistic, divided into two unequal parts, a body that was physical and lower and a soul that was spiritual and higher. Embedded in that presumption, James Nelson correctly notes, was an approach to bodiliness, which "distrusted, feared, and discounted our bodies."[33] Sandra Lipsitz Bem shows how that distrust and fear of our bodies and their perceived inadequacies is manifested in our real lives in our endless attempts to improve them.[34] Those attempts, we underscore, are motivated more by our desire to improve our *gendered* bodies rather than our *physiological* bodies. Nowhere was that distrust and fear more in evidence than in matters related to sexuality. The Christian tradition has always been suspicious of embodied sexuality and has regarded it in general as "objectively disordered," as a consequence of original sin.[35] This negative tradition about the body seriously impacted ethical judgments on the dignity of embodied men and women and led to strict sexual norms that restricted sexual activity only to marriage between a man and a woman. As far back as the fifth century, Saint Augustine of Hippo taught that virginity was to be preferred to marriage,[36] and that even in marriage "in these days no one perfect in piety seeks to have children other than spiritually."[37]

After the horrors of the Second World War, that presumption began to wane and was replaced by a developing and widespread theological opinion that human existence—"even in the sphere of the Spirit—is essentially

---

[32]*Dignitatis Humanae*, no. 3.

[33]James Nelson, *Body Theology* (Louisville, KY: Westminster/John Knox, 1992), 9.

[34]Sandra Lipsitz Bem, *The Lenses of Gender: Transforming the Debate on Sexual Inequality* (New Haven, CT: Yale University Press, 1993), 159–62.

[35]Mark Jordan, *The Silence of Sodom: Homosexuality in Modern Catholicism* (Chicago: University of Chicago Press, 2000), 34.

[36]Augustine, *De Bono Coniugali*, III, 3, in *Patrologiae Cursus Completus: Series Latina*, ed. J. P. Migne, 40, 375. This work throughout the rest of the book will be abbreviated as *PL* and its Greek companion as *PG*. The Council of Trent taught the same thing. See *Catechism of the Council of Trent*, trans. John A. McHugh and Charles J. Callan (New York: Wagner, 1945), 338–43.

[37]Augustine, *De Bono Coniugali*, *PL* 40, 387.

bodily existence."[38] So fundamental to human existence and anthropology is corporeality that contemporary Catholic theologians tend to say not that men and women *have* bodies but that they *are* bodies. The distrust and fear of the human body that once controlled the Christian traditions, and that so diminished human dignity, has given way to a positive evaluation of the human body, embodiedness, and their essential place in human reality that has greatly enhanced human dignity. That enhancement calls for a reevaluation, we argue in this book, of the Catholic norms that control sexual ethics.

Third, through his/her body a human person is essentially a person-in-relationship, with himself/herself, with other embodied persons, with the material world, and with God. Psychological studies repeatedly indicate that one of the greatest threats to healthy human development is poor self-esteem, and the Christian tradition has not always done an adequate job of emphasizing healthy self-esteem or self-love. Jesus's great commandment is well known: "You shall love the Lord your God with all your heart, with all your soul, with all your mind, and with all your strength." The second is this: "'You shall love your neighbor as yourself" (Mk 12:28–34; Mt 22:34–40, 46b; Lk 10:25–28). Not so well known is the fact that there are *three* commandments in this text: love God, love neighbor, *and* love self. Typically, the Christian tradition has interpreted self-love as egocentric and antithetical to the love of the gospel. While this certainly *can* be the case, and the cultures of Western countries that emphasize radical individualism encourage egocentric love, that love is not the healthy self-love demanded by the gospel. Authentic self-love first affirms oneself as a good, valuable, and lovable self-in-God and then, in alliance with neighbor-love, turns toward others and gives this good, valuable, and lovable self-in-God unconditionally to them.[39] If humans do not truly and fully accept and love themselves, in both their wholeness and their brokenness, they can neither give themselves fully to another person nor fully accept the other person.

Humans are also in relation to each other. Who is our neighbor and how are we called to love him/her? As the gospels make clear, our neighbor can be anyone, at any time, at any place. Some of the most challenging parables, that of the good Samaritan, for example, concern those whom we would least likely consider to be our neighbor: "Samaritans"; homosexuals; people with AIDS; capital criminals; the poor; the outcasts of society; and visibly, in our day, refugees. Yet, it is these very people that Jesus commands us to love and to treat with compassion and mercy. The possibilities of fulfilling this command in both disposition and action are infinite and complex, but

---

[38]Rudolph Bultmann, *Theology of the New Testament* (London: SCM, 1952), 1:192.

[39]See Darlene Fozard Weaver, *Self-Love and Christian Ethics* (Cambridge: Cambridge University Press, 2002).

it is beyond doubt that the core of Christian ethics is that we first recognize this demand and then act on it with neighbor-love and neighbor-justice.

Humans are also in relationship to the *material world*. As embodied persons, we recognize our need for clean air and water, shelter, and healthy living conditions, and this recognition conveys also a responsibility to care for the material world. This responsibility for our environment is a crucial issue in contemporary ethics. As the world population continues to grow and the science of climate change continues to reveal calamitous effects on our environment and the survival of the human species, if we do not act soon to reduce carbon emissions, this issue requires urgent attention. We need to utilize technology to develop what Schillebeeckx refers to as a "meta-cosmos" that rescues humans "from their animal limitations and offers an opening for new possibilities."[40] Technology can be a negative or positive tool for humanization. It can produce an atomic bomb or it can produce clean and reusable energy, though not without risk, as we saw at Chernobyl, Three Mile Island, and Fukushima, Japan.[41] It can help us harness solar and wind energy, conserve energy, and preserve natural resources to reduce carbon emissions, thereby slowing climate change. We must acknowledge both that there are a limited number of natural resources and that limited resources require not only conservation but also fair and equitable distribution throughout the world. Social and environmental ethics both rely heavily upon this dimension of human reality and dignity.[42]

Humans are also, and importantly, in relationship with God, and this relationship will be important throughout this book as we seek to articulate a Christian ethics for the third millennium. "Created in the image of God, the human person is called to know and worship [God] . . . and to glorify [God] in all his attitudes and activities."[43] Christians believe in a loving Creator-God, that they are in a profound relationship with this Creator-God, and that their dispositions and actions impact their relationship with this Creator-God. If they freely accept relationship with God, as they can, then they accept also that they find their ultimate well-being/doing and dignity in this relationship. This relationship, however, is not a divinely exclusive one; it is reflected broadly in all our human relationships. Our relationship with God and neighbor is dialectical. Pope Francis reminds us that "You cannot love God without loving your neighbor and you cannot love your

---

[40]Schillebeeckx, *Christ*, 735.

[41]See Osamu Takeuchi, "Nature, Human Beings, and Nuclear Power in Japan," in *Just Sustainability: Technology, Ecology, and Resource Extraction*, ed. Christiana Z. Peppard and Andrea Vicini (Maryknoll, NY: Orbis Books, 2015), 23–26.

[42]See Pope Francis, *Laudato Si'*. See also Richard Miller, ed., *God, Creation, and Climate Change* (Maryknoll, NY: Orbis Books, 2010); and Peppard and Vicini, *Just Sustainability*.

[43]Janssens, "Artificial Insemination," 9.

neighbor without loving God."[44] God's love for us and our love for God is foundational for all being-in-relationship. It invites us to live a life of faith and hope in self-love and neighbor-love embodied in care for ourselves, for others, and for the material world we share.

Our relationship with God includes various mysteries that shape a Christian perspective. These mysteries may not lead to different anthropological or normative conclusions of what is right and wrong, but they do provide distinct perspectives. We are committed to the particularity of the Christian community and its distinct perspectives and contributions to ethical discourse. Here, we briefly outline those mysteries. In Chapter 3, we explain how these mysteries impact the selection, interpretation, prioritization, and integration (SIPI) of the four sources of ethical knowledge to define human dignity and formulate and justify norms that facilitate and do not frustrate attaining human dignity in the areas of environmental and sexual ethics.

Charles Curran argues that perspective, which he calls "stance," is drawn from "the visual experience and expresses the way we look at something that puts everything else into focus."[45] A foundational question to be asked of Christian ethical method, then, is what perspective or stance guides Christian ethicists in their perception of reality. Metaethical objectivism justifies the claim that the good can be defined, and faith in the living Christ provides the perspective or hermeneutical lens to formulate and justify both that definition and the norms that facilitate its attainment. Drawing from what he calls the "fivefold Christian mysteries," Curran formulates a Christian perspective that serves as a paradigm and point of departure for Christian ethical method.[46] James Gustafson judges that "Curran's stance demonstrates the significance of 'postethical' levels of moral discourse or, in other words, of background beliefs and loyalties that provide a larger framework of justification and orientation for ethics without being a sufficient condition for determining particular moral action."[47] Curran proposes that the following mysteries are inherent in a Christian perspective: creation, sin, incarnation, redemption, and resurrection destiny.[48]

[44]Pope Francis, *The Infinite Tenderness of God: Meditations on the Gospels* (Frederick, MD: The Word Among Us Press, 2016), Meditation 47.

[45]Charles Curran, *The Catholic Moral Tradition Today* (Washington, DC: Georgetown University, 1999), 30.

[46]Charles Curran, *Moral Theology: A Continuing Journey* (Notre Dame, IN: University of Notre Dame Press, 1982), 38–44; Curran, *The Catholic Moral Tradition Today*, 30.

[47]James M. Gustafson, "Charles Curran: Ecumenical Moral Theologian Par Excellence," in *A Call to Fidelity*, 225–26.

[48]Other scholars (James M. Gustafson, *Christ and the Moral Life* [New York: Harper and Row, 1968], 242–48; James T. Bretzke, *A Morally Complex World* [Collegeville, MN: Liturgical Press, 2004], 33–35) have proposed Christ as the foundational stance for Christian ethics. While Christ is the *norma normans non normata*, proposing him as foundational stance begs the question of Christology. We concur with Curran that, given the complexity of Christological questions and the danger of a narrow

The mystery of creation nurtures the belief that God has created the universe and everything in it, including rational human beings, and that God's creation is fundamentally good. Since human nature is a clearly discernible *rational* nature, to act according to their nature, humans are required to act rationally, and through rational reflection on the created world, they have the capacity to discern ethical truth, that is, to discern the behavior that facilitates the attainment of human dignity. Unfortunately, however, long historical experience shows that humans do not always act rationally, and sin is a demonstrable reality of their existence together; it came into creation through human actions contrary to their rational nature. Though the mystery of sin does not destroy the basic goodness of God's creation, it does deform it. It impacts human reason, diminishing the ability to discern the meaning of human existence, the recognition of and respect for human dignity, and the call to wholeness or holiness. The mystery of incarnation asserts that Jesus is both fully human and fully divine, thereby supporting and strengthening the fundamental goodness of everything human. If sin deforms the human image God created, the mystery of redemption, "the successful struggle of Jesus against the power of sin and evil," restores that image. "Resurrection destiny" and the triumph of Jesus over evil, sin, and death, historically exist in the tension between the "already" and "not yet." Christian ethics must "live with an eschatological tension between the present time of redemption and the unrealized future of resurrection destiny."[49] We point to something here that is important to note in a materialistic world: one need not accept that these religious mysteries are true in any scientifically verifiable way to accept them as satisfying and beneficial to a life in community with other human beings. Philosopher Owen Flanagan, who certainly does not believe they are true and who asserts that "thinking about our lives in ways that incorporate superstition and wishful thinking is childish and unbecoming to rational social animals like us,"[50] still accepts them as supporting a way of social life that is "noble, honest, and worthy."[51]

For Curran, perspective "serves as an interpretive tool in understanding the basic mysteries of Christian life."[52] For Philip Keane, it "is a creative, integrating, imaginative grasp of the meaning of life."[53] The Christian

---

Christology (*The Catholic Moral Tradition Today*, 31–32) and further, given that the mysteries that Curran cites are directly related to questions of Christology, these mysteries may adequately account for a Christian stance.

[49]Curran, *The Catholic Moral Tradition Today*, 33–34.

[50]Owen Flanagan, *The Really Hard Problem: Meaning in a Material World* (Cambridge, MA; MIT Press, 2007), 108.

[51]Ibid., 190.

[52]Curran, *Moral Theology*, 43.

[53]Philip S. Keane, *Christian Ethics and Imagination* (New York: Paulist Press, 1984), 65.

theological perspective that Christian ethicists share, the selection, interpretation, prioritization, and integration of these five mysteries, shapes their moral perspective and guides the process of their formulating a definition of human dignity and the norms that facilitate its attainment. Often times, their perspective is implied rather than stated in their writings. Drawing attention to perspective, however, is crucial to Christian ethical method. It may shift the focus from the formulation and justification of specific norms for the moral life, which is often polarizing and not necessarily conducive to dialogue among Christian ethicists, to perspectives on creation, sin, incarnation, redemption, and resurrection destiny and how those mysteries shape a perspective, provide common ground for open, constructive, and charitable dialogue, and build community. Calls from Vatican II and from the International Theological Commission[54] for constructing interdisciplinary theological methods could foster such dialogue.

We concur with Curran's proposal of the fivefold Christian mysteries that constitute the Christian perspective or stance: creation, sin, incarnation, redemption, and resurrection destiny. The selection, prioritization, interpretation, and integration of those mysteries depend on the specific area of applied ethics or specific ethical issue being addressed. Christian ethical perspectives largely agree on some issue, such as environmental ethical issues; they largely disagree on other issues such as sexual ethical issues.

Fourth, each corporeal human being, the Christian traditions universally hold, is brought into existence by the creative act of God. "So God created man in his own image, in the image of God He created him; male and female He created them" (Gn 1:27). Each corporeal human being, male and female alike, is created by God in the image and likeness of God. That human image and likeness of God introduces a very important, and much ignored, dimension of human dignity, namely, its historical dimension. Contemporary Catholic theology looks upon God as both transcendent *mystery* and, on the basis of God's creation of all there is, *as* present in and to the world as the ground of its existence.[55] This mystery is revealed to humans, not from outside but from inside their world and history, especially from inside the history of the man Jesus of Nazareth. It is communicated to every person created and born into the world and remains embedded in their world as a "supernatural existential"[56] at the very heart of their history. Divine mystery

[54]International Theological Commission, *Theology Today: Perspectives, Principles and Criteria* 5, www.vatican.va/roman_curia/congregations/cfaith/cti_documents/rc_cti_doc_20111129_teologia-oggi_en.html.

[55]See, for instance, Michael H. Barnes, *In the Presence of Mystery: An Introduction to the Story of Human Religiousness* (Mystic, CT: Twenty-Third Publications, 1984); Elizabeth A. Johnson, *She Who Is: The Mystery of God in Feminist Theological Discourse* (New York: Crossroad, 1992).

[56]See Karl Rahner, *Theological Investigations* (Baltimore: Helicon, 1954), 1:297–346.

is not above the historical process but at its very heart, in and through history's unfolding forward movement.

When men and women cooperate with this divine mystery, they can be converted, changed existentially, intellectually, and ethically, and move forward to a more responsible and ethical stance toward both their fellow humans and the God who created them. It is here that the mystery of God present in and to God's creation makes existential contact with the mystery of the human created by God. Created in the image and likeness of divine mystery, the human is herself/himself mystery to be plumbed to an always greater depth. The human is not complete at creation, but a being waiting to be completed, waiting to grow gradually into what the Creator-God intended her/him to become: humanly, relationally, intellectually, ethically, and spiritually. That dynamic of the human waiting for gradual growth and completion means that everything that can be said at any given time in history about her/him is partial, tentative, and waiting to gradually evolve as humans themselves evolve. The full comprehension of the mystery of humanity, Christian theologians teach, is eschatological, that is, it is achieved only at the end.[57]

Fifth, humans are universally acknowledged to be essentially historical beings, and any credible understanding of them and of their dignity must recognize the impact of history on them. This impact and its implications for defining human dignity, however, are interpreted differently according to different theoretical perspectives. Some theologians focus on a classicist, universal, and essential understanding of basic goods like life, knowledge, self-integration, practical authenticity, justice and friendship, marriage, and religion or holiness. Others focus on a historically conscious, particular, and existential understanding of these same goods. While acknowledging the universal inclination of human beings toward basic goods, the latter also recognize their particularity. As aspects of universal human dignity, the basic goods are universal; as existential instantiations of goods that provide human beings with a rational basis for ethical choice, they are particularized by history, culture, social context, and relationships. We agree with Lisa Sowle Cahill. The basic goods are universal as "shared framing experiences and moral common ground" in that there is "shared human being in the world;"[58] they are particular in that the "shared is achieved not beyond or over against particularity but in and through it."[59] Historical consciousness recognizes that there is not a single, absolute perspective or

[57]Schillebeeckx, *Christ,* 731.

[58]Lisa Sowle-Cahill, *Sex, Gender, and Christian Ethics* (Cambridge: Cambridge University Press, 1996), 51.

[59]Ibid., 55.

definition of human dignity, but rather plural partial, adequate, and reliable perspectives that are shaped by an ongoing dialogue in the present, with the past, directed toward the future.

The sixth dimension of the human is that each and every human, corporeal person is unique in herself/himself and equal to all other human persons. This dimension is universally acknowledged, and we see no need to delay on it, except to emphasize that however unique every person might be, not one of them is ever as fully developed and formed as she/he can be. An essential honoring of their dignity, therefore, will mean allowing them to grow and develop gradually in every facet of their lives, as both Popes John Paul II and Francis teach.[60]

An essential prerequisite before entering into any of the many dialogues in this book is to be clear about how we understand what is ethical: what is ethical or good or right is what facilitates these dimensions of the human person and of human dignity, what is unethical or evil or wrong frustrates them. Ethical challenges abound when, as is inevitable, our actions facilitate some dimensions of human dignity but conflict with others. We can travel, for example, to a theological conference to discuss important ethical issues surrounding climate change and possible theological and scientific responses to it. In one sense, this facilitates our relationships with colleagues-neighbors, the impact we can have on religious and political groups, and perhaps creates an overall positive impact on our relationship with the material world. In another sense, however, the material resources we use to travel to the conference by car or plane, and the services provided by workers in hotels and restaurants who are often not paid a just and living wage, can have a negative impact on the material world and human relationships we are hoping to improve. Such is the ethical complexity of every genuine human act.

NEUROSCIENCE

Two colleagues who kindly read our original manuscript suggested that this section should be placed elsewhere in our book. We just as kindly disagree and have decided to keep it here because we see it as intimately related to, and a major deepening of, the description of human dignity we have just given. We introduce it at this point, therefore, and will return to it throughout our book, sometimes explicitly, sometimes implicitly, a relatively new science developed in the past sixty years. That new science is neuroscience, a branch of science that deals with the anatomy, physiology,

[60]*Familiaris Consortio*, no. 34 (hereafter *FC*); *AL*, no. 295.

biochemistry, and psychology of the human, bicameral brain and especially with its relation to learning and behavior. Neuroscience comes in various incarnations: neuroanatomy; neurophysiology; neuropsychology; and, perhaps most important for our purposes, neurocognitive science. Since it is intimately concerned with learning and behavior, it must be concerned with ethical learning and behavior, and therefore intimately related to theological ethics. Psychiatrist/neuroscientist Andrew Newberg writes of the interaction between neuroscience and theology in what he calls neurotheology, "a unique field of scholarship and investigation that seeks to understand the relationship specifically between the brain and theology, and more broadly between the mind and religion."[61] Echoing Pope John Paul II's call for an intense dialogue between science and theology, "a common interactive relationship," in which each discipline is "open to the discoveries and insights of the other" while still retaining its own integrity,[62] Newberg writes that "neurotheology should strive to foster dialogue between science and religion in order to better understand both perspectives."[63]

John Paul insists that the church values scientific research "when it proves helpful in understanding the historical context in which pastoral action has to be developed and when it leads to a better understanding of the truth."[64] We agree with the pope and suggest that neuroscience data on the bicameral brain is enormously helpful in leading to a deeper understanding of ourselves, our emotions, thoughts, dispositions, and possibilities for action in the world, and that, therefore, it should be of interest to theological ethicists. Ethicist Neil Messer advises that "theologians would be ill-advised to dismiss neuroscience as irrelevant to Christian ethics." If Christian ethics, he argues, "is concerned with what it means to live well as an embodied human creature before God, in company with others, in the physical world we inhabit," all elements of our description of human dignity, "it seems unwise simply to ignore areas of scientific inquiry that make claims about the conditions of such physically embodied moral lives."[65] We enter one caveat: in any interaction between neuroscience and theology, neuroscience must remain rigorously science and theology must remain rigorously theology with no "dumbing down" of either.

We offer four reasons why theological ethicists should pay attention to the data of neuroscience. First, every theological ethics, including the

---

[61] Andrew B. Newberg, *Principles of Neurotheology* (Burlington, VT: Ashgate, 2010), 1.

[62] John Paul II, "The Relationship of Science and Theology: A Letter to Jesuit Father George Coyne," *Origins* 18 (November 17, 1988): 377.

[63] Newberg, *Principles of Neurotheology*, 53.

[64] *FC*, no. 5.

[65] Neil Messer, *Theological Neuroethics: Christian Ethics Meets the Science of the Human Brain* (New York: Bloomsbury T. and T. Clark, 2017), 7–8.

virtue ethics we will propose, presupposes an understanding of the human person and of the working of the person's brain. Neuroscience in its various incarnations is now a major source of understanding how the human brain *really* works and, therefore, how the human person *really* thinks, judges, and acts. It is crucial, therefore, to the construction of a realistic theological and virtue ethics.

Second, in the early days of emotion research, it was assumed that emotion and cognition resulted from separate brain processes, and theological ethicists, accepting that assumption, have privileged reason over emotion. Contemporary neuroscience has now exploded that assumption and has shown "the overlap between circuitry involved in cognitive and affective [emotional] processing."[66] That overlap led neuroscientists to conclude that "emotion really amounted to cognition, in the definition of cognitive neuroscience, because emotion entailed information processing and transformation."[67] There is mounting evidence that emotion is "constitutive of, and not separate from, the reasoning and decision-making that people do about their own values and the preferences and values of others."[68] Emotion serves to guide, control, and even on occasion inhibit attention. The brain, Newberg writes, "places functional restrictions on all thought processes, and hence [on] how we experience religion, spirituality, and theology."[69] It is an essential element in every consideration of the ethical human person, placing restrictions on the understanding, judging, and deciding that is involved in every human choice of ethical action.

Third, the human self, we argue in this book, is essentially an interpersonal, relational self and the data of neurocognitive research show that persons with deficits in the right frontal lobe but not the left undergo a personality change that includes an incapacity for empathy,[70] "the ability spontaneously to reconstruct in oneself what another is feeling, thinking, and intending."[71] Pope Francis correctly insists that mercy, preceded necessarily by empathy, must always be pastorally active when judging moral situations.[72] Empathy, therefore, must also be active in theological ethicists when they seek to formulate principles and norms for the facilitation of human dignity.

---

[66]Richard J. Davidson, "Seven Sins in the Study of Emotion: Correctives from Affective Neuroscience," *Brain and Cognition* 52 (2003): 129.

[67]Michael L. Spezio, "The Neuroscience of Emotion and Reasoning in Social Contexts: Implications for Moral Theology," *Modern Theology* 27 (2011): 339–56, at 346.

[68]Ibid., 342.

[69]Newberg, *Principles of Neurotheology*, 84.

[70]Richard J. Perry et al., "Hemispheric Dominance for Emotions, Empathy, and Social Behavior: Evidence from Right and Left Handers with Frontotemporal Dementia," *Neurocase* 7 (2001): 145–60.

[71]Spezio, "The Neuroscience of Emotion," 351.

[72]*Evangelii Gaudium*, no. 44 (hereafter *EG*); *AL*, nos. 308–11.

Fourth, neurotheology fashions a theological method that opens the insights of one virtue ethicist to the insights of others, thereby eliminating the unnecessary, unhelpful, and sometimes downright un-Christian polarity that presently separates them.[73] For theological ethicists to ignore neuroscience and its data is to ignore a sure foundation in which to root their ethical theories. In a short Introduction we cannot possibly deal with neuroscience and its data in intimate detail, and we choose to deal only with phenomena we judge to be critical to any theological ethics: attention, emotion, free will, and experience.

It is now a demonstrated and universally accepted neuroscientific fact that the human brain is divided into two interconnected hemispheres. There is undoubted unity, one brain, but also division, two connected but functionally different hemispheres. Despite the popular generalization that the hemispheres perform exclusive, subject-specific, and different functions, that the left hemisphere deals exclusively with reason and language, for instance, and the right hemisphere deals exclusively with emotion and imagination, neuroscience has demonstrated that both hemispheres deal with the same realities, though in functionally different ways. Contemporary neuroscience is moving away from the idea that the brain is right or left globally dominated to the idea that "lateralization is a property of individual nodes or local subnetworks"[74] called hubs. There are nodes or hubs in both hemispheres for a particular function and these hubs are connected across neural pathways. Jared Nielson has demonstrated that "left- and right-lateralized networks are homogeneously stronger among a constellation of hubs in the left and right-hemispheres, but that such connections do not result in a subject-specific global brain lateralization difference that favors one network [or hub] over the other," though there clearly are left-dominated connections associated with language and perception of internal stimuli and right-dominated connections associated with attention to external stimuli.[75] The right-hemisphere hub underwrites breadth of attention; the left-hemisphere hub underwrites narrow, focused attention. This has the related consequence that the right hemisphere sees things whole and *in their context* and the left hemisphere sees things divided into parts and abstracted from their context and *re-presents* in concepts its own "divided whole," something different from the whole the right hemisphere sees.[76]

[73]At the November, 2016 Consistory creating new Cardinals, Pope Francis called polarity "a virus that compromises the universality of the Church."

[74]Jared A. Nielson et al., "An Evaluation of the Left-Brain vs. Right-Brain Hypothesis with Resting State Connectivity Magnetic Resonance Imaging," *PLoS One* 8, no. 8 (August 14, 2013).

[75]Ibid.

[76]Iain McGilchrist, *The Master and His Emissary: The Divided Brain and the Making of the Western World* (New Haven, CT: Yale University Press, 2009), 27–28.

A right parietal hub is involved in a holistic approach to things, and the left parietal hub is involved in more reductionist and analytic processes.[77]

In the 1980s, data derived from functional electroencephalogram studies (fEEG) showed that both hemispheres, the entire brain, were involved in every mental process, and scientists interpreted this data to mean that there were no substantive differences in function between the two hemispheres. More sophisticated research has shown this conclusion to be false. The right hemisphere, it has been shown, predominantly thinks in images and metaphors, includes empathy in its decision making, is where metaphorical and parable experience is attended to and interpreted, and is comfortable taking risks. The left brain, in contrast, predominantly "relies on self-reflective knowing, is language-dependent and logical, removes experience from its context by constructing abstract, static *re-presentations* of data, controls its environment with power derived from knowledge comprehended through practical, strategic, efficient, sequenced planning."[78] Despite these functional differences, we emphasize, both hemispheres are active in every brain activity, and both are always engaged. If we say, therefore, the right hemisphere does this and the left hemisphere does that, it is to be understood as a statement of predominance, that a hemisphere hub is *predominantly*, not exclusively, active in the function involved.

The issue of attention, "the selective prioritization of the neural representations that are most relevant to one's current behavioral goals,"[79] is an important issue in both science and theology. Prioritization is necessary, for despite its billions of neurons, the human brain is a limited information system and external and internal stimuli compete for its limited resources. Attention resolves that competition in favor of the data that is most relevant to the task and goal at hand. It is also, as we shall see in a moment, an essential element of free will and choice. The one brain, attending to reality in two different functional ways, orients knowledge of two different "worlds." One is "the live, complex, embodied, world of individual, always-unique beings, forever in flux, a net of interdependencies, forming and reforming wholes, a world with which we are deeply connected." The other is a world we experience in a *re-presented* version that is "static, separable, bounded, but essentially fragmented entities."[80] The former is the world attended to and perceived by the right hemisphere; the latter is the world attended

[77]Newberg, *Principles of Neurotheology*, 77.

[78]Brian Curtis, "Rebalancing the Bicameral Brain: A Return to Art for Life's Sake." Paper delivered at the SECAC Conference, Greensboro, NC, October 31, 2013, www.brian-curtis.com/text/confer-pape_bicameral.html, emphasis added.

[79]Timothy J. Buschman and Sabine Kastner, "From Behavior to Neural Dynamics: An Integrated Theory of Attention," *Neuron* 88 (2015): 127.

[80]McGilchrist, *The Master and His Emissary*, 31, emphasis added.

to and perceived by the left hemisphere. The latter is presumed to yield knowledge, and since knowledge enables us to control reality, including *verbal* theological reality, also power. Something important to remember here is that an integral part of any scholarly discipline is the assumptions scholars bring to their investigations and conclusions. "Assumptions are highly dependent on language, emotion, and social interaction,"[81] and it is important for both scientists and theological ethicists to identify not only the assumptions of others, which they readily seek to do, but also their own, which they do not so readily seek to do. This identification is a complex and highly emotional process, which takes time, patience, and a commitment to the kind of constructive, honest, and charitable dialogue that Pope Francis so appreciated at the 2014 Synod on Marriage and the Family and characterized as "a spirit of collegiality and synodality."[82]

Early neuropsychological literature distinguished several types of attention, two of which are important for our purposes here, sustained attention and focused attention,[83] and the research showed some broad, consistent differences in hemispheric-hub dominance. Experimental data indicated that sustained attention is predominantly right-hemisphere–hub reliant, and focused attention is predominantly left-hemisphere–hub reliant, but remember that it is a question of predominance and that the lateral hubs are connected. Scanning studies clearly indicate that focused attention is reliant on a hub in the left frontal cortex[84] and that left-hemisphere lesions lead to deficits in focused attention.[85] Selective attention, what I choose to attend to, is also reliant on the left hemisphere,[86] and obviously what I selectively choose to attend to will always be at work in any human, contextual situation and the ethical choices for it. There is also evidence of right-hemisphere–hub predominance for broad, global attention.[87] Since

---

[81]Newberg, *Principles of Neurotheology*, 78.

[82]Speech at the conclusion of the 2014 Synod on Marriage and the Family, en.radiovaticana.va. The English word *synod* derives from two Greek words, *sun* meaning together and *hodos* meaning journeying. It means, therefore, journeying together.

[83]Adriaan H. van Zomeren and Wiebo H. Brouwer, *Clinical Neuropsychology of Attention* (Oxford: Oxford University Press, 1994).

[84]Maurizio Corbetta et al., "Selective and Divided Attention during Visual Discriminations of Shape, Color, and Speed: Functional Anatomy by Positron Emission Tomography," *Journal of Neuroscience* 11 (1991): 2383–402.

[85]Walter Sturm and André Büssing, "Einfluss der Aufgabenklomplexität auf hirnorganische Reaktionsbeeinträchtigungen—Hirnshädigungs oder Patienteneffkt?," *European Archives of Psychiatry and Neurological Sciences* 235 (1986): 214–20.

[86]Olivier Godefroy and Marc Rousseaux, "Divided and Focused Attention in Patients with Lesions of the Prefrontal Cortex," *Brain and Cognition* 30 (1996): 155–74; Marc Rousseau et al., "Analyse et évolution des deficits cognitifs après rupture des anéurysmes de l'artère communicante antérieure," *Revue Neurologique* 152 (1996): 678–87.

[87]Richard B. Ivry and Lynn C. Robertson, *The Two Sides of Perception* (Cambridge, MA: MIT Press, 1998); Lynn C. Robertson et al., "Effects of Lesions of Temporal-parietal Junction on Perception and

many brain areas may be active simultaneously and sometimes conflictually, any conflict will need to be resolved "to maintain a coherent direction of behavior." They are resolved by what is called *executive attention*, which has been associated with the anterior cingulate and prefrontal cortex areas of the brain.[88] In functional imaging studies, the anterior cingulate cortex has been shown also to modulate sensory input. It is not difficult to imagine executive attention at work in the process of discernment involved in making a practical judgment of conscience in a situation.

We raise here a question that is centrally important in both social neuroscience and theology, the question of the connection of cognitive and emotional brain activation. In the early days of emotion or affect research, it was assumed that emotion and cognition resulted from separate brain processes, an assumption Richard Davidson, drawing on contemporary studies, dubs the first sin in the study of emotion. Davidson's correction emphasizes the more recent hypothesis of "the overlap between circuitry involved in cognitive and affective [emotional] processing,"[89] a view that demonstrates that "emotion really amounted to cognition, in the definition of cognitive neuroscience, because emotion entailed information processing and transformation."[90] There is mounting evidence that emotion is "constitutive of, and not separate from, the reasoning and decision-making that people do about their own values and the preferences and values of others."[91] As noted earlier, emotion serves to guide, control, and even on occasion inhibits attention. This insight has profound implications for how emotion impacts virtue, which we investigate in Chapter 2. Recall Newberg's judgment: the brain "places functional restrictions on all thought processes, and hence [on] how we experience religion, spirituality, and theology."[92]

The age-old question of free will, so crucial in judging ethical responsibility, arises at this point. Free will implies the human ability to choose one thing rather than another, and is the *sine qua non* of ethical decision making. Without free will, we would not have the ability to freely choose our actions and would consequently have no ethical responsibility for them. Our actions would be determined and we would never be culpable or, as in the Judeo–Christian tradition, guilty of sin. Neuroscience raises new and serious questions about free will. Many brain studies show an association between volitional processes and increased energy in the brain's frontal

Attentional Processing in Humans," *Journal of Neuroscience* 8 (1988): 3757–69.

[88]Michael I. Posner, *Attention in a Social World* (New York: Oxford University Press, 2012), 19–21, and the other researchers cited there.

[89]Richard J. Davidson, "Seven Sins in the Study of Emotion: Correctives from Affective Neuroscience," *Brain and Cognition* 52 (2003): 129.

[90]Spezio, "The Neuroscience of Emotion and Reasoning," 346.

[91]Ibid., 342.

[92]Newberg, *Principles of Neurotheology*, 84.

lobes. "Right here," researcher Jeffrey Schwartz asserts, "you can say while pointing to the bright spots on the PET scan, volition originates."[93] The critical question, of course, is which comes first, the increased frontal lobe energy that causes free will or the act of will that causes the frontal lobe activity. If the brain energy comes first, then it can be argued that our actions are determined by our brains; if the act of will comes first, then we exercise free will. As a result of his extensive experiments with obsessive compulsive disorder (OCD) patients, whom he found can be trained to choose and to have thoughts other than their obsessive ones, Schwartz argues that humans do have free will and are responsible for their actions. He explains his choice by arguing for what he calls mental force, "a physical force generated by mental effort," which is "the physical expression of will . . . [and] . . . physically efficacious."[94] Mental force enables humans to make a free choice of this action or that. There is no determinism.

Schwartz traces the cause of this mental force to the outcome of what is called, in neurocognitive science, effortful attention. He marvels that at the end of the nineteenth century, without any of the modern neuroscientific research tools, psychologist William James had already reached the same conclusion. "Effort of attention," James wrote, "is thus the essential phenomenon of will." Schwartz responds that "The causal efficacy of will is a higher-level manifestation of the causal efficacy of attention. To focus attention on one idea, on one possible course of action among the many bubbling up inchoate in our consciousness, is precisely what we mean by volition."[95] Volition acts through attention that focuses on and makes predominant one thought or one action out of the many that are possible. Attention, however, is only the first part of what "will" means. There is a second part, James argued and Schwartz has shown to be true, namely, consent to the reality that is attended to. Schwartz found in his experiments that "for the stroke victim, the OCD patient, and the depressive, intense effort is required to bring about the requisite refocusing of attention—a refocusing that will, in turn, sculpt anew the ever-changing brain."[96] This is true also, we suggest, for the person pondering an ethical choice. It is his/her effortful attention that generates the mental force that will produces lasting changes in his/her plastic brain. Effortful *attention* leads to efficacious *intention*.

The brain is a physical organ open to being changed, and it can be trained to focus attention on one thing rather than on another. It is not the brain, however, that has free will but the person whose brain it is and whose

---

[93]Jeffrey M. Schwartz and Sharon Begley, *The Mind and the Brain: Neuroplasticity and the Power of Mental Force* (New York: Harper, 2002), 294.

[94]Ibid., 295.

[95]Ibid., 324–25.

[96]Ibid., 360.

mental force prescribes and achieves the necessary focused attention and intention. Michael Gazzaniga pursues this line of argument in his explanation of free will. Brains are physical realities built up of genes, and we do not and cannot speak of physical realities being free. "People are free and therefore responsible for their actions; brains are not responsible."[97] Neurocognitive scientist Philippe Rochat notes an important human social propensity. "Humans have a propensity toward social actions that might be unique among other animals. Our social life revolves round the perception of shared intention leading to unique collaboration, cooperation, and helpful behaviors."[98] People with plastic brains live in relationship with other people with plastic brains, and in the cultural experience of living together and producing rules for living together, of learning to pay attention to those rules, and of intending to follow them in the appropriate contexts, people, not brains, become personally responsible. Humans "are the result of the most complex collaborative project in history, whose two equal partners are our biology and the human culture we are immersed in."[99] We will see when we deal with virtue ethics that the human experience of exemplary role models is important in the learning of virtuous habits;[100] plastic brains can be trained in the virtues of personal and social responsibility.[101]

The foregoing suggests several important conclusions for theologians. What is new is present first to the global and sustained attention of a right-hemisphere hub before it can be present to the narrow, focused attention of a left-hemisphere hub. New experience triggers a release of noradrenaline, predominantly in the right hemisphere,[102] and induces change in the right hippocampus but not in the left.[103] Not just new experience but also new information, new analysis, and new skills engage the attention of the right hemisphere more than that of the left,[104] even if the new information is

---

[97]Michael Gazzaniga, *The Ethical Brain* (New York: Dana Press, 2005), 89.

[98]Philippe Rochat, "Self-Consciousness and the Origin of an Ethical Stance," in Rastogi Kar, *Cognition and Brain Development* (Washington, DC: American Psychological Association, 2013), 157; Michael Tomasello, *Origins of Human Communication* (Cambridge, MA: MIT Press, 2008).

[99]Steven Quartz and Terrence Sejnowski, *Liars, Lovers, and Heroes: What the New Brain Science Reveals about How We Become Who We Are* (New York: Harper Collins, 2002), 31.

[100]For the general relationship of human experience and theological ethics, see Michael G. Lawler and Todd A. Salzman, "Human Experience and Moral Theology," *Irish Theological Quarterly* 76 (2011): 35–56.

[101]See Gazzaniga's account of the effect of training the brain in *The Ethical Brain*, 55–70

[102]Elkhonon Goldberg, *The Executive Brain: Frontal Lobes and the Civilized Mind* (Oxford: Oxford University Press, 2001); Gerald Edelman and Giulio Tononi, *A Universe of Consciousness: How Matter Becomes Imagination* (New York: Basic Books, 2000).

[103]Akaysia C. Tang, "A Hippocampal Theory of Cerebral Lateralization," in *The Asymmetrical Brain*, ed. Kenneth Hugdahl and Richard J. Davidson (Cambridge, MA: MIT Press, 2003), 37–68.

[104]Roger W. Sperry, "Consciousness, Personal Identity, and the Divided Brain," in *The Dual Brain: Hemisphere Specialization in Humans*, ed. D. Frank Benson and Eran Zaidell (New York: Guilford Press, 1985), 11–26; Howard Gardner, *The Shattered Mind* (New York: Knopf, 1974).

verbal, in which area the left hemisphere is predominant.[105] There is no scientific doubt that the apprehension[106] of anything new occurs first in the right hemisphere,[107] and that then, once the new has become familiar, it becomes the concern also of the left-hemisphere interpreter.[108] The right hemisphere alone, therefore, can bring us something new, something that we do not already know, some new theological method, fact, or hermeneutic, for instance; the left hemisphere deals with and interprets what it knows and prefers what it knows.[109] This makes it more efficient than the right hemisphere, in situations when knowledge is routine, but less efficient when knowledge might have to be revised, as in any developing field of knowledge like theology.[110] Twenty years ago Vilayanur Ramachandran demonstrated a tendency for the left hemisphere to deny discrepancies that do not fit its accepted scheme of things, even to accept absurdities like the assertions that the practice of slavery is perfectly ethical and that any claim of religious freedom is perfectly unreasonable and therefore unethical; the right hemisphere, in contrast, in its alerting role, is actively alert for discrepancies.[111] It will be alert also, of course, for any new theological information, and there is a neuroscientific message here for Catholic traditionalists.

It is neuroscientifically clear that, notwithstanding the overlap between emotional and cognitional brain circuitries, emotional understanding occurs strongly in a right-hemisphere hub;[112] the left hemisphere is not as concerned about others and their feelings. Neuropsychologist Larry Schutz demon-

---

[105]Debra L. Mills et al., "Language Acquisition and Cerebral Specialization in 20-Month-Old Infants," *Journal of Cognitive Neuroscience* 5 (1993): 317–34; Donna J. Thal et al., "Early Lexical Development in Children with Focal Brain Injury," *Brain and Language* 40 (1991): 491–527.

[106]Our students are always tempted to misunderstand this word, reading it in its common dictionary meaning of fear or dread rather than in its standard cognitive meaning, namely, taking something in to the cognitive process.

[107]The evidence here is vast. We cite only two sources: Goldberg, *The Executive Brain*; Elkhonon Goldberg et al., "Lateralization of Frontal Lobe Functions and Cognitive Novelty," *Journal of Neuropsychiatry and Clinical Neurosciences* 6 (1994): 371–78.

[108]See Goldberg, *The Executive Brain* and Gazzaniga, *The Ethical Brain*, 148–51.

[109]Kenneth Podell et al., "The Cognitive Bias Task and Lateralized Frontal Lobe Functions in Males," *Journal of Neuropsychiatry and Clinical Neurosciences* 7 (1995): 491–501; Elizabeth A. Phelps and Michael S. Gazzaniga, "Hemispheric Differences in Mnemonic Processing: The Effects of Left Hemisphere Interpretation," *Neuropsychologia* 30 (1992): 293–97.

[110]Raymond Molloy et al., "Discourse Comprehension by Right-Hemisphere Stroke Patients: Deficits of Prediction and Revision," in *Discourse Ability and Brain Damage: Theoretical and Empirical Perspectives*, ed. Yves Joanette and Hiram H. Brownell (New York: Springer-Verlag, 1990), 113–30; Hiram H. Brownell et al., "Inference Deficits in Right Brain-damaged Patients," *Brain and Language* 27 (1986): 310–21.

[111]Vilayanur S. Ramachandran, "Phantom Limbs, Neglect Syndromes, Repressed Memories, and Freudian Psychology," *International Review of Neurobiology* 37 (1994): 291–333; see also Vilayanur S. Ramachandran and Diane Rogers-Ramachandran, "Denial of Disabilities in Anosognosia," *Nature* 382 (1996): 501.

[112]Georg W. Alpers, "Eye-catching: Right-hemisphere Attentional Bias for Emotional Pictures," *Laterality* 13 (2008): 158–78.

strated that, absent the right hemisphere, "social intercourse is conducted with a blanket disregard for the feelings, wishes, needs, and expectations of others."[113] Recall that persons with deficits in the right frontal lobe but not the left undergo a personality change, which includes an incapacity for empathy,[114] and that Pope Francis insists that mercy, which is preceded by empathy, must always be pastorally active when judging ethical situations.[115] The virtues of empathy and mercy, therefore, must be active also in theological ethicists. If emotions rely more strongly on the right hemisphere, explicit, logical reasoning relies more strongly on the left hemisphere, though the less explicit reasoning that is involved in science and theology is a right-hemisphere activity. The noted French physicist, Henri Poincaré, judged that the subliminal right-hemisphere self is in no way inferior to the conscious left-hemisphere self. It is capable of discernment, and knows how to intuit and choose.[116] Poincaré wrote at the beginning of the twentieth century, but there is now an extensive body of research showing that insight and problem solving is associated with activation in the right anterior temporal area.[117]

Another misinformed stereotype is the exclusive association of the left hemisphere and language; the left hemisphere, it is believed, is where language is exclusively at home. Again, the stereotype is wrong. The left hemisphere is more strongly associated with language, but the right hemisphere has associations with it, too, just not as strong associations. An alerting right-hemisphere hub first makes external realities present in their contextual wholeness and then transmits this whole image to a left-hemisphere hub, which divides it into parts, *re-presents* those parts in abstract concepts that it names, and then deals with the named abstractions as explicit "things" it can control and manipulate. Newberg delivers a chilling judgment on this process. "We are trapped within our brain peering out into the world and reconstructing it as best we can [including theologically]. We inherently experience a 'second-hand' rendition of the world."[118] The right hemisphere's language strength is in understanding meaning as a whole and in context. It is with the right hemisphere that we understand the meaning of a story or

---

[113]Larry E. Schutz, "Broad-perspective Perceptual Disorder of the Right-hemisphere," *Neuropsychology Review* 15 (2005): 11–27.

[114]Richard J. Perry et al., "Hemispheric Dominance for Emotions, Empathy, and Social Behavior: Evidence from Right and Left Handers with Frontotemporal Dementia," *Neurocase* 7 (2001): 145–60.

[115]*EG*, no. 44; *AL*, nos. 308–11.

[116]Brewster Ghiselin, ed., *The Creative Process* (Berkeley: University of California Press, 1992), 28.

[117]John Kounios et al., "The Origins of Insight in Resting-state Brain Activity," *Neuropsychologia* 46 (2008): 281–91; Simone Sandkühler and Joydeep Bhattacharya, "Deconstructing Insight: EEG Correlates of Insightful Problem Solving," *PLoS One* 3 (January 23, 2008): 1459.

[118]Newberg, *Principles of Neurotheology*, 252.

a biblical parable,[119] or of any nonliteral meaning,[120] including analogical and metaphorical theological language.[121] Patients with right-hemisphere damage have trouble understanding metaphor, which underlies all forms of understanding in theology, philosophy, and science.[122] Most of our theological expressions, indeed almost all our language expressions, are analogical and metaphorical, and they are grasped predominantly in the right hemisphere. One final hemispheric fact is of the greatest importance for theological ethicists: besides the virtue of empathy, the virtues of justice and mercy are also predominantly reliant on the right hemisphere.[123] The two hemispheres, however, we insist, are in continuing, overlapping dialogue, and it is as a result of this dialogue that humans come to know and understand. There is a natural dialogical lesson here, we suggest, for theological ethicists of different methodological persuasions and consequently different ethical conclusions.

OUR THESIS GOING FORWARD

The Second Vatican Council's *Gaudium et Spes* reflects a fundamental shift in method for doing theological ethics. The method evolved from a focus on law, acts, and biology to a focus on persons, relationships, and the meaning and value of acts for persons and their relationships. With the revival of virtue ethics, method has evolved again to include the virtues as an essential dimension of persons and a focal point to adequately consider the meaning and value of acts for persons and relationships. The tradition of Catholic theological ethics is a gradually evolving not a static tradition and, as a gradually evolving tradition, there is never a clear break with the past that informs and shapes the present, and this fact has both positive and negative implications. The positive implications are that there is demonstrated continuity in the natural law tradition stemming from Plato, Aristotle, the Stoics, and Aquinas to the contemporary versions of natural law we will consider in Chapter 1. The negative implications are that some

---

[119]Paolo Nichelli et al., "Where the Brain Appreciates the Moral of a Story," *NeuroReport* 6 (1995): 2309–13.

[120]Simone G. Shamay-Tsoory et al., "Impaired 'Affective Theory of Mind' Is Associated with Right Ventromedial Prefrontal Damage," *Cognitive and Behavioral Neurology* 18 (2005): 324–37.

[121]See David Tracy, *The Analogical Imagination: Christian Theology and the Culture of Pluralism* (New York: Crossroad, 1981).

[122]David Anaki et al., (1) "Cerebral Hemisphere Asymmetries in Processing Lexical Metaphors," *Neuropsychologia* 36, no. 4 (1998): 353–62; David Anaki et al., (2) "Cerebral Hemisphere Asymmetries in Processing Lexical Metaphors," *Neuropsychologia* 36, no. 7 (1998): 691–700.

[123]Daria Knoch et al., "Diminishing Reciprocal Fairness by Disrupting the Right Frontal Cortex," *Science* 314 (2006): 829–32.

distorted perceptions of natural law, for example, the focus on acts and bad biology, can continue to influence contemporary versions of natural law in method, anthropology, and normative content. The positive and negative implications will be demonstrated throughout this book.

One of the facts about Catholic theological ethics is that there are methodological divisions among Catholic theological ethicists. Dialoguing about these divisions and proposing a method grounded in virtue to resolve them is, we believe, a productive venture to move the church forward from polarized and intractable normative ethical debates. The Catholic tradition, as Pope Francis has recently noted, is that there is always *more* to be understood about God, God's will, and God's words, always yet another interpretation to be offered of them, and that the church and her theologians must always refer back to Vatican II to proclaim "the Gospel in a new way."[124] This is precisely why religious believers and their theologians must eschew mutual condemnations and embrace the way of dialogue in charity marked out by Popes Francis and John Paul II. This dialogue is not to be confused with debate in which participants *defend* their versions of Christian truth and try to convert their opponents to their opinion. Dialogue, rather, in the words of John Paul II, is a mutual seeking after truth "in a manner proper to the dignity of the human person" in which participants *explain* "to one another the truth they have discovered, or think they have discovered, in order thus to assist one another in the quest for truth."[125] Pope Francis advises the participants in any dialogue to "keep an open mind. Don't get bogged down in your own limited ideas and opinions, but be prepared to change or expand them." He sees no problem in plural partial truths for, he judges, "the combination of two different ways of thinking can lead to a synthesis that enriches both." The unity we seek, he adds, "is not uniformity, but a unity in diversity."[126]

A long-standing Catholic tradition argues that every human agent's free, informed, discerned judgment of conscience is the ultimate and inviolable authority of every ethical judgment, decision, and act. The theological ethicist's free, informed, discerned judgment of conscience, grounded in a virtuous perspective, is the ultimate foundation of his/her methodological, anthropological, and normative ethical claims to truth. The truth of those claims and their impact on Catholic doctrinal teaching and pastoral application must be determined by the communal conscience of the whole communion church. This is a gradual process that takes time, virtue, prayerful

[124]Pope Francis, "Audience with Members of the Italian Theological Association, 29.12.2017," *Holy See Press Office*.

[125]*Ut Unum Sint*, no. 18 (hereafter *UUS*).

[126]*AL*, no. 139.

discernment, and commitment to the "dialogue of charity" initially recommended by Pope John Paul II[127] and recently reiterated by Pope Francis.[128] Our intention in this book is that we provide a methodological–ethical roadmap, grounded in a virtuous perspective, that moves the church forward in its ongoing discernment of ethical truth and that, like Pope Francis in *Amoris Laetitia*, changes the primary focus in Catholic theological ethics from a law-based, act-centered ethics of doing to a virtue-based, person-centered ethics of being.

[127]*UUS*, nos. 17, 51, 60.
[128]*AL*, no. 305.

1

Catholic Ethical Method

An Overview

James Keenan has highlighted the importance of ethical method for Catholic theological ethics in the twenty-first century.[1] We agree with his judgment, adding only the importance of making one's ethical method transparent. Also, the International Theological Commission recognizes a "plurality of theologies,"[2] and specifies a plurality of perspectives, principles, and methodological criteria, for doing theology.[3] There is also a consistent call from the community of Catholic theological ethicists for an ongoing "faithful reconstruction"[4] of moral theology and its transformation into a holistic "theological ethics."[5] All this suggests a need for reflection on the method of such a reconstructed ethics. Method is a fundamental variable in Catholic theological ethics and different virtuous perspectives shape the different methods that are at the root of many anthropological, ethical, and normative differences dividing Catholic ethicists. It is imperative, then, to investigate Catholic ethical method, and in this chapter we do so with two specific purposes: first, to elucidate our own method and, second, to issue an invitation to all Catholic theological ethicists to Pope John Paul II's

[1] James F. Keenan, "Note: Vatican II and Theological Ethics," *Theological Studies* 74 (2013): 162–90.

[2] International Theological Commission, *Theology Today*, 5 (2012), www.vatican.va.

[3] This pluralism extends to the application of principles and is reflected in the USCCB's document *The Challenge of Peace* (Washington, DC: USCCB, 1983), i: "the pastoral letter makes specific applications, observations and recommendations which allow for diversity of opinion on the part of those who assess the factual data of a situation differently."

[4] Bryan Massingale, "Beyond Revisionism: A Younger Moralist Looks at Charles E. Curran," in *A Call to Fidelity: On the Ethical Theology of Charles E. Curran*, ed. James J. Walter et al. (Washington, DC: Georgetown University Press, 2002), 253–72, at 267.

[5] Norbert Rigali, "On Presuppositions of Theological Ethics," *Horizons* 38, no. 2 (2011): 211–29, at 211–12.

dialogue in charity.[6] Such dialogue is mandated, we believe, by faithfulness to the biblical injunction not to "quench the Spirit" (1 Thes 5:19), by the present unhelpful divisions among Catholic ethicists and by the need to clarify different but legitimate Catholic ethical methods.

There are plural Catholic ethical methods, but for the sake of focus and clarity we isolate here the two major ones, which we will call *conservative* and *progressive.* We choose *conservative* for the first group because they seek to conserve and protect Catholic tradition as interpreted by the Magisterium. They give priority to tradition among the four sources of Catholic moral knowledge, which we will address in Chapter 3, namely, scripture, tradition, science, and experience. We choose *progressive* for the second group because, forewarned by notorious errors in Catholic teaching in the past, they accept tradition as a source but not uncritically. They employ a dialectic among the four sources of moral knowledge to uncover the truth attuned to present reality that can then progress into the future as the best account of truth presently achieved. We have already outlined our method in the Introduction and in this chapter we enlarge on that outline. Our method is historically conscious, open to the Catholic theological ethical tradition; follows natural law contemporarily reinterpreted; is based on and seeks to facilitate human and sexual dignity; is rooted in the human person rather than in his/her acts; is articulated from a Christian perspective; accepts the four moral sources articulated in the Wesleyan Quadrilateral; is inductive rather than deductive; is virtue ethical; and accepts the authority and inviolability of a properly informed conscience. Our method aligns with a progressive method, following the direction mapped out by Bernard Lonergan: it is "a normative pattern of recurrent and related operations yielding cumulative and progressive results."[7]

As noted in the introduction, the operations alluded to occur on four levels and are themselves fourfold. On the empirical level, we experience and pay attention to our experience; on the intellectual level, we seek to understand that experience instructed by scripture, tradition, and science; on the rational level, we judge our experience for its truth; and on the responsible level, we decide to act on our judgment. To construct an ethical normative pattern, ethical method must account for both epistemic claims about how we know ethical truth and normative claims about the content of that truth. We begin by offering an expanded definition of method: *Catholic ethical method is a normative pattern of recurrent and related theological operations that proposes an epistemology for reaching ethical truth, and*

[6] *Ut Unum Sint*, no. 17.

[7] Bernard J. F. Lonergan, *Method in Theology* (Toronto: University of Toronto Press, 2003), 4.

seeks both a definition of human dignity and the formulation and justification of moral norms for its flourishing.

RELATIVISM OR PERSPECTIVISM?

We explore and address at the outset the charge of ethical relativism leveled by the Catholic Magisterium against Catholic ethicists whose ethical method leads to normative conclusions different from those of the Magisterium and, drawing from Bernard Lonergan, we propose perspectivism as an epistemological tool that accounts for the plurality of Catholic ethical methods while maintaining an objectivist metaethic. Cardinal Ratzinger, in his homily at the opening of the 2005 papal conclave, spoke of the "dictatorship of relativism," which *"does not recognize anything as definitive and whose ultimate standard consists solely of one's own ego and desires."*[8] In this chapter, we are specifically concerned with ethical relativism, which denies the existence of universal, objective ethical truth. Such objective truth is necessary, the Magisterium argues, as the foundation for absolute norms, which assert that certain acts—murderous, contraceptive, and homosexual acts, for example—are intrinsically evil and can never be morally justified regardless of intention, context, or circumstance. Concern about relativism is warranted in the twenty-first century. It is critical, however, to discern the difference between *relativism*, which rejects all objective ethical truth, and *perspectivism*, which acknowledges objective ethical truth but argues that, since it is truth from a specific perspective, as is our approach in this book, it is always partial truth. Legitimate theological pluralism, which the International Theological Commission's document *Theology Today* advances as an essential criterion of Catholic theology, derives from different perspectives or lenses. We consider relativism and perspectivism in turn.

Relativism

We begin by defining relativism both negatively and positively. Relativism is defined negatively in contrast to other philosophical positions: it denies universalism, the position that there can and ought to be universal agreement on matters of truth and goodness; it denies objectivism, the position that truth and goodness are independent of both individual and communal human judgment; it denies absolutism, the position that truth and

---

[8]Joseph Ratzinger, "Cappella Papale Mass 'Pro Eligendo Romano Pontifice' Homily of His Eminence Card. Joseph Ratzinger of the College of Cardinals," www.vatican.va.

goodness are timeless and immutable; and it denies monism, the position that there is only one correct judgment about truth and goodness. Relativism is defined positively by its claim that truth and goodness and the proposition "X is true" depend not only on the objects to which the ascriptions are being made but also on the humans who are making them.[9] As the thinker who is regarded as the father of relativism, the Greek philosopher Protagoras, famously said, "man is the measure of all things."[10]

In 2002, Barna Research Group conducted two national American surveys, one among adults and one among teenagers, which asked participants if they believed that there are unchanging moral absolutes or that moral truth is relative to contextual circumstances. In the adult group, 64 percent responded that truth is always relative to the person and his/her situation; in the teenage group, 83 percent responded that truth is always relative to the person and situation, and a mere 6 percent responded that moral truth is absolute.[11] Though we have not conducted any controlled scientific study to uncover data, the Barna data reflect our experience with students; relativism is now as common in the classroom as laptops and cellphones. Relativism is not a new doctrine in the world; it has been around a long time. So much so that philosophical ethicist Alasdair MacIntyre concludes that relativism "is one of those doctrines that have by now been refuted a number of times too often. Nothing is perhaps a surer sign that a doctrine embodies some not-to-be-neglected truth than that in the course of the history of philosophy it should have been refuted again and again." He goes on to make the defensible assertion that "genuinely refutable doctrines need to be refuted once."[12]

In modern times, ethical relativism has been the subject of much Catholic concern. Pope Pius XII condemned "situation ethics" as a form of relativism that denies universal ethical truth.[13] Pope Paul VI warned of ethical relativism that claims that "some things are permitted which the Church had previously declared intrinsically evil," and that this vision "endangers the Church's entire doctrinal heritage."[14] Pope John Paul II warned of the

[9]See Maria Baghramian, *Relativism* (London: Routledge, 2004), 2–3.

[10]We have little direct knowledge of Protagoras since there remain only fragments of his writing; we know him only indirectly through Plato and Aristotle, both of whom are antirelativists.

[11]Barna Research, "Americans Are Most Likely to Base Truth on Feelings" (2002), www.barna.com.

[12]Alasdair MacIntyre, "Relativism, Power, and Philosophy," *Proceedings and Addresses of the American Philosophical Association* 59 (1985): 5–22, at 22.

[13]See Pius XII, "Allocution to the Fédération mondiale des jeunesses féminines Catholiques," *Acta Apostolicae Sedis* 34 (January 18, 1952): 413–19 (hereafter AAS); Radio Message about the Christian conscience, AAS 34 (1952): 270–78; and Instruction of the Holy Office, February 2, 1956, in *Enchiridion Symbolarum Definitionum et Declarationum de Rebus Fidei et Morus*, 33rd ed., ed. Heinrich Denzinger and Adolf Schönmetzer (Rome: Herder, 1965), 3918.

[14]Paul VI, "'Address' to Members of the Congregation of the Most Holy Redeemer," *AAS* 59 (1967): 962.

dangers of relativism that detaches human freedom from any objective foundation and proposes certain methods "for discovering the moral norm" that rejects absolute and immutable norms and precepts taught by the Magisterium. Some Catholic ethicists complain that in his encyclical *Veritatis Splendor* John Paul accused them, falsely, of "canonizing relativism."[15] In a 1993 speech to the presidents of the Asian Bishops' conferences[16] and again in a 1996 speech to the presidents of the doctrinal commissions of the Bishops' conferences of Latin America,[17] Cardinal Ratzinger warned of the dangers of a relativism that denies the existence of objective truth, calling it "the gravest problem of our time."[18] This concern with relativism and its impact on morality continued to be a central concern of his pontificate as Benedict XVI. We agree with the popes that relativism is a concern in the twenty-first century but not with their failure to distinguish between relativism and legitimate theological disagreement on objectivist claims to ethical truth. They mistakenly conflate, we suggest, legitimate doctrinal pluralism and relativism. Philosophical ethics can aid in discernment here.

The Second Vatican Council's *Decree on Priestly Formation,*[19] and more recently the International Theological Commission's *Theology Today*,[20] highlight the essential importance of philosophy for doing theology. Philosophical ethical theory distinguishes three levels of ethical discourse, namely, moral judgments, normative ethics, and metaethics.[21] These distinctions shed light on understanding whether a claim that a particular ethical position is an expression of relativism is accurate. As subjects endowed with reason and the ability to choose freely, humans make moral judgments on the basis of what they judge is right or good. This is the realm of daily moral decision making. When asked, for instance, "Where have you been?" and I reply, "I have been at the gym," my reply is truthful and moral if I have, indeed, been at the gym. Such truthfulness is required not only as fulfillment of the commandment, "Thou shalt not bear false witness" but also because the social good of living together in society would be impossible without it. These daily moral decisions serve as the source for both normative eth-

[15]Maura Anne Ryan, "'Then Who Can Be Saved?': Ethics and Ecclesiology in *Veritatis Splendor*," in *Veritatis Splendor: American Responses*, ed. Michael E. Allsopp and John J. O'Keefe (Kansas City, MO: Sheed and Ward, 1995), 1–15, at 11.

[16]Cardinal Joseph Ratzinger, "Christ, Faith and the Challenge of Cultures," www.ewtn.com/library/CURIA/RATZHONG.HTM.

[17]Cardinal Joseph Ratzinger, "Relativism: The Central Problem for the Faith Today," www.ewtn.com/library/CURIA/RATZRELA.HTM.

[18]Ratzinger, "Christ, Faith and the Challenge of Cultures."

[19]*Optatum Totius*, no. 15.

[20]*Theology Today*, 64–66.

[21]See Henry J. McCloskey, *Meta-Ethics and Normative Ethics* (The Hague: Martinus Nijhoff, 1969), 7; John D. Arras et al., "Ethical Reasoning in the Medical Context," in *Ethical Issues in Modern Medicine*, 5th ed., ed. John D. Arras and Bonnie Steinbock (London: Mayfield, 1999), 1–40.

ics and metaethics. It is the obligation in conscience of all rational human beings to make moral judgments in light of what they judge is good or bad, right or wrong. It is the task of theological ethicists to critically reflect upon, analyze, and develop these moral judgments into a systematic normative ethics and metaethics. Normative ethics formulates and justifies norms that prescribe right actions and good intentions and proscribe wrong actions and bad intentions. Metaethics, which literally means beyond (normative) ethics, is the foundation of all normative ethics and daily moral action. It asks two foundational questions. First, do ethical terms like *good* and *right* have any meaning; second, if they do have meaning, how is that meaning justified?

Modern metaethical inquiry emerged in the early part of the twentieth century with G. E. Moore's seminal work, *Principia Ethica*,[22] and since then various metaethical theories on the meaning of ethical terms have been developed. Nihilism claims that ethical knowledge and truths do not exist and that, therefore, ethics is a meaningless discipline.[23] Emotivism asserts that ethical terms are defined by individual emotions and desires; for emotivism, there is no objective truth since emotions are relative to each individual.[24] Relativism claims there are no objective truths; ethical truths are defined either socially or personally. Social or cultural relativism claims that moral judgments are nothing more than descriptions of customs or practices of a society or culture.[25] Personal relativism or subjectivism claims that moral judgments are nothing more than judgments about one's personal emotions.[26] This latter is the type of relativism castigated in Cardinal Ratzinger's claim that relativism's ultimate goal consists solely of one's own ego and desires. Both social and personal relativism deny that the good can be defined objectively and, therefore, they assert that there is no objective basis on which to justify claims to objective truth and absolute norms or intrinsically evil acts.

Objectivist metaethical theories claim that ethical terms do have meaning and that their meaning can be justified.[27] In Catholic theological ethics, the ethical terms *good* and *right* are defined in relation to *human dignity*,

[22]George E. Moore, *Principia Ethica* (Cambridge: Cambridge University Press, 1903, repr. 1968).

[23]Gilbert Harman, *The Nature of Morality: An Introduction to Ethics* (New York: Oxford University Press, 1977), 11.

[24]For a discussion of emotivism, see Charles L. Stevenson, *Ethics and Language* (New Haven, CT: Yale University Press, 1944).

[25]Robert Veatch, "Does Ethics Have an Empirical Basis," *Hastings Center Studies* 1 (1973): 50–65, at 52–53. See also David F. Kelly, *Contemporary Catholic Health Care Ethics* (Washington, DC: Georgetown University Press, 2004), chap. 9.

[26]Veatch, "Does Ethics," 55.

[27]William K. Frankena, *Ethics*, 2nd ed. (Englewood Cliffs, NJ: Prentice Hall, 1973), 97–102. Veatch distinguishes between four types of absolutist theories: supernatural, rationalist, intuitionist, and empirical. Catholic natural law is considered an empirical absolutist theory. See Kelly, *Contemporary Catholic*, 81–85.

human flourishing, or some cognate formulation. What is good or right facilitates human dignity and flourishing: the recognition and concession, for instance, of the inviolable freedom, including freedom of religion, of every person. What is evil or wrong frustrates human dignity and flourishing: slavery, for instance, or the denial of employment and a just wage. Virtually every Catholic theological ethicist espouses an objectivist metaethics and defines the good or right on the basis of what facilitates human dignity. There are, however, among them a variety of theological anthropologies and understandings of human dignity, and this variety explains the different formulations and justifications of norms facilitating or frustrating human dignity. Sometimes these formulations and justifications are at variance with magisterial formulations and justifications.

For example, whereas the Magisterium teaches that artificial contraception within a marital relationship frustrates human dignity and is, therefore, intrinsically immoral, social scientific data clearly show that the vast majority of Catholic couples approve of artificial contraception and, by implication, do not accept either that it frustrates human dignity or that it is intrinsically immoral.[28] Reflecting on the reasoned and conscientious experience of these Catholic couples, we could formulate an alternative moral norm to the Magisterium's as follows. Whether artificial contraception facilitates or frustrates human dignity depends on the reasons for choosing it and on how it impacts one's relationships with oneself, one's spouse, and one's God. The difference between the Magisterium's formulation and justification of a moral norm that facilitates human dignity and alternative formulations and justifications may or may not indicate metaethical relativism, but whether it does or not can be determined only by careful discernment of the arguments and reasons for these formulations and justifications.

If there is a difference of opinion about specific norms that facilitate or frustrate human dignity, this does not *eo ipso* indicate a relativistic metaethical theory. To prove relativism, it is not sufficient simply to demonstrate that basic moral judgments or norms are different. One also needs to demonstrate, William Frankena notes, that these moral judgments or norms "would still be different even if they were fully enlightened, conceptually clear, shared the same factual beliefs, and were taking the same point of

[28] Studies in the United States indicate 75–85 percent of American Catholics, who consider themselves good Catholics, approve of a form of contraception forbidden by the church. See William V. D'Antonio, et al., *Laity American and Catholic: Transforming the Church* (Kansas City, MO: Sheed and Ward, 1996), 131; James D. Davidson, et al., *The Search for Common Ground: What Unites and Divides Catholic Americans* (Huntington, IN: Our Sunday Visitor, 1997), 131. For a similar situation in England, see Michael Hornsby-Smith, *Roman Catholicism in England: Customary Catholicism and Transformation of Religious Authority* (Cambridge: Cambridge University Press, 1991), 177. A 2010 survey of English Catholics reveals that "just 4 per cent of Catholics believe the use of artificial contraception is wrong." See Christopher Lamb, "Few Now View Contraception as Immoral," *The Tablet* (September 18, 2010): 45.

view."[29] Such a standard is high and, for this reason, Frankena believes metaethical relativism has not been proven. The fact that people disagree with the Magisterium on basic moral norms, such as the absolute norm forbidding artificial contraception, in and of itself proves nothing. It may be that people deny the existence of objective truth, in which case they are certainly relativists. It may simply be that they have a different objective definition of human dignity and the norms that facilitate or frustrate it, in which case they would be not relativists but objectivists. Objectivism does not per se eliminate difference in either definitions of human dignity or in the formulation and justification of norms that facilitate its attainment, as the Magisterium's documented evolution in its own moral teachings related to slavery, usury, religious freedom, and torture well illustrate.[30] These are clear examples of the Magisterium's evolution of its understanding of human dignity, frequently assisted by the scholarly contributions of theologians and accompanied by a corresponding evolution in the formulation and justification of norms. Catholic ethicists can espouse and defend metaethical objectivism and still disagree on the objective definition of human dignity and the norms that facilitate or frustrate it. What accounts for this variability is the second question of metaethics, namely, the epistemic justification of the definition of ethical terms. Bernard Lonergan proposes *perspectivism* as a theory that justifies truth claims and contrasts it with relativism.

Perspectivism

Lonergan's theory of perspectivism, which says that different truths derive from different theoretical perspectives, reliably and adequately accounts for different definitions of human dignity and the norms that facilitate or frustrate it. It also addresses charges of relativism aimed at those who disagree with some of the absolute norms the Magisterium offers. Writing on the nature of historical knowledge, he states "Where relativism has lost hope about the attainment of truth, perspectivism stresses the complexity of what the historian is writing about and, as well, the specific difference of historical from mathematical, scientific and philosophic knowledge."[31] Relativism concludes to the falsity of a judgment. Perspectivism concludes to its *partial* but reliable and adequate truth and, therefore, also to the further development of that truth toward its fullness. Sandra Lipsitz Bem, a leading theorist on sex and gender, also argues for cultural perspectivism

[29]Frankena, *Ethics*, 110.

[30]See John T. Noonan, "Development in Ethical Doctrine," *Theological Studies* 54 (1993): 662–77, at 674–75; Bernard Hoose, *Received Wisdom?: Reviewing the Role of Tradition in Christian Ethics* (London: Chapman, 1994).

[31]Lonergan, *Method in Theology*, 217.

in the understanding of gender, though she speaks of *cultural lenses* that shape the human perception and understanding of gender.[32] Throughout this book we will speak of both perspectives and lenses through which we perceive and understand reality.

Lonergan offers three factors that give rise to perspectivism in human knowledge, including ethical knowledge. First, human knowers are finite, the information available to them at any given time is incomplete, and they cannot attend to or master all the data available to them. Second, the knowers are selective, given their different socializations, personal experiences, and range of data offered to them. Third, knowers are individually different, and we can expect them to have different interpretations of the data available to them. The theologian-knower immersed in the philosophy of Plato, Augustine for instance, will achieve different understanding, make different judgments, and act on different decisions from the theologian-knower immersed in the philosophy of Aristotle, Aquinas for instance. Augustine and Aquinas produce legitimate but different theologies, both of which are necessarily partial and incomplete explanations of complex theological reality. They are like two viewers at fourth-story and thirteenth-story windows of the Empire State Building; each gets a different, but no less partial, reliable, and adequate view of what lies outside their windows. We could expect that if they both ascended to a higher story they would get a different, but no less partial, reliable, and adequate view.

Every human judgment of truth, including every judgment of moral truth, is a limited judgment based on limited data and understanding. "So far from resting on knowledge of the universe, [a judgment] is to the effect that, no matter what the rest of the universe may prove to be, at least *this* is so."[33] It is precisely the necessarily limited and, as neuroscience teaches us, sometimes inhibited nature of human sensations, understandings, judgments, and decisions that leads to perspectivism, not as to a source of falsity but as to a source of partial, reliable, and adequate truth. Though he said it on the basis of his understanding of God's incomprehensibility, Augustine's restating of earlier Greek theologians, cited in the International Theological Commission's *Theology Today*, is à propos and accurate here: "*Si comprehendis non est Deus*, if you understand, what you understand is not God."[34] Aquinas articulates the same judgment, though differently:

---

[32]Sandra Lipsitz Bem, *The Lenses of Gender: Transforming the Debate on Sexual Inequality* (New Haven, CT: Yale University Press, 1993).

[33]Bernard J. F. Lonergan, *Insight: A Study of Human Understanding* (London: Longmans, 1957), 344, emphasis added. See also Lonergan, *Method in Theology*, 217–19.

[34]*Sermon* 117, *PL* 38, 360; *Theology Today*, 97. For a detailed analysis, see Victor White, *God the Unknown* (New York: Harper, 1956); William Hill, *Knowing the Unknown God* (New York: Philosophical Library, 1971).

"Now we cannot know what God is, but only what God is not; we must, therefore, consider the ways in which God does not exist rather than the ways in which God does."[35]

No single objectivist definition of human dignity, including ours given in the Introduction, comprehensively captures its full truth. Perspectivism accounts for the plurality of partial truths embedded in different definitions. It is a theory of knowledge that presents human persons as they exist, that attends to those dimensions of the human person deemed most important for defining human dignity, that interprets and prioritizes those dimensions if and when they conflict, and that formulates and justifies norms that facilitate, and do not frustrate, the attainment of human dignity. The only way for humans to achieve truth is via perspectives that are partial and particular.[36] It is focus on and effortful attention to different particular perspectives that leads to both different and partially true definitions of human dignity and the formulation of different norms that facilitate or frustrate it.

In summary, there is broad metaethical agreement within Catholic theological ethics. First, it accepts some version of metaethical objectivism; there *are* objective definitions of human dignity. Second, it defines the ethical terms *good* and *right* in relation to some objective definition of human dignity. Third, given different perspectives and theological lenses, Catholics can and sometimes do disagree on both the specific definition of human dignity and the formulation and justification of norms that facilitate or frustrate its attainment. Fourth, Lonergan's theory of perspectivism and Bem's theory of cultural lenses, which recognize the inherent limitations of humans to know, account for the different definitions of human dignity and the different formulations and justifications of norms that facilitate or frustrate it. Fifth, the variability that arises from perspectivism is an essential part of an objectivism that recognizes universals; the good is *objectively* defined as human dignity. Different objective definitions of human dignity are not to be taken *eo ipso* as forms of a relativism that denies universals.

Theology Today: *Perspectives, Principles, and Criteria*

Theology Today illustrates Lonergan's insight into and perspectivist method of reaching ethical truth and its justification. The method can account for the difference in objectivist definitions of the *good* and the *right* defined as human dignity and the difference in the norms that facilitate or frustrate it. We consider each in turn.

The word *perspectives* in *Theology Today*'s subtitle highlights the reality

[35]Thomas Aquinas, *Summa Theologiae*, 1, 3, preface (hereafter *ST*).

[36]Massingale, "Beyond Revisionism," 258.

of a "plurality of theologies" in Catholic theology which are "undoubtedly necessary and justified."[37] The document distinguishes between the "legitimate pluralism of theology" as a rational enterprise, which "can be evaluated in relation to a common universal truth,"[38] and relativism, which does not recognize any common universal truth. With the long tradition of Catholic theology, it cautions that theology cannot know the fullness of divine truth; only God can. The plurality "results primarily from the abundance of divine truth itself, which human beings can only ever grasp under its specific aspects [partially] and never as a whole, and moreover never definitively, but always, as it were, with new eyes,"[39] through new lenses. Searching for unity among the plurality of theologies, *Theology Today* formulates the following criterion to guide this search. Catholic theology "attempts to integrate a plurality of enquiries and methods into the unified project of the understanding of faith, and insists on the unity of truth and therefore on the fundamental unity of theology itself. Catholic theology recognizes the proper methods of other sciences and critically utilizes them in its own research. It does not isolate itself from critique and welcomes scientific dialogue."[40] In the case of Catholic theological ethics, however, this criterion leaves an unanswered question: What truly constitutes the unity of ethical truth? Is it a truth reflected in a univocal definition of human dignity and corresponding univocal norms that facilitate its attainment? Or is it a more perspectival account of truth reflected in plural definitions of human dignity that recognize and embrace the difference in fourth-story, thirteenth-story, and twenty-first-story views on human dignity and the difference in the formulation and justification of norms that facilitate its attainment?

Theology Today and Catholic tradition give some indication of the answers to these questions. The document's Chapter 2, part 4, entitled "Responsible adherence to the ecclesiastical Magisterium," discusses, first, the nature and authority of the various levels of the Magisterium and magisterial teaching and, then, the proper relationship between the Magisterium, theologians, and theologies. This section ends with a call for responsible adherence to the Magisterium, but it also recognizes the importance of dialogue between theologians and the Magisterium and the "chronic collisions or contrasts" that can threaten this relationship.[41] That is part of the inevitable tension in relationships "wherever there is genuine life."[42] And "while 'dissent' towards the Magisterium has no place in Catholic theology, investigation

[37]*Theology Today*, 77.
[38]Ibid., 78.
[39]Ibid., 77.
[40]Ibid., 75.
[41]Ibid., 42.
[42]Ibid.

and questioning is justified and even necessary if theology is to fulfill its task."[43] We must distinguish between *dissent in principle* from the Magisterium as an authoritative teaching body and *reasoned dissent* from what it teaches. Catholic theological tradition justifies the latter, never the former.

The young Joseph Ratzinger underscores the need for the investigation and questioning of what is taught. "Not everything that exists in the Church must for that reason be also a legitimate tradition. . . . There is a distorting, as well as a legitimate tradition . . . [and] . . . consequently tradition must not be considered only affirmatively but also critically."[44] Thanks to changing sociohistorical perspectives that provide new lenses, there has been a major evolution in the Catholic tradition of the definition of human dignity, and this evolution has been reflected in Catholic moral norms about what facilitates or frustrates the attainment of human dignity. At one time, the tradition approved slavery; later it condemned it as violating human dignity. It condemned the taking of interest on loans and then approved it. It approved torture and then condemned it. It condemned religious freedom and later approved it as an inviolable human right.[45] These developments in Catholic moral teaching are intrinsically linked to the evolution in methods and theologies, guided by evolving historical, cultural, and spiritual perspectives and lenses. The definition of human dignity is part of that development as is the corresponding formulation and justification of norms that facilitate its attainment.

All contemporary Catholic theological ethicists can agree that the good and the right are defined in principle in terms of human dignity, but human dignity itself is subject to plural Catholic objectivist definitions guided by theological perspectives, principles, and criteria that recognize the understanding of human dignity as an evolving reality. Formulating and justifying norms that facilitate or frustrate the attainment of human dignity must be done as a communion church through John Paul II's dialogue in charity, recognizing that there will be partial truths and disagreements on concrete definitions of human dignity and the particular norms that facilitate or frustrate its attainment. These disagreements, however, we repeat again, are not to be automatically labeled as relativism; rather they reflect a perspectival objectivism. Such perspectival objectivism, which we have claimed as part of our ethical method, is well within the parameters of both a pilgrim church in search of practical ethical truth and *Theology Today*'s "plurality of theologies."

---

[43]Ibid., 41.

[44]Joseph Ratzinger, "The Transmission of Divine Revelation," in *Commentary on the Documents of Vatican II*, ed. Herbert Vorgrimler (New York: Herder and Herder, 1969), 3:170–98, at 185.

[45]See Michael G. Lawler, *What Is and What Ought to Be: The Dialectic of Experience, Theology, and Church* (New York: Continuum, 2005), 127–29.

NATURAL LAW

We have already asserted that our ethical method employs the natural law contemporarily reinterpreted. It is time to explain precisely what we mean by that assertion. There are two broad interpretations of natural law in the Catholic ethical traditions, one natural/biological, the other social/personal. The biological interpretation, which was the interpretation widespread in neo-Thomism and the Manuals of Moral Theology used by confessors, views nature as "already, out, there, now, real." It is *already* for it is prior to any human attention to it; it is *out* for it is outside human consciousness; it is *there* for it is spatially located; it is *now* for it exists and is attended to in time; it is *real* for it is bound up with real human living and acting "and so must be just as real as they are."[46] The personal interpretation is well described by a variety of theoretically diverse ethicists.

In the medieval world, where we may reasonably begin, the Scholastics in general considered human nature to be specifically distinct from all other animal natures by being *rational*. They considered reason to be the human characteristic *par excellence* and frequently speak of the natural law as being tantamount to reason. Thomas Aquinas, for instance, argues that what is distinctive about the human person is the capacity for rational self-direction[47] and that, while every creature *acts* in accordance with principles established by the creator, only rational creatures are capable of *discerning* rational principles and rationally following them.[48] His teacher, Albert the Great, observes that, therefore, only rational creatures can be said to be under *obligation*.[49] This Thomistic stance, Jean Porter notes, is encapsulated in the phrase "reason as nature, which appears to have been first used by Philip the Chancellor."[50] In 1188, the distinguished medieval canonist, Huguccio of Ferrara, sums up this stance nicely. "The natural law is said to be reason, that is to say, a natural power of the soul by which the human person distinguishes between good and evil, choosing good and rejecting evil. And reason is said to be a law because it commands, also because it binds." It is said to be natural "because reason is one of the natural goods, or because it agrees with the highest nature, and does not dissent from it." It is "a judgment of reason, that is to say, a motion proceeding from reason, directly or indirectly, that is, any work or operation to which one is obliged

[46]Lonergan, *Method in Theology*, 263.

[47]*ST*, I-II, 1, 6.

[48]*ST*, I-II, 91, 2, ad 3.

[49]Thomas Aquinas, *De bono*, V, 1, 2, ad 12.

[50]Jean Porter, *Natural and Divine Law: Reclaiming the Tradition for Christian Ethics* (Grand Rapids: Eerdmans, 1999), 87.

by reason, as to discern to choose, to do good."[51] To embrace reason, itself a natural good, as a source of moral wisdom, Huguccio says, is to embrace the natural law, and this is precisely what many contemporary Catholic theological ethicists do.

After two hundred years of neo-Thomist fixation on physical nature, a variety of contemporary and prominent ethicists are reclaiming this Scholastic rational tradition. Martin Rhonheimer describes natural law as "the *law of the practical reason*, and this is why a theory of the *lex naturalis* is precisely a theory of the practical reason."[52] We cannot draw direct conclusions from what *is* to what morally *ought to be*, from the presumed physical structure of the sexual act, for example, to sexual moral obligation, for even after determining what *is*, we still have to rationally determine whether it is right or wrong. To draw a conclusion from physical fact to moral obligation is a logical fallacy, a "naturalistic fallacy" Moore calls it,[53] a "theological fallacy" we call it. All we can understand from nature is the naked physical facticity of a reality, sexual intercourse for instance, nothing else. Nature reveals to our attention, understanding, judgment, and decisions only its naked facticity, not our moral obligation. Everything beyond nature's facticity is the result of rational interpretation by attentive, understanding, reasonable, and responsible human beings.[54]

Jean Porter, who might reasonably be described as the leading contemporary Catholic natural law theorist, notes that, in contradistinction to the neo-Thomists of the past two centuries, medieval natural law theorists, including Aquinas, "did not attempt to derive ethical principles from a supposedly self-evident and fixed conception of human nature." For them, "the natural law in its primary sense was identified either with reason or with the most basic principles of action, which were in turn linked to the image of God, that is, the capacity for moral judgment found in all men and women."[55] Following Aquinas, Germain Grisez and John Finnis argue that the human is essentially *homo rationalis,* a rational agent whose choices actualize and realize certain basic goods. Finnis summarizes his position thus: "By a simple act of [rational] non-inferential understanding one grasps that the object of the inclination one experiences is an instance of a general form of good, for oneself (and others like one)."[56] Catholic ethical theory has

[51]Odon Lottin, *Le droit naturel chez saint Thomas D'Aquin et ses prédécesseurs*, 2nd ed. (Bruges, Belgium: Beyart, 1931), 109.

[52]Martin Rhonheimer, *Natural Law and Practical Reason: A Thomistic View of Ethical Autonomy* (New York: Fordham University Press, 2000), viii–ix.

[53]Moore, *Principia Ethica, 64.*

[54]See Jean Porter, *Nature as Reason: A Thomistic Theory of Natural Law* (Grand Rapids: Eerdmans, 2005), 123–25.

[55]Porter, *Natural and Divine Law*, 17.

[56]John Finnis, *Natural Law and Natural Rights: Fundamentals of Ethics* (Washington, DC: George-

largely moved away from a focus on a fixed "human nature" to an evolving "human person." That is to say, the once physicalist understanding of human nature and natural law in the two past centuries is in the process of being transformed into a contemporary personalist, rational understanding. The former defines the ethics of acts based on the physical structure of those acts; the latter defines the ethics of acts based on the meaning of those acts for persons. Brian Johnstone describes this shift as "a move from a 'physicalist' paradigm to a 'personalist' paradigm."[57] Charles Curran and Richard McCormick comment that "from the viewpoint of moral theology or Christian ethics anyone who admits human reason as a source of moral wisdom adopts a natural law perspective."[58]

Jean Porter judges that "a contemporary appropriation of the Scholastic concept of the natural law would undoubtedly go beyond the Scholastics in recognizing the element of human construction in the development of social practices and mores." This judgment applies also to those precepts of the natural law revealed by God, which "cannot be translated directly into social practices without a considerable degree of interpretation," that is, without some human construction.[59] It is inevitable that different groups of equally rational human beings, embedded in different cultural, social, and personal contexts and, therefore, viewing reality through different lenses, may offer different interpretations of nature and moral obligation deriving from nature, and that any given interpretation may be wrong. That is a fact that has been demonstrated time and again in Catholic history.[60] It is also something taken for granted in the social scientific enterprise known as the sociology of knowledge.

One of the founders of the sociology of knowledge, Alfred Schutz, presents its widely taken-for-granted principle: "It is the *meaning* of our experiences and not the *ontological structure* of the objects that constitute reality."[61] "The potter, and not the pot," Alfred North Whitehead adds metaphorically, "is responsible for the shape of the pot."[62] The uninterpreted experience of nature, as of every other objective reality, is restricted to the noting of its facticity and is void of meaning, a quality that does not inhere in nature but is assigned to it by rational beings in interpretive and

town University Press, 1983), 34.

[57]Brian V. Johnstone, "From Physicalism to Personalism," *Studia Moralia* 30 (1992): 71.

[58]Charles Curran and Richard A. McCormick, *Readings in Ethical Theology No.7: Natural Law and Theology* (Mahwah, NJ: Paulist Press, 1991), 1.

[59]Porter, *Natural and Divine Law*, 307.

[60]See John T. Noonan, Jr., *A Church That Can and Cannot Change: The Development of Catholic Ethical Teaching* (Notre Dame, IN: University of Notre Dame Press, 2005); Lawler, *What Is and What Ought to Be*, 127–129.

[61]Alfred Schutz, *Collected Papers* (The Hague: Martinus Nijhoff, 1964–67), 1:230.

[62]Alfred North Whitehead, *Symbolism: Its Meaning and Effect* (New York: Putnam's, 1959), 8.

constructive acts. The decisive criterion for the meaning of any human action, including any moral action, is the intention of the actor.[63] Meaning is what is or was meant by the *actor*, who is always to be understood not as an Enlightenment radical *individual* but as an Aristotelian–Thomistic radically *social person*. The Catholic natural law tradition is committed to an objectivist ethic grounded in human nature and reason. Yet it also recognizes the particularity of these foundations, which are influenced by history, culture, familial relations, and power structures.[64] Not only the Catholic tradition but also the human condition, Pope John Paul II notes, "finds itself between these two poles—universality and particularity—with a vital tension between them."[65]

If the decisive criterion for the meaning of any action, including any moral action, is the meaning assigned to it by social actors, an immediate question arises. Different actors in different cultural groups may define the meaning of an action in radically different ways and, then, a question arises as to which definition is true. Common sense suggests that something is the "same" for each and every individual actor, but common sense cannot determine how that sameness is to be understood. Only critical research, interpretation, history, and dialectic can do that.[66] Consider the following.

You see a young man rushing toward an old woman and pushing her to the ground. You are first tempted to judge that this is an act of violence. But then you notice that there is a large truck coming up behind the old woman and she is about to step, unaware, in front of it. You now realize the young man has saved her life. Now you are tempted to judge his action as charitably heroic. The physical action is the same in both scenarios, but the *meaning* of the action is far from the same. It is radically different, and it is utterly futile to point out to committed actors the "objective" meaning of the act, for the objective meaning is the meaning assigned to the act by the actor, not the naked, uninterpreted, physical facticity of the act. The goodness of human nature, the *created* goodness Christians would say, is the ground for the value of human morality but, as Porter notes, human nature also "under-determines morality." There can be, she points out, "more than one natural morality. Indeed, there are many such, because every indigenous ethical tradition should be considered as a distinctive form of natural morality." This concept, she further points out, "implies

[63]See, for example, Thomas Luckmann, *The Invisible Religion: The Transformation of Symbols in Industrial Society* (New York: Macmillan, 1967); Peter L. Berger and Thomas Luckmann, *The Social Construction of Reality: A Treatise in the Sociology of Knowledge* (New York: Doubleday, 1966).

[64]See Todd, A. Salzman, "Natural Law and Basic Goods: Particular to Someone Everywhere," in *Ethical Theology: New Directions and Fundamental Issues*, ed. James Keating (Mahwah, NJ: Paulist Press, 2004), 252.

[65]Pope John Paul II, "The Fabric of Relations among People," *Origins* 25 (October 19, 1995): 297.

[66]See Lonergan, *Method in Theology*.

a particular set of normative commitments that should guide the ongoing development of Christian morality, as well as offering a starting point for assessing other moral traditions."[67]

The natural law arises, we argue, from a dialectical and constructive interaction between material and rational natures. What, then, we may ask, about the objects and objectivity of nature? Bernard Lonergan supplies a rational answer. He distinguishes two kinds of objects. There is the material object in the immediate world, the object that is "already, out, there, now, real" before anyone asks, "what is it?" and before anyone answers with a name, "it is an apple" or "it is sexual intercourse." There is also the object in the world mediated by meaning. This object is what becomes socially apprehended, understood, judged, and decided in answer to the questions: What is it? It is an apple, with all the varied meanings assigned to apples. It is sexual intercourse, with all the varied meanings assigned to sexual intercourse. There are, in short, objects independent of human rational activity and objects that are the result of such activity. The two should never be confused or, still less, isolated from one another. Not all "objects" are absolutely independent of human rational operation and construction. The philosopher of science, Norwood Russel Hanson, asserts truly that "all facts are theory-laden,"[68] and the physicist, Werner Heisenberg, explained that our knowledge of reality is never purely objective but is always conditioned by the knowing subject. Joseph Ratzinger comments, in an essay on the place of history in biblical exegesis, that "where human beings are concerned, or where the mystery of God makes itself visible, all of this [consideration of the impact of history] is even more important."[69]

True objective knowledge, therefore, is a third thing that results from the dynamic interaction of the already, out, there, now, and real material object and the attending, understanding, judging, and deciding subject. It derives, not from material, ontological structure alone but from the interaction of a material object and a rational human subject socially constructing reality, meaning, value, and truth. What is frequently called *objective* reality by noncritical common sense is more properly called *social reality* or reality humanly invested with *social* existence, meaning, value, and truth. Objective knowledge, Theodore Roszak argues, is "an arbitrary construct in which a given society in a given historical situation has invested its sense of meaningfulness and value."[70] Such an approach to the relationship of

[67]Porter, *Natural and Divine Law*, 308.

[68]See, for example, Norwood Russell Hanson, *Patterns of Discovery: An Inquiry into the Conceptual Foundations of Science* (Cambridge: Cambridge University Press, 1958); Norwood Russell Hanson, *Observation and Explanation: A Guide to Philosophy of Science* (New York: Harper and Row, 1971).

[69]Joseph Ratzinger, "100 Years: The Magisterium and Exegesis," *Theology Digest 51* (2004): 7.

[70]Theodore Roszak, *The Making of a Counter Culture* (New York: Doubleday, 1969), 215.

being, meaning, value, and truth in the human world precludes their absolute connection with empirical, ontological being alone and explains why plural meanings and truth about the "same" reality abound in the human world. Plural meanings, values, and truths, all of which are deemed objective by the actors who subscribe to them, derive inevitably from the plural sociohistorical perspectives and lenses that abound in the human world.

This epistemological overview of object, objectivity, and perspectivism has profound implications for how we understand nature and the norms and principles we derive from that understanding. First, depending on the meaning derived from the dialectic of interdependence between an object and a social subject, nature includes a variety of meanings and partial truths. These meanings must be judged morally, as *Gaudium et Spes* notes,[71] in light of the human person who is a rational, relational, embodied, enculturated, historical subject. These epistemological considerations caution against positing a one-size-fits-all morality deduced from so-called objective nature, and they have implications for the norms we formulate to guide moral sexual persons. They lead us to a position in complete agreement with Jean Porter when she writes of the Scholastic concept of the natural law that it

> does not force us to judge ways of life different from our own as intrinsically iniquitous or sinful. Nor does it lead to the conclusion that any moral code that is incompatible with Christian ideals is *ipso facto* to be condemned. Rather, it allows for a positive theological assessment of diverse human mores, seen as expressions of human nature bearing their own integrity and value, even when they are not compatible with a Christian way of life.[72]

When we do encounter disagreement with our own point of view, it is critical to the search for truth that we do not assume that our view is the right view. We really have no ground for such an assumption without further and unbiased inquiry.[73]

Second, Josef Fuchs allies our foregoing discussion of nature to moral norms in the following manner. He asks what is meant by the objectivity of moral norms and gives two answers. First, he provides a negative answer: "objectivity does not derive from formal revelation, tradition, or the authentic documents of the Magisterium." Second, he provides a positive answer: "if the norms of moral rightness derive from a process of knowledge, evalu-

---

[71] *Gaudium et Spes*, no. 51 (hereafter *GS*).

[72] Porter, *Natural and Divine Law*, 311.

[73] See Alasdair MacIntyre, "Intractable Ethical Disagreements," in *Intractable Disputes about the Natural Law: Alasdair MacIntyre and His Critics*, ed. Lawrence Cunningham (Notre Dame, IN: University of Notre Dame Press, 2009), 20.

ation and judgment [and with Lonergan and us, he assumes they do], then it must be admitted that they are determined not only by the elements of the world-object but also by elements of the judging-subject that necessarily enter into this process."[74] Human subjects cannot make genuinely moral judgments without careful hermeneutics, that is, without attention to and understanding, judgment, and affirmation of, both the world and themselves in the world. "It is only in this way that a norm is truly objective—whether it is discerned by society or by a single person."[75] This concept of objectivity is different from the one that calls a norm "objective," if it is generally accepted in a society, the Church for example, or is proposed by a social authority, the Magisterium for example. It is, however, the only concept of objectivity that takes account of the true nature of not only physical acts but also the rational subject who performs the acts.

We agree with the majority of Catholic theological ethicists that an absolute moral norm exists and that such an absolute norm dispels all possible confusion. We agree also, however, with ethicist, Dietmar Mieth, that the only absolute norm is that "good is to be done and evil left undone,"[76] and that every other moral norm requires interpretive judgment.[77] Fuchs agrees. "There is no discrepancy of theories and opinions within Catholic moral theology about the one moral *absolutum,* the translation of the moral *absolutum* into the [concrete] *material plurality* of human reality is, however, a different matter."[78] Norbert Rigali makes a standard philosophical distinction: "Formally, [human nature] is a principle, in every human being, of embodied spiritual self-transcendence in culture; and in this respect it is universal and unchanging. Materially, however, it is a principle, in every human being, of a particular, historical mode of embodied spiritual self-transcendence, possible within the limits of a particular culture [and perspective]; and in this respect human nature is particular, historical, and variable."[79] Neither truth nor moral law are objects "already, out, there now, real" over against a subject. They exist, rather, Rigali writes, *in* a moral subject "when the interrelation between a moral subject and a moral object is known in and by the moral subject (conscience) itself."[80]

---

[74]Josef Fuchs, *Ethical Demands and Personal Obligations* (Washington, DC. Georgetown University Press, 1993), 103.

[75]Ibid., 104.

[76]See *ST*, I-II, 94, 2, for this first principle of practical reasoning.

[77]Dietmar Mieth, *Ethical und Erfahrung. Beitrage zur theologisch-ethischen Hermeneutik* (Freiburg, Germany: 1977), 34.

[78]Fuchs, *Ethical Demands and Personal Obligations*, 27, emphasis in original.

[79]Norbert Rigali, "Christian Morality and Universal Morality: The One and the Many," *Louvain Studies* 19 (1994): 29.

[80]Norbert Rigali, "The Unity of Ethical and Pastoral Truth," *Chicago Studies* 21 (1982), 224–35, emphasis added.

"The scholastics grounded human dignity positively," Porter comments, "in the capacity for moral discernment and self-direction enjoyed by each rational adult." They are far from claiming, she further comments, as does John Paul II in *Veritatis Splendor*,[81] that men and women must depend on their "bishops and pastors" for knowledge of the moral laws. The Second Vatican Council agrees with her general claim. Laypersons, it taught, are not to imagine that their pastors "are always such experts that to every problem which arises, however complicated, they can readily give a concrete solution, or even that such is their mission." The clear implication is that they are not. The Council goes on to advise laypersons, "enlightened by Christian wisdom and giving close attention to the teaching authority of the Church,"[82] to take on their own distinctive role. That distinctive role, it teaches with regard to the moral norms of married life, is to reach objective judgments based on the nature not only of physical acts but also of the human person.[83] Acknowledging the evident plurality of objective moral judgments in the modern world, the Council enjoins "the entire People of God, especially pastors and theologians, to hear, distinguish, and *interpret* the many voices of our age, and to judge them in the light of the divine word. In this way, revealed truth can always be more deeply penetrated, better understood, and set forth to greater advantage."[84] The divine word and its truth, however, the Catholic tradition consistently teaches, are fully accessible only to God; it is never fully but only partially accessible to limited human beings.

VIRTUE ETHICS AND NEUROSCIENCE

It is accepted as a historical truism today that Catholic ethics have developed and changed over the years.[85] In the last century, Lonergan was convinced that something new was happening in history and that, since a living morality and virtuous life ought to be part of what was happening, humans were living in a new age that required a new moral approach. That new approach, he prophesied correctly, would be necessarily historical and empirical/scientific. Lonergan's distinction between a classicist and an historical notion of culture has itself become classical. "The classicist

---

[81] *Veritatis Splendor*, no. 117.

[82] *GS*, no. 43.

[83] *GS*, no. 51.

[84] *GS*, no. 44, emphasis added.

[85] See Noonan, *A Church That Can and Cannot Change*; Charles E. Curran, *The Development of Ethical Theology: Five Strands* (Washington, DC: Georgetown University Press, 2013); Lawler, *What Is and What Ought to Be*, 127–29.

notion of culture was normative: at least *de iure* there was but one culture that was both universal and permanent." The historical notion of culture was "the set of meanings and values that informs a way of life. It may remain unchanged for ages. It may be in the process of slow development or rapid resolution."[86] Classicist culture is static; historical culture is dynamic. Ethics, which is necessarily part of culture, mirrors this distinction.

In its classicist mode, ethics is a static, permanent achievement that anyone can learn as they learn algebra; in its historical mode, it is a dynamic, ongoing process requiring an attentive, understanding, discerning subject. The classicist understanding, Fuchs writes, conceives of the human person as "a series of created, static, and thus definitively ordered temporal facts." The historical understanding conceives of the person as a subject in process of "self-realization in accordance with a project that develops in God-given autonomy, that is, along a path of human reason and insight, carried out in the present with a view to the future."[87] Classicist ethics sees moral norms coming from the past as once and for all definitive; virtue norms enunciated in the fifth or sixteenth centuries continue to apply absolutely in the twenty-first century. Historical ethics sees the moral norms of the past, not as absolute facts for uncritical acceptance but as partial insights that provide moral foundations for further critical attention, understanding, judgment, and decision in the present. What Augustine and his medieval successors knew, for instance, about human sexuality can never be the absolute and exclusive basis for a moral judgment about sexuality today. Since there are plural communities of culture and meaning in history and since they are always evolving in dialectic with new situations and information, historical ethics is necessarily evolving and pluralistic. We shall return to this assertion later.

In early twentieth-century ethics, two normative approaches to determining the morality of an action held the field. One was Jeremy Bentham's and John Stuart Mill's utilitarian approach, which says that the moral action is the one that maximizes utility for the maximum number of persons. The other was Immanuel Kant's deontological approach, in which the moral action is the one that accords with laws, obligations, and duties. Toward the end of the century a "new" approach, which was actually an old approach of Aristotle's recovered, was introduced as another option, namely, virtue ethics, which gives precedence, not to the actions of agents but to their personal characters formed in their respective ethical traditions and learned through the imitation of respected exemplars in those traditions. We share with philosophers Philippa Foot and Alasdair MacIntyre the judgment that neither utilitarianism nor deontology offers an adequately comprehensive

[86]Lonergan, *Method in Theology*, xi.

[87]Fuchs, *Ethical Demands*, 39.

ethical theory, indeed that, because of them, "we have—very largely if not entirely—lost our comprehension, both theoretical and practical, of morality."[88] We join with them and the many other modern ethicists who advance virtue ethics over normative ethics as a more promising approach to the moral life than utilitarianism or deontology.[89] We shall consider virtue *ethics* in detail in Chapter 2; here we consider virtue *reality* as a quasi-introduction to that virtue ethics.

We have already explained our notion of *virtue* in the Introduction, and so there is no need to repeat it here. Here we seek an answer to the question, how is virtue learned? We answer together with prominent contemporary virtue ethicist, Linda Zagzebski, who enthrones exemplars as the primary tool for learning both virtue and virtue ethics. For Zagzebski, both virtue and the good are defined in terms of paradigmatic exemplars. To be a virtuous, and therefore moral, person is to imitate and be like a virtuous exemplar or "saint," and a moral act is the kind of act a "saint" would do in a similar situation. This exemplarist approach was already clearly implied in Aristotle[90] and in Christian hagiography. Alasdair MacIntyre assigns a crucial role to the influence of exemplary adults in the moral formation of children. The teacher's role in the education of the young is not only didactic but also exemplary,[91] and it is exemplary, he adds, and both Zagzebski and we agree, not only intellectually but also emotionally and behaviorally. The paradigmatic exemplars are generally well known: Socrates, Jesus Christ and his saint-followers, Buddha and his *bodhisattvas*. Lesser known, but by no means less exemplary in virtue, are the rescuers of Jews during the Nazi pogroms in Germany, the first responders of 9/11, and the many carers in the widespread l'Arche community today, all of whom, at considerable cost to themselves, put empathy with, compassion for, and service of others before their own selfish concerns. Gregory Peterson judges: "That I am a fully-formed moral agent capable of engaging in wise decision-making is rendered possible by my years of ethical formation by those who were themselves morally wise within the community, who engaged both in active instruction and who set an example of what a morally exemplary life looks like."[92]

---

[88]MacIntyre, *After Virtue*, 2. See also G. E. M. Anscombe, "Modern Ethical Philosophy," in *Philosophy* 33 (1958): 1–19; Philippa Foot, "Ethical Beliefs," in *Proceedings of the Aristotelian Society* 59 (1958–59): 83–104.

[89]In addition to Foot and MacIntyre, whom most judge to be the preeminent modern virtue theorists, other important theorists in the field of virtue ethics will be introduced as the chapter unfolds.

[90]Aristotle, *Nichomachean Ethics*, 10, 5 and 9 (hereafter NE).

[91]Alasdair MacIntyre, *Dependent Rational Animals: Why Human Beings Need the Virtues* (Chicago: Open Court, 1999).

[92]Gregory R. Peterson, "Exemplarism: Some Considerations," in *Theology and the Science of Ethical Action: Virtue Ethics, Exemplarity, and Cognitive Neuroscience*, ed. James A. Van Slyke et al. (New

In both utilitarianism and deontology, and in ethical theory in general, moral decision making has traditionally been deductive, from universal moral principles to moral action. Exemplarist virtue ethics offers an alternative approach. Personal discernment, judgment, and decision making remain central to ethics, but in virtue ethics they are a discernment, a judgment, and a decision to imitate and be like an exemplar. Michael Spezio asserts that "reflection on and study of moral exemplars should form the proper basis of moral theorizing, and that insights gleaned from the lives of moral exemplars provide the resources, the data on which moral theorists can reflect."[93] He offers an analogy from sports, where study of superior athletes like Pele, Muhammad Ali, Michael Jordan, and Serena Williams can help us understand athletic excellence. "Similarly, we might expect that studying moral exemplars would produce insights into moral functioning and that this would aid in the process of moral education and formation."[94]

Humans are great imitators, of skills, of virtues, of actions, and this gives them the singular advantage that they do not have to learn everything by self-experience. A Pele or a Serena Williams, of course, does not emerge merely from the imitation of an exemplar; they need hours and hours of practice for their skills to become habitual. Influential philosopher Owen Flanagan comments that, given the human, indeed primate, propensity to imitate, "much of what any human does or knows is determined horizontally, by what other members of his social world are doing and thinking."[95] Neuroscientist Michael Gazzaniga introduces an important caveat: "Elite performance results from intense, demanding practice, and those who excel are more willing than their peers to engage creatively in this regimen for countless hours. It is their drive [and not simply their genes or their dispositions] that produces talent."[96] The same argument applies to virtuous persons. As for Pele and Ali, so also for Jesus, Buddha, Gandhi, Mother Teresa, and their modern imitators: practice in virtue makes perfect. The study of exemplars is, of course, both historical and empirical/scientific, verifying Lonergan's prophecy encountered earlier.

A second verification of Lonergan's prophecy that twenty-first century ethical theory would be historical/empirical has come into ethical theory in the past thirty years. Those years have witnessed the burgeoning of the sciences, especially the neurosciences introduced in the Introduction, and have spawned a renewed interest in what we may call the science of

York: Routledge, 2013), 91.

[93]Michael L. Spezio, "Relating Political Theory and Virtue Sciences: A Reflection on Human Dignity, Empathy, and the Capabilities Approach," in *Theology and the Science of Ethical Action*, 85.

[94]Ibid., 87.

[95]Owen J. Flanagan, Jr., *The Science of the Mind* (Cambridge, MA: MIT Press, 1984), 268.

[96]Michael S. Gazzaniga, *The Ethical Brain* (New York: Dana Press, 2005), 59.

ethics. That interest has led to a reexamination of David Hume's famous "no-ought-from-is" principle, that no moral ought can be derived from any natural is. That, in turn, has further led to a reexamination of the relationship between descriptive scientific accounts of morality and ethical theory. Josef Fuchs highlights the need for this reexamination. While the facts of nature do not declare morality, "they remain relevant for arriving at valid ethical statements about concrete, worldly conduct."[97] Neurophilosopher Sarah Churchland goes further and has no hesitation in judging that "morality seems to me to be a natural phenomenon—constrained by the forces of natural selection, rooted in neurobiology, shaped by the local ecology [including virtuous exemplars], and modified by cultural developments."[98]

We underscore the import of Churchland's final phrases: local ecology and culture are involved in the natural phenomenon that is ethics. We can agree with her claim, adding only the notion of "tradition," either as an addition to or a specification of "culture," for a moral life is also a social life. That social and moral behavior is moderately supported by the neuroscientific data showing that "whether a subject sees a merely social event or a conventionally 'moral' event, the same regions of the prefrontal cortex show increased activity."[99] Contemporary sociobiology offers the evolutionary thesis that we are more likely to behave altruistically to kin than nonkin, to those more closely attached to us than those not attached, to our in-group rather than to our out-group, and this for the ultimate purpose of perpetuating our genes.[100] Attachment "refers to the dispositions to extend care to others, to want to be with them, and to be distressed by separation."[101] At the root of all human moral practices, Churchland judges, "are the social desires; most fundamentally, these involve attachment to family members, care for friends, the need to belong. Motivated by these values, individually and collectively we try to solve problems that can cause misery and instability and threaten survival."[102] Owen Flanagan adds his weight to that judgment, arguing that every prominent feature of human ethics rests on some biological feature. "A necessary condition of articulating a moral code is having linguistic ability; a necessary condition of giving the moral code

---

[97]Josef Fuchs, SJ, "Natural Law or Naturalistic Fallacy?" in Josef Fuchs, *Moral Demands and Personal Obligations*, trans. Brian McNeil (Washington, DC: Georgetown University Press, 1993), 41.

[98]Patricia S. Churchland, *Braintrust: What Neuroscience Tells Us about Morality* (Princeton, NJ: Princeton University Press, 2011), 191.

[99]Ibid., 60.

[100]See Celia Deane-Drummond, *The Wisdom of the Liminal: Evolution and Other Animals in Human Becoming* (Grand Rapids: Eerdmans, 2014), 194–237; Markus Mühling, *Resonances: Neurobiology, Evolution, and Theology Evolutionary Niche Construction* (Göttingen, Germany: Vandenhoeck and Ruprecht, 2014), 137–64.

[101]Churchland, *Braintrust*, 16

[102]Ibid., 12.

meaningful semantic content is having intelligence; the widespread nature of moral codes makes sense only on the assumption that we are a social species also afflicted by a certain amount of selfishness; and the specific content of certain widespread moral precepts, such as those prohibiting murder or assault, presuppose a natural fear of death and bodily harm."[103]

Discerning the impact of science in general, and neuroscience in particular, on knowledge and ethical theory is an ongoing project and further highlights the historical nature of knowledge in general and moral knowledge in particular. Insight into scientific knowledge must also be integrated with classic ethical concepts, such as the concept of love, to which we now turn.

VARIETIES OF LOVE

We conclude this chapter with a consideration of altruism and love, the pertinence of which will become clear. Altruism is "an action favoring other individuals at the expense of the altruist,"[104] a definition that favors action or "the helping agent's awareness of the need of another and the intention to be of assistance."[105] There is a debate about two kinds of altruism. The first kind is kin altruism, altruism toward one's kin, which evolutionary sociobiologists explain as an activity to ensure the successful continuation of one's genes. It is exemplified most obviously in the protective behavior of parents toward their children, which, long before Darwin, had been recognized by both Aristotle and Aquinas. Aristotle judged that "in common with other animals and with plants, mankind has a natural desire to leave behind them an image of themselves."[106] Aquinas argues that once paternal recognition is assured, perhaps by spousal trust or by physical resemblance or both, the dynamics of kin altruism leads to deeper investment by fathers in their children as a way of continuing themselves. Man, he argues, "naturally desires to be assured of his offspring, and this assurance would be altogether nullified in the case of promiscuous copulation."[107] The second kind of altruism is reciprocal altruism, or cooperation between unrelated individuals, which is not without some self-interest and is popularly described as "you scratch my back and I'll scratch yours." Our concern here is not to provide an extended analysis of altruism but to relate it to the universal virtue of love.

---

[103]Flanagan, *The Science of the Mind*, 272.

[104]Edith Wyschogrod, "Pythagorean Bodies and the Body of Altruism," in *Altruism and Altruistic Love: Science, Philosophy, and Religion in Dialogue*, ed. Stephen G. Post et al. (Oxford: Oxford University Press, 2002), 29.

[105]Jerome Kagan, "Morality, Altruism, and Love," in Post, *Altruism and Altruistic Love*, 43.

[106]Aristotle, *Politics*, I, 2.

[107]Thomas Aquinas, *Summa Contra Gentiles*, III, 2, 115.

There are four Greek words that are translated into English as "love": *agape, eros, philia,* and *storge.*[108] *Agape* is the word for love frequently found in the Christian scriptures, most famously in the writings of Paul; it has been interpreted, particularly in Protestant theology, as unconditional or self-sacrificing love or un-self-interested altruism. *Eros* is self-interested love, love of another person for some benefit, though not exclusively, to oneself. *Philia* is mutual love between two persons for the benefit of both; it is what we commonly call friendship and is a species of reciprocal altruism. *Storge* is familial love, best exemplified, perhaps, by the natural or instinctual love of parents for their children. Here, we are particularly interested in *agape* and *philia* and their interrelationship.

Even the most egocentric of persons recognize that they cannot achieve human flourishing and dignity without other people. That is why our ethical method embraces the element of relation. If I do not associate with other people, assist them, see to their needs and let them see to mine, I will fail to become the full human being I could become. I will not, of course, allow everyone into my life—that project is too vast; and not everyone will allow me into their lives. Those few I do let into my life, and who reciprocate by letting me into theirs, will be special and specially named. They will be named *friends*, without whom, Aristotle wrote, "no one would choose to live, even if he had all other goods."[109] Aristotle offers three reasons why we need friends and why our lives would not be complete without them. First, honest friends are a crucial source of self-understanding. The best way to come to an understanding of myself, Aristotle knew before any modern evolutionary psychologist, is to see myself reflected in the unedited mirror of an honest friend. Second, friends help us sustain even the most necessary activities, including the pursuit of the morally good life. I need virtuous friends with whom I can share and learn virtuous acts (a premodern argument for exemplarity). Third, I cannot become morally good except in relation to another, because virtue cannot be attained alone.[110]

Aristotle was not the only ancient to write about friendship. The Roman philosopher Cicero also wrote about it, and his *De Amicitia* became an influential book about friendship in the Western world. The Roman agrees with the Greek. Friendship, "a complete accord of feeling on all subjects, divine and human, accompanied by kindly feeling and attachment,"[111] is to be preferred "to all human possessions."[112] Genuine friendship requires

[108]See the classic C. S. Lewis, *Four Loves* (New York: Harcourt, Brace, Jovanovich, 1960).

[109]*NE*, 8.1.

[110]See John M. Cooper, "Aristotle on Friendship," in *Essays on Aristotle's Ethics*, ed. Amelie Oksenberg Rorty (Berkeley: University of California Press, 1980), 301–40.

[111]Cicero, *Friendship* (Chicago: Albert and Scott, 1890), 17.

[112]Ibid., 15.

testing. The prudent man checks "the impetus of his kindly feeling as he would his chariot, that we may have our friendships fully proved."[113] Hypocrisy is the death of friendship, "for it destroys all truth, without which the name of friendship can avail nothing."[114]

Early Christian writers sought to Christianize Cicero. In his *Confessions*, Augustine reflects on the death of a dear friend, a man "sweet to me above every other sweetness," and confesses that their early friendship was not a true friendship. True friendship "cannot be unless you solder it together in those who unite to one another by the love poured forth in our hearts by the Holy Spirit who is given to us."[115] For Aristotle and Cicero, friends are brought together by the good or virtue they see and value in one another; for Augustine, friends are brought together by God and they grow together in God until they attain true friendship. The twelfth-century monk, Aelred of Rievaulx, made an even more concerted attempt to Christianize Cicero.[116] For Aelred, true friendship is spiritual, when other persons are loved not for what they can give back in terms of material goodness or erotic pleasure, but for what they are in themselves, images of God and reflections of the love of Christ.[117] As with Cicero, friendship must be tested before it is accepted with good will and mutual esteem.[118]

If friendship was such a significant aspect of virtue and goodness for pagan Aristotle and Cicero, why has it never been a significant part of virtue for Christians? The answer lies in an interpretation of the words of Jesus reported in the gospels: "Love (*agape*) your enemies and pray for those who persecute you, so that you may be the sons of your Father who is in heaven" (Mt 5:44–47). The nineteenth century Anglican theologian, Jeremy Taylor, explained what happened to *philia* and *agape*. "When friendships were the noblest things in the world," as in the days of Aristotle and Cicero, "charity (*agape*) was little."[119] When Christianity created a shift in the culture of Europe, charity became the noblest thing in the world and friendship was demoted. The problem lies in the understanding of the two words.

Philia, the word Aristotle uses for friendship, is the particular, preferential, and reciprocated love of a friend over all others. And there is the Gordian knot: *philia* is particular, preferential, and reciprocal love. *Agape* is the universal, nonpreferential, and not-necessarily-reciprocated love of others, the love commanded by Jesus: "love your neighbor as yourself"

---

[113]Ibid., 40.

[114]Ibid., 56.

[115]Augustine, *Confessions* (Garden City, NY: Doubleday, 1960), 97.

[116]See Todd A. Salzman, "Friendship as Virtue," *Chicago Studies* 37 (August 1998): 209–27.

[117]Aelred of Rievaulx, *Spiritual Friendship* (Scranton, PA: University of Scranton Press, 1994), 1:38.

[118]Ibid., 3:119–27.

[119]Jeremy Taylor, "Discourse on the Nature and Offices of Friendship," in *Works*, vol. 1, ed. R. Heber, revised and corrected C. P. Eden (London: 1847), 72.

(Mk 12:31) and even "love your enemies" (Mt 5:44). *Agape* is what God shows when God makes the "sun to rise on the evil and the good" (Mt 5:45); it is what God is said to be in the metaphor "God is love" (1 Jn 4:8). *Philia* is a reciprocally preferential love based on the valued goodness of the individual friend; *agape* is nonpreferential and universal love, love that is to be shown even to an enemy who can never be expected to reciprocate. *Philia* is a love subject to change, as every ended friendship verifies, though it can be argued, as Aelred argues, that friendship that ends was never true friendship. *Agape*, by definition, is love that "never ends" (1 Cor 13:8). Though there is evidence that the early Christians referred to themselves as "friends (*philoi*) of God," perhaps applying to themselves what Isaiah said of Abraham (Is 41:8), it was not a designation that stuck. It was quickly superseded by "children of God," which might have been judged to be more familial and intimate.[120]

The relationship between *philia* and *agape* became problematic when the latter was prioritized as Christian love, the love that makes perfect "as your heavenly Father is perfect" (Mt 5:48), leaving *philia* to languish as a lesser love that does not measure up to all that is required of the Christian. Friendship may be a good and powerful love, it may even be necessary and very useful in every human life. It is just not specifically Christian and does not lead to God as does *agape*. Søren Kierkegaard enunciated the standard argument in two statements. "Love of one's neighbor . . . is self-renouncing love, and self-renunciation casts out all preferential love just as it casts out all self-love."[121] Christianity has misgivings about erotic love and friendship because "preference in passion or passionate preference is really another form of self-love."[122] There, in a nutshell, is the problem as Kierkegaard enunciates it. Neighbor-love is Christ-like selflessness; friendship-love is disguised selfishness and, therefore, anathema to followers of the Christ. In his seminal treatment of *agape* as equal regard, Gene Outka takes a less restrictive approach, arguing that *agape* permits "special relations" as long as they do not violate the demands of equal consideration for all.[123] It may not be as clear, then, as Kierkegaard argues, that *agape* and *philia* are separate and unconnected.

---

[120]See Adolph Harnack, "Friends," in *The Mission and Expansion of Christianity* (New York: Harper Torchbooks), 421.

[121]Søren Kierkegaard, "You Shall Love Your Neighbor," in *Other Selves: Philosophers on Friendship*, ed. Michael Pakaluk (Indianapolis, IN: Hacket Publishing, 1991), 242.

[122]Søren Kierkegaard, *Works of Love,* trans. Howard and Edna Long (New York: Harper and Row, 1964), 65–66.

[123]Gene Outka, *Agape: An Ethical Analysis* (New Haven, CT: Yale University Press, 1972). See also his "Universal Love and Impartiality," in *The Love Commandments: Essays in Christian Ethics and Ethical Philosophy*, ed. Edmund N. Santurri and William Werpehowski (Washington, DC: Georgetown University Press, 1992).

The problem in history is that *agape* was enthroned as the norm of all love, and *philia* did not measure up to that norm. *Agape*, however, is not the norm of love; God is the norm of love, both *agape* and *philia*. Friendship by itself is not a non-Christian love; friendship *without God and Christ* is a non-Christian love. Human friendship-love and *agape*-love both originate in and are images of the love of God. Paul Wadell puts it well. "Once it is acknowledged that both Christian friendship and *agape* originate in the same love, not only are they reconcilable they are also inseparable . . . we not only know why *agape* is not opposed to friendship, we also know why it is friendship's most perfect expression."[124] Friendship, then, is reciprocated *agape*.

Both *agape* and *philia* are extolled in biblical writings. Jesus summed up Torah in the commandments to love God and to love (*agapeseis*) one's neighbor as oneself (Mk 12:29–31; Mt 22:37–40; Lk 10:27). That double commandment is the sacred root of the Christian demand for universal neighbor-love (*agape*). John reports, however, that Jesus, the paradigmatic neighbor-lover, called his disciples friends (*philoi*) (15:15), and loved Lazarus so particularly and so obviously that onlookers could comment "see how he [Jesus] loved (*ephilei*) him" (11:36). John 15:15 was a decisive factor leading Aquinas to identify *agape* and *philia*.[125] The demands of universal neighbor-love do not displace or negate particular friendship-love and the special relationship it implies. Rather, the virtues of *agape* and *philia* are related and mutually nourish one another.

The tension between the universal, inclusive love of all and the particular, preferential love of some is retained in the Pauline instruction to the followers of Jesus in Galatia: "As we have opportunity, let us do good to all men, and *especially* to those who are of the household of faith" (Gal 6:10). The virtue of Christian love is both universal ("all men") and legitimately particular ("especially"). The particularity is made even more exclusive, the relation even more preferential, in the post–Pauline Letter to Timothy: "If anyone does not provide for his relatives, and *especially* for his own family, he has disowned the faith and is worse than an unbeliever" (1 Tm 5:8). The virtue of Christian love is both universal (*agape*) and particular (*philia*), it requires inclusive and exclusive covenants, and neither the abstract universal nor the concrete particular dimension excludes the other. The universal love of all comes easiest when the particular love of some, spouse, parents, children, fellow-Christians, comes first. Newman is con-

[124]Paul J. Wadell, *Friendship and the Ethical Life* (Notre Dame, IN: University of Notre Dame Press, 1989), 83.

[125]For an extended discussion of friendship in the New Testament, see Alan C. Mitchell, "'Greet the Friends by Name': New Testament Evidence for the Greco-Roman Topos on Friendship," in *Greco-Roman Perspectives on Friendship*, ed. John T. Fitzgerald (Atlanta: Scholars Press, 1997), 225–62.

rect: "the best preparation for loving the world at large, and loving it duly and wisely, is to cultivate an intimate friendship and affection toward those who are immediately about us."[126] Stephen Post, however, may have said it best. "The moral [and virtuous] agent is a social animal. . . . Because there are degrees of relatedness and proximity, [universal] Good Samaritanism provides only a partial vision of love."[127] *Agape* is only one facet of the love to which Christians are called.

We conclude this chapter with an assertion common to all Christian theological ethicists, namely, that love of God and neighbor, both *philia* and *agape*, is the root of our human cooperation with and journey toward God.[128] Christian virtue ethics is not so much obeying God as loving God who first loved us. The first principle of Christian ethics is "Love the Lord your God." The second flows from this: because you love God do good and avoid evil—in other words, be virtuous. We turn now to a specific consideration of virtue ethics.

[126]John Henry Newman, *Parochial and Plain Sermons*, Sermon 5, 258.

[127]Stephen G. Post, *A Theory of Agape: On the Meaning of Christian Love* (Lewisburg, PA: Bucknell University Press, 1990), 104.

[128]See, for instance, Margaret A. Farley, *Just Love: A Framework for Christian Sexual Ethics* (New York: Continuum, 2006); Edward Collins Vacek, *Love, Human and Divine: The Heart of Christian Ethics* (Washington, DC: Georgetown University Press, 1994).

2

Virtuous Perspective

In contemporary ethics, as introduced in the previous chapter, there are three normative approaches to determining the morality of an action. There is the utilitarian approach, in which the moral action is the one that maximizes utility for the maximum number of persons. There is the deontological approach, in which the moral action is the one that obeys rules and obligations. Finally there is the renewed virtue-ethical approach, in which the moral action is the one that gives precedence, not to the actions of agents but to their personal characters formed in their moral communities. We share with Philippa Foot and Alasdair MacIntyre the judgment that neither utilitarianism nor deontology offers an adequately comprehensive ethical theory, and we join with them and many other contemporary ethicists who advance virtue ethics as a normative ethics more promising to the moral life than utilitarianism or deontology.[1] We have already given an account in the Introduction of our virtue *theory*. In this chapter, we give an account of our virtue *ethics* based on that theory.

VIRTUE EPISTEMOLOGY

That virtue includes an intellectual, deliberative, and decisive dimension means that some epistemological theory is required for its full understanding. To act rightly in choice and action follows from to know and to judge rightly. To understand the process of human knowing, we espouse the epistemological theory established by Bernard Lonergan in his magisterial *Insight*, for we believe that epistemology fully elucidates the process of both coming to know and to judge and coming to virtue. "All human beings," Aristotle teaches, "desire to know by nature."[2] Lonergan agrees, arguing that

[1]In addition to Foot, and MacIntyre, whom most judge to be the preeminent modern virtue theorists, other important theorists in the field of virtue ethics will be introduced as this chapter unfolds.

[2]Aristotle, *Metaphysics*, ed. Joseph Sachs (Santa Fe, NM: Green Lion Press, 1990), 980a20.

human knowing begins in the "pure desire to know."[3] Human knowing is not simply "taking a look" at reality. It is endlessly discursive, cycling and recycling through various levels of cognitive activity until truth is reached in the judgment, deliberated on, and a decision is made for action according to the truth.[4] I judge, quickly through habit, we hope, that a homeless person sleeping on the street is the right person in the right situation for compassion, and I decide to help her/him find accommodation. It is in my rational judgment and only in my rational judgment, that truth about her/his situation is achieved. This judgment may be followed by a decision to act, and it is at the moment of decision and action that ethics enters in.

Perception is critical in the process of coming to know. Perception is a function of a subject's relationship to an object, the subject's active patterning of the object in the phenomenal world. No phenomenal object simply impresses itself upon rational subjects, as it impresses itself upon nonrational animals, nor do rational subjects simply construct or project the phenomenal object. Rather, objects nakedly "out, there, now, and real" in the phenomenal world are shaped by the subject's attention, short- and long-term interests and goals, the intensity of his/her emotional interactions with the object, and in general the character lens through which he/she views the object.[5] The world that persons consciously encounter and attend to is not a world of sense data objectively and nakedly "out, there, now, real,"[6] but rather a world shaped by their subjective interpretations called perceptions. Perception is an exercise of practical reason leading to choice; what we "see" is a function of who we are. As philosopher of science Norwood Russell Hanson wittily notes, "there is more to seeing than meets the eyeball."[7] This claim has implications for virtue ethics.

What does perception have to do with virtue ethics? Aristotle writes that "we become just by first performing just acts."[8] We pose two questions to that assertion. First, how do we know which actions are just and to be performed? Second, what motivation might we have for performing those just actions? The first question is easily answered. We learn, as we saw in the previous chapter, what are just acts, compassionate acts, and so on from respected exemplars: parents, teachers, mentors, friends, saints, whom we hold as virtuous and moral. We judge an action right and moral if it is one

[3]Bernard J. F. Lonergan, *Insight: A Study of Human Understanding* (London: Longmans, 1957), 74, 372–75.

[4]Ibid., 273–774.

[5]Ibid., 190.

[6]Ibid., 251; see also Bernard J. F. Lonergan, *Method in Theology* (Toronto: University of Toronto Press, 2003), 263.

[7]Norwood Russell Hanson, *Patterns of Discovery: An Inquiry into the Conceptual Foundations of Science* (Cambridge: Cambridge University Press, 1958), 7.

[8]Aristotle, *Nichomachean Ethics*, II, 1103a31–1103b2 (hereafter *NE*).

that a virtuous person would do in the circumstances, and it is by imitation of virtuous persons that we learn which actions are right, moral, and virtuous. We need to be careful, however, how we understand the word *learning*.

Words will never make anyone virtuous, for virtues are habits or dispositions learned only by repeated performance. It is via habituation, critically questioned and requestioned in the cycle of attention, perception, understanding, judgment, and decision that we come to learn and value the truth and goodness of justice and compassion and of just, compassionate, and virtuous actions in general. The perception of ethical relevance is the product of both experience and habituation but, we repeat, there is no real morality until that ethical relevance is judged to be true in the personal judgment of truth and then followed by personal decision and action. Aristotle is pointing at this critical approach to learning virtues when he claims that "a morally praiseworthy act must be done in full awareness of *what* we are doing and *why* we do it. It must be an act freely chosen and not done from coercion."[9] It must be, in contemporary ethical language, an act of practical judgment that the Catholic tradition calls *conscience*. There is no moral action prior to my choice to do this action, nor is there any moral praise to be earned from simply imitating another person. "We are ethically obliged," Robert Fitterer writes, "not only to *act* well but also to *think* well."[10] That thinking well, Aristotle and Lonergan agree, requires moral agents to be open to ongoing inquiry and consequent reflective grasp of their attention, perception, understanding, judgment, and decision, for personal bias and pleasure can distort them and may need to be corrected.[11]

Virtues are *learned* and can be learned only within particular communities; they can be *sustained* only in those communities; they get their *content* from those communities; they get their value from and in community; and they *act back* on communities to sustain them.[12] Humans are not absolutely the autonomous persons they are claimed to be. Persons who are "role-figures"[13] first exemplify what it means to be just, loving, and so on, and then by personal repetition of acts of justice and love an individual establishes those virtues as personal character states, habits, or dispositions. As habits are stabilized, both the virtuous exemplars and the acts of virtue learned from them need to be more and more purified by critical examination and reexamination in the process of knowing that issues in the practical judg-

---

[9]Robert J. Fitterer, *Love and Objectivity in Virtue Ethics: Aristotle, Lonergan, and Nussbaum on Emotions and Moral Insight* (Toronto: University of Toronto Press, 2008), 6, emphasis in original.

[10]Ibid., emphasis in original.

[11]*NE*, II, 1109b1–12; Lonergan, *Insight*, 225–42.

[12]See Lawrence Bloom, "Community and Virtue," in *How Should One Live?: Essays on the Virtues*, ed. Roger Crisp (Oxford: Clarendon Press, 1998), 231–50.

[13]Daniel Statman, "Introduction to Virtue Ethics," in *Virtue Ethics: A Critical Reader*, ed. Daniel Statman (Washington, DC: Georgetown University, 1997), 15.

ment of truth, decision, and action. This process of critical examination and reexamination not only purifies the agent and his/her virtues but also leads him/her nearer to the self-determination and authenticity that establish his/her full morality.[14] MacIntyre is correct when he asserts that "separated from the *polis* [community and culture] what could have been a human being becomes instead a wild animal."[15]

Caroline Walker Bynum enters an important caveat to this discussion of role models, warning us that "medieval hagiographers pointed out repeatedly that saints are not even primarily 'models' for ordinary mortals; the saints are far too dangerous for that."[16] The saint, James Keenan adds, "has always been an original, never an imitation,"[17] a judgment that is empirically supported by a quick scan of what Jennifer Herdt calls "the rainbow cast of [Christian] saints. . . . All are understood as having imitated Christ, but they are nevertheless a far cry from carbon copies of one another."[18] Augustine is not Maria Goretti, Thérèse of Lisieux is not Theresa of Calcutta, Francis is not Dorothy Day. The saints are all originals; they became virtuous and moral in their own way, and so, too, must all moral agents become virtuous and morally excellent in their own way. They must become authentically and virtuously themselves, not simply clones of Augustine or Thérèse. Yet we do learn from those whom we judge to be virtuous. The virtuous role model from whom we learn virtue by imitation offers a respected, historical account of human well-being/doing and a demonstration that the virtues are both means to and constituents of that well-being/doing. "We ought to attend to the undemonstrated sayings and opinions of experienced and older people or of people of practical wisdom not less than to demonstrations," Aristotle writes, "for, because experience has given them an eye, they see aright."[19] Their lenses, in the metaphor running through this book, are 20/20.

As we learn from role models, we must also submit them, their character, and their virtue to critical attention, perception, understanding, and the practical judgment that this role model is or is not a truly good, virtuous person and his/her virtues are means to his/her goodness and will be to ours

---

[14]Jennifer Herdt, in her *Putting on Virtue: The Legacy of the Splendid Vices* (Chicago: University of Chicago Press, 2008), gives a splendid account of the historical travails of this mimetic approach to learning virtue and ultimately comes down in its favor.

[15]Alasdair MacIntyre, *Whose Justice? Which Rationality?* (Notre Dame, IN: University of Notre Dame Press, 1988), 98.

[16]Caroline Walker Bynum, *Holy Feast and Holy Fast* (Berkeley: University of California Press, 1987), 7.

[17]James F. Keenan, "Proposing Cardinal Virtues," in *Theological Studies* 56 (1995): 709–29, at 713.

[18]Herdt, *Putting on Virtue*, 8.

[19]*NE*, VI, 11, 1143b10–13. The Council of Trent also urged the imitation of the lives and morals of saints for the cultivation of personal piety and virtue. See *Enchiridion Symbolarum Definitionum et Declarationum de Rebus Fidei et Morus*, 33rd ed., ed. Heinrich Denzinger and Adolf Schönmetzer (Rome: Herder, 1965), 1824 (hereafter DS).

in our own ways. The child's virtue is not *his/her* virtue but the virtue of the one who is his/her role model or is in authority over him/her. To become authentic and authentically virtuous and good the child must develop into *his/her* authenticity, *his/her* virtue, and *his/her* adult good. The virtuous life, like human life itself, is essentially developmental. As each person has an original way of being human, so also each has an original way of being virtuous. Neither the original human nor the original virtuous character can be ultimately created by imitating past models. They can be shaped by imitating past models but finished only by personal articulation. The dynamic of virtue begins with imitation of role models or exemplars but concludes with authentic goodness and morality through personal decision and responsibility.

EMOTIONS

We consider emotion in a section of its own because since Kant and his categorical imperative of invariant duty, it has been philosophically fashionable to dismiss human emotions as of no ethical value. Only rationality, specifically the rational appetite or will, Kant and his followers insist, is of importance for ethics. Modern virtue ethicists judge that to be a mistake. Martha Nussbaum, for instance, argues that emotions "are forms of *evaluative* judgments that ascribe to certain things and persons outside a person's own control great importance for the person's own flourishing or well-being/doing."[20] They are ways of perceiving objects as "invested with value or importance"[21] for me. We agree that emotions have a share in rationality to the extent that they signal initial cognitive content of the value of persons, objects, and situations as salient for a person's own well-being and doing. Structurally, however, Nussbaum is a neo-Stoic; for her, emotions are forms of thought. Structurally we are Thomists; for us emotions are appetitive motions,[22] initially of the sensory appetite and ultimately of the intellectual appetite or will.[23] We make a distinction between the *apprehension* of value and the *judgment* of value.[24] Emotions, we suggest, apprehend the *possible* value or disvalue of an object or situation for me,

[20]Martha C. Nussbaum, *Upheavals of Thought: The Intelligence of Emotions* (Cambridge: Cambridge University Press, 2001), 22, emphasis added. For more on the evaluative character of emotions, see Michael Stocker, "How Emotions Reveal Value and Help Cure the Schizophrenia of Modern Ethical Theories," in *How Should One Live?*, 173–90.

[21]Nussbaum, *Upheavals of Thought*, 30.

[22]Thomas Aquinas, *Summa Theologiae*, I-II, 13, 1 (hereafter *ST*).

[23]See Thomas Aquinas, *De Veritate,* 25, 1.

[24]See Fitterer, *Love and Objectivity*, 64.

tend toward or away from that object or situation,[25] and after the cognitive process outlined above, respond positively to *actual* value or negatively to *actual* disvalue.[26] The sensory appetite, exercised through the five senses, tends toward or away from an object or situation because persons apprehend it as suitable or unsuitable for their personal well-being.[27]

We agree with the claims Nussbaum makes about the cognitive content of emotions, but not with the language in which they are articulated. We agree that emotions are "central to the apprehension of value and the judgment of value,"[28] but we believe a distinction must be made between the *apprehension* of value and the *judgment* of value. Given the epistemology we have elaborated, we cannot agree with Nussbaum's description of emotion as a *judgment* of value, for we restrict the word *judgment* to the rational judgment of truth and value. That judgment is not merely an apprehension of value but the outcome of the cognitive process of apprehension, perception, understanding, and judgment that this emotion, of justice, compassion, or hatred, is a feeling that signals something genuinely salient for my well-being/doing. We are willing to describe emotion as a *proto-judgment* of value[29] but such *proto*-judgments are no more than apprehensions of *possible* value that must be refined through the cognitive process before any judgment or choice of *actual* value can be made and acted upon. Only in the rational judgment of truth and value can the possible value that emotion initially signals be judged and chosen as an actual value or disvalue for my well-being/doing. Only in this rational choice is an emotion something for which I am morally responsible.

In my cultural upbringing I may have learned hatred of people of another race and, when I encounter one, I may experience a spontaneous emotion of hatred. I am not to be blamed for that spontaneous emotion; only when I discern the emotion and consciously choose it am I in any way guilty of the moral wrong of hatred. The virtuous person is always the one whose emotions and desires are under the control of reason, particularly of the intellectual appetite or will.[30] The child and the animal do not have the capacity to be fully virtuous, Aristotle tells us, for they do not have the deliberative capacities for choice and action required for virtue.[31] They lack the judg-

---

[25]On emotion as a mode of tending, see *ST*, I-II, 22, 1.

[26]See a similar structure of emotion in Edward Collins Vacek, *Love, Human and Divine: The Heart of Christian Ethics* (Washington, DC: Georgetown University Press, 1994), 12.

[27]*ST*, I, 81, 2 ad 2.

[28]Fitterer, *Love and Objectivity*, 64.

[29]Ibid., 80. Antonio R. Damasio, *Looking for Spinoza: Joy, Sorrow, and the Feeling Brain* (Orlando, FL: Harcourt, 2003), 60–61, locates the initial triggering of both fear and anger in the amygdala in the right temporal lobe of the brain.

[30]*ST*, I, 82, 4.

[31]*NE*, III, 2, 1111a25–26, 1111b8–9; VI, 13, 1144b8.

ment that can control desires.[32] Aquinas also knows what human experience regularly demonstrates, namely, that as reason can control emotion, so also can strong emotion sometimes control reason so that it can "become remiss or altogether impeded."[33] That fact enters into virtue ethics for any judgment of guilt. That is why Pope Francis urges that in every situation, given "our awareness of the weight of mitigating circumstances—psychological, historical, even biological," we must avoid "unduly harsh or hasty judgments."[34] That consideration leads him to fully approve the gospel injunction not to judge or condemn (cf. Mt 7:1; Lk 6:37).

The second and third assertions above, that emotions are salient for a person's own individual goodness and well-being/doing are central to any consideration of virtue. The value I initially apprehend in an emotion is not a general value for every human person but a particular value perceived as salient for *my* particular good and well-being/doing. Emotions, Nussbaum claims and we agree, "contain an ineliminable reference to me."[35] They are the world apprehended specifically from *my* perspective. It is a culturally universal value, let us assume, that mothers are to be loved. When *your* mother dies, then, I might feel emotions of love and grief, but my love and grief will be nothing compared to yours. Nor will my love and grief at the death of your mother be as powerful as my love and grief when *my* mother dies. The fact that it is *my* mother who has died is not just an accidental fact of *my* life but a fact that essentially structures the entire experience for me and concentrates my keen attention on it. When that attention is cognitively processed through to the judgment of truth, my emotions reveal my deepest values and goals not only to me but also to any attentive observer.

If emotions are so self-centered, does training individuals to be attentive to them and the values they reveal not promote selfishness? It does promote selfishness, we respond, but not a selfishness that is self-centered and self-enclosed but a self-ishness that is self-attention, self-understanding, self-judgment, and self-responsibility that might lead to self-correction and greater outward-looking toward neighbors in the world. Aquinas teaches that "every nature desires its own being and its own perfection,"[36] but Michael Slote adds a caveat: "self-concern should not dwarf concern for others, but neither should the latter dwarf self-concern."[37] We agree with both Aquinas and Slote. Self-knowledge can enable a conversion from who I presently

[32]*NE*, VII, 3, 1147b5.

[33]*ST*, I-II, 77, 1.

[34]*Amoris Laetitia*, no. 308 (hereafter *AL*).

[35]Nussbaum, *Upheavals of Thought*, 52.

[36]*ST*, I, 48, 1; see also I, 5, 1.

[37]Michael Slote, "Self-Regarding and Other-Regarding Virtues," in David Carr and J. W. Steutel, eds., *Virtue Ethics and Moral Education* (New York: Routledge,1999) 97.

am to who I can become, and the more I become who I can become, the more I become of good character and virtue, the more I am enabled to deal virtuously with my neighbors, whenever, wherever, and in whatever guise I might find them.

There is a Christian consideration here. When asked which commandment was the first of all, Jesus replied: "You shall love the Lord your God with all your heart . . . the second is this, you shall love your neighbor as yourself" (Mk 12:30–31). That injunction is well-known, but perhaps not so well understood. It contains, we suggested in the Introduction, three separate injunctions: love God, love your neighbor, and love yourself. Since Augustine, Jesus's saying has been interpreted in Christian teaching as grounding a wholly legitimate and virtuous self-love.[38] John Mahoney articulates the common judgment of theologians that human reality is essentially relational when he says that, "as in God, so in his human creatures made in his image, reality is essentially relational . . . the fullness of personal identity is found only in *interpersonal* identity."[39] My relationships exercise a strong formative influence on me, my emotions, my practical judgments, and my actions. This is especially true for those who are in a loving relationship that so enhances the personal value of both the lover and the beloved that each becomes more distinctively herself/himself.[40] We assert here a commonplace assertion for Christian theologians, namely, that our love for God responding to God's love for us is the foundation of a moral life. Self-love that encloses me in myself is certainly not virtuous, for it ignores all the real relationships I have in the real world. Self-love, however, that empowers me to the understanding of my-self and my right place in those relationships, and inserts me justly and lovingly into them, is as virtuous as any love of neighbor and is, indeed, a necessary precondition for genuine love of both neighbor and God.

Margaret Farley issues an insightful warning here: "love is the problem in ethics, not the solution."[41] It is the problem, we argue, because it is usually contentless, and so we seek to give it content. Novelist Toni Morrison asserts that "You do not deserve love. . . . You can only earn [it] by practice and careful contemplation. . . . Love is not a gift. It is a diploma."[42] We suggest you earn the diploma by following an ancient definition: to love is

---

[38]See, for example, *ST*, II-II, 25, 4.

[39]John Mahoney, *The Making of Moral Theology* (Oxford: Clarendon Press, 1987), 319, emphasis added.

[40]For an extended treatment of this idea, see Michael G. Lawler, *Marriage and the Catholic Church: Disputed Questions* (Collegeville, MN: Liturgical Press, 2002), 140–61.

[41]Margaret A. Farley, "An Ethic for Same-Sex Relations," in *A Challenge to Love: Gay and Lesbian Catholics in the Church*, ed. Robert Nugent (New York: Crossroad, 1983), 93–106, at 100.

[42]Toni Morrison, *Paradise* (New York: Plume Book, 1999), 141.

to will the good of another.[43] Love is an activity of a person's will, a will for the well-being of another person. Love of another person is ecstatic; in love I go out of myself to seek the good and well-being of another equal and unique self. That there are two equal selves in any loving relationship introduces the cardinal virtue of justice, "the virtue according to which, with constant and perpetual will, someone renders to someone else her or his due rights."[44] There is, therefore, in right love always an integration of love and justice. There is always, in Farley's apposite phrase, "just love."[45] In self-love, willing my own good, I go into myself to come to self-knowledge and self-acceptance, not, however, to stay self-enclosed but to then go out from myself to will the good of another, equal self with full self-knowledge and responsibility. We argue that not only is right self-love both humanly and Christianly legitimate but also that it is the basis of all other right love, of neighbor and of God, for if humans do not fully accept themselves, neither can they give themselves fully to another person or fully accept that other person.[46]

We summarize our position on the ethical significance of emotions in a passage borrowed from Hursthouse: "1. The virtues (and vices) are morally significant. 2. The virtues (and vices) are all dispositions not only to act, but to feel emotions, as *re*actions as well as impulses to action . . . 3. In the person with the virtues, these emotions will be felt on the *right* occasions, towards the *right* people or objects, for the *right* reasons, where 'right' means 'correct.'"[47]

Neuroscience provides us with important information here. It demonstrates that a serious hemispheric asymmetry exists with respect to emotion and that the apprehension, discernment, and understanding of emotion are all predominantly associated with a right-hemisphere hub. With the single exception of anger, which is left-hemisphere dependent,[48] the right frontal lobe is critical for every other kind of emotional expression.[49] The right

---

[43]See *ST*, I-II, 28, 1c.

[44]*ST*, II-II, 58, 1.

[45]Margaret Farley, *Just Love: A Framework for Christian Sexual Ethics* (New York: Continuum, 2006).

[46]For more detail on the question of self-love, see Stephen Pope, "Expressive Individualism and True Self-Love: A Thomistic Perspective," in *Journal of Religion* 71 (1991): 384–99; Stephen Pope, *The Evolution of Altruism and the Ordering of Love* (Washington, DC: Georgetown University, 1994).

[47]Rosalind Hursthouse, "Virtue Ethics and the Emotions," in *On Virtue Ethics* (Oxford University Press, 1999), 108, emphases in original.

[48]Eddie Harmon-Jones, "Contributions from Research on Anger and Cognitive Dissonance to Understanding the Motivational Functions of Asymmetrical Frontal Brain Activity," *Biological Psychology* 67 (2004): 51–76; Tim Indersmitten and Robert C. Gur, "Emotion Processing in Chimeric Faces: Hemispheric Asymmetries in Expression and Recognition of Emotions," *Journal of Neuroscience* 23 (2003): 3820–25.

[49]Bryan Kolb and Ben Milner, "Performance of Complex Arm and Facial Movements after Focal Brain Lesions," *Neuropsychologia* 19 (1981): 491–503.

orbitofrontal cortex is essential to emotional understanding and regulation[50] and to the appreciation of the emotional significance of events.[51] Despite the left hemisphere's widely presumed predominance for language, the right hemisphere is even superior at understanding and expressing emotion in language.[52] In sum, there is clear neuroscientific evidence that humans rely predominantly on the right hemisphere for apprehending and discerning emotion, whether sensually or intellectually expressed.[53] This neuroscientific data has important, and almost-always ignored, implications for ethical method.

To recognize, understand, and interpret any human experience objectively requires both global right-brain as well as narrowly focused left-brain, attention, for objective human experience is almost always accompanied by one emotion or another. Emotions, we argued, are *proto-judgments* of value or disvalue critical for my goodness and well-being/doing. Such proto-judgments, we further argued, are apprehensions of *possible* value or disvalue to me and must be refined through the cognitive process that culminates in the rational judgment that this action at this time and in this situation is an *actual* value that can be morally acted upon. Every moral action, then, involves both the right hemisphere, which without any rational analysis apprehends an action as a value or disvalue for me and for my well-being/doing, and the left hemisphere, which analyzes this apprehension in a rational process that culminates in the practical judgment that this action, at this time, and in this situation is the good and moral thing to do.[54] The *Catechism of the Catholic Church* is completely correct in its assertion that "By his emotions a man [or a woman] *intuits* the good and suspects evil."[55] It ought to go further and assert that the initial intuition is followed by a rational process that ends in the judgment of truth that this intuited action is truly either good or evil.

---

[50]Nicole A. Roberts et al., "The Impact of Orbito-prefrontal Cortex Damage on Emotional Activation to Unanticipated and Anticipated Acoustic Startle Stimuli," *Cognitive, Affective, and Behavioral Neuroscience* 4 (2004): 301–16.

[51]Helena Barbas et al., "Serial Pathways from Primate Pre-frontal Cortex to Autonomic Areas May Influence Emotional Expression," *BMC Neuroscience* 4 (2003): 25.

[52]Teow-Chong Sim and Carolyn Martinez, "Emotion Words Are Remembered Better in the Left Ear," *Laterality* 10 (2005): 149–59; Barbara A. Cicero et al., "Emotional Versus Non-emotional Lexical Perception in Patients with Right and Left Brain Damage," *Neuropsychiatry, Neuropsychology and Behavioral Neurology* 12 (1999): 255–64.

[53]John Stirling et al., "Dichotically Presented Emotionally Intoned Words Produce Laterality Differences as a Function of Localisation Task," *Laterality* 5 (2000): 363–71; Hulya Erhan et al., "Identification of Emotion in a Dichotic Listening Task: Event-related Brain Potential and Behavioral Findings," *Brain and Cognition* 37 (1998): 286–307.

[54]For a similar explanation, see Ronald De Sousa, *Rationality of Emotion* (Boston: MIT Press, 1987); Ronald De Sousa, *Emotional Truth* (Oxford: Oxford University Press, 2011). See also Edward Collins Vacek, "Orthodoxy Requires Orthopathy: Emotions in Theology," *Horizons* 40 (2013): 218–41.

[55]*Catechism of the Catholic Church*, no. 1771, emphasis added (hereafter *CCC*).

Moral psychologist Jonathan Haidt proposes a similar position to the one we have just articulated. According to Haidt, humans operate on two different cognitive systems, a fast, effortless, and nonconscious *intuitive* system and a slow, effortful, conscious *reasoned* system. The function of the reasoned system, he argues, is to provide justifications for judgments already made by the intuitive system.[56] Neuroscientist Joshua Greene concludes from his research data to a dual-process model of human moral cognition similar to Haidt's. Greene's research focused on the brain activity of subjects responding to thought experiments related to Philippa Foot's trolley problems. There are two basic trolley problems. The first is that five men are walking along a railroad track unaware that a runaway trolley is coming behind them and will kill all five when it hits them. Another man sees the situation and is in a position to switch the trolley to another track on which a person is sitting. The moral question posed is whether the man should switch the trolley, saving the five men but killing the one person. The second scenario is that a man is standing together with a second heavy man on a bridge over the track. If he throws the heavy man over the bridge and stops the trolley, he will save the five men on the track but will kill the heavy man. The moral question posed is whether he should throw the heavy man into the track of the trolley. Greene asked his subjects to resolve these moral dilemmas and assessed the activity of various brain regions using functional magnetic resonance imaging (fMRI). He found that in the first scenario, switching the track of the trolley, the brain activity was in areas involved in cognitive processing and took longer, and in the second scenario, throwing the man off the bridge, the brain activity was in areas involved in emotional processing and was quicker. He concluded that these findings support a dual-process model of moral cognition similar to the one proposed by Haidt in which the different fMRI responses arise from two different subsystems in the brain.[57]

We do not necessarily agree with all of either Haidt's or Greene's conclusions, but we do agree with their major conclusion: there are two systems of moral cognition in the human brain, one emotional and intuitive, the other rational and reasoned. How the two systems are related is still a matter for debate, but we believe that there is no debate over our primary concern here, namely, that Catholic theological ethicists must learn to pay more attention to neuroscience, the human brain, human emotions and the

[56]Jonathan Haidt, "The Emotional Dog and Its Rational Tail: A Social Intuitionist Approach to Moral Judgment," *Psychological Review* 108, no. 4 (2001): 813–34; Jonathan Haidt, *The Righteous Mind: Why Good People Are Divided by Politics and Religion* (London: Penguin, 2012).

[57]Joshua D. Greene, "The Neural Bases of Cognitive Conflict and Control in Ethical Judgment," *Neuron 44* (2004): 389–400; Joshua D. Greene, *Moral Tribes: Emotion, Reason, and the Gap between Us and Them* (London: Atlantic Books, 2014).

sometimes-functional restrictions they place "on all thought processes, and hence [on] how we experience religion, spirituality, and theology."[58]

THREE STAGES OF THE CONCEPT OF A VIRTUE

Alasdair MacIntyre's *After Virtue* presents three successive logical steps in his account of virtue—practice, narrative order of a single human life, and moral traditions. We investigate these to shed light on different virtuous perspectives. MacIntyre explains "practice" as any coherent and complex form of socially established cooperative human activity through which goods internal to that form of activity are realized in the course of trying to achieve those standards of excellence that are appropriate to, and partially definitive of, that form of activity, with the result that human powers to achieve excellence, and human conceptions of the ends and goods involved, are systematically extended.[59] Practice is not the simple act of throwing a football with skill but the broader and more complex game of football itself with its rules, strategies, and players, not the act of moving a pawn on a chessboard but the complex game of chess itself with its rules, strategies, and players. The game of human life is also a practice with its rules defined in particular cultures.

Practice includes "the creation and sustenance of various forms of human community such as nations, cities, and families,"[60] and requires standards of excellence and obedience to rules, like the rules of football and the rules of living together with others. Goods can be either external or internal. External goods, such as power, fame, and wealth, are objects of competition within practices where there are winners and losers. Michael Jordan, Peyton Manning, and Arnold Palmer are judged winners within their practices and, to equally excel, individuals are to imitate them. Internal goods, such as skill and excellence, are also the result of competition to excel, and their achievement can benefit whole communities. Saint John Paul II, Mother Teresa, and Mahatma Gandhi are declared excellent and winners within their life practices, and they also are exemplars to be imitated in the quest for a life of excellence. MacIntyre situates virtues within practices, and they are essential for gaining and nourishing internal goods. He defines virtue as "an acquired human quality the possession and exercise of which tends to enable us to achieve those goods which are internal to practices and the lack of which

---

[58]Andrew B. Newberg, *Principles of Neurotheology* (Burlington, VT: Ashgate, 2010), 84.

[59]MacIntyre, *After Virtue*, 187.

[60]John S. Grabowski, *Sex and Virtue: An Introduction to Sexual Ethics* (Washington, DC: Catholic University of America Press, 2003), 149.

effectively prevents us from achieving any such goods."[61] That a practice is a "socially established cooperative human activity" signals the importance of membership in, and the influence of, a community and culture on both virtue and the individual learning virtue. The form of "socially established cooperative human activity" is the search for virtue or goodness, and "goods internal to that form of activity" are the virtues themselves as defined in a particular cultural perspective. It is a central claim of virtue theory from Aristotle to MacIntyre that virtues are shaped in a community and culture by narratives and exemplary models judged to be virtuous.

MacIntyre qualifies the notion of a practice. A practice has a history that, though it is not immune to criticism and often requires development, serves as a standard for evaluating present practices. When we begin to play football, for example, we measure our practice on the basis of the established rules, excellent players who have been role models up to that point, and standards of excellence.[62] However, the rules and role models are never stagnant. "Practices never have a goal or goals fixed for all time . . . but the goals themselves are transmuted for all times."[63] Rules of the game change to improve the game, and new role models of excellence emerge to redefine the nature of perfection or prowess within the sport itself. Records are made to be broken and breaking records indicates that the practice evolves and changes within a set of parameters. Virtue accounts for these parameters, the continuum mean between excess and defect. Within this continuum mean, there are many ways the goods in the game can be realized.

The particularity of practices is set within the context of "the narrative order of a single human life,"[64] which is a "unity of a narrative quest."[65] MacIntyre explains that the medieval concept of a quest helps to explain narrative and includes two features. First, it requires some understanding of a final *telos* or good. Second, the quest is a *search for* a particular definition of the universal good that coincides with one's lived narrative, not a *discovery of* a predefined definition of the good for all people, times, and cultures. Virtues sustain both practices and those who follow them in their quest for the good. The quest is for individuals with multiple narratives that particularize the universal good; it is also for communities who pursue the good but also refine its meaning and nature. There are, again, continuum mediums for the individual and community about what does and does not fulfill the good. "If the narrative of our individual and social lives is to continue intelligibly . . . it is always both the case that there are constraints

[61]MacIntyre, *After Virtue*, 191.
[62]Ibid., 190.
[63]Ibid., 194.
[64]Ibid., 187.
[65]Ibid., 219.

on how the story can continue and that within those constraints there are indefinitely many ways that it can continue."[66] Within the continuum mediums, and this is crucial for our discussion of virtues, "one and the same segment of human behavior may be correctly characterized in a number of different ways."[67] A person running and pushing an old man to the ground could be attacking him or he could be pushing him out of the way of an oncoming car. A person practicing Natural Family Planning (NFP) could be practicing the virtue of responsibility or the vice of a contralife attitude. The reality in both cases depends on intention, circumstances, and the context of the narrative being followed by the person pushing the old man to the ground or the person practicing NFP.

The third stage of the concept of virtue, which sustains the other two stages, is tradition. "A living tradition . . . is an historically extended, socially embodied argument precisely in part about the goods which constitute that tradition."[68] MacIntyre explains the relationship between a practice, narrative, and tradition. "The history of a practice in our time is generally and characteristically embedded in and made intelligible in terms of the larger and longer history of the tradition through which the practice in its present form was conveyed to us; the [narrative] of each of our own lives is generally and characteristically embedded in and made intelligible in terms of the larger and longer histories of a number of traditions." When a tradition is living, it involves "continuities of conflict"[69] to refine and redefine definitions of the good and the cultural and contextual continuum mean of its definitions. Since individual histories, cultures, and contexts are always particular within a universal good, there can be differences of the meaning of an act between an individual in a given practice or narrative and another individual in another practice or narrative.

What is the interrelationship between MacIntyre's three stages? He himself argues that "each later stage presupposes the earlier, but not *vice versa*." He explains that "each earlier stage is both modified by and reinterpreted in the light of, but also provides an essential constituent of, each later stage. The progress in the development of the concept [of virtue] is closely related to, although it does not recapitulate in any straightforward way, the history of the tradition of which it forms the core."[70] In the evolution of practice, narrative, and tradition, there is a dialectical relationship between them; the practice is modified and reinterpreted by the narrative, and the practice and narrative are further modified and reinterpreted by the tradition. The practice

---

[66]Ibid., 216.
[67]Ibid., 206.
[68]Ibid., 222.
[69]Ibid., 222.
[70]Ibid., 187.

of playing football is modified by the narrative of an individual who plays football and also engages in other practices, like being a son or daughter, husband or wife, teacher or student, that shape and impact the level and degree of commitment he/she can make to the practice of playing football in relation to all those others. The different practices have a combination of virtues that sustain them, but they may also conflict with virtues in other practices and impact the realization of the internal goods associated with that practice. A person's individual and communal narratives and the multiple practices within those narratives impact the realization of the goods within a particular practice and may put the virtues that sustain conflicting practices into conflict. Prominent virtue ethicist Rosalind Hursthouse refers to this situation as "the conflict problem" between virtues.[71] Such a conflict problem is evident, for example, between the virtue of chastity that sustains the practice of NFP for regulating fertility in marriage and the virtue of justice that sustains the practice of responsible parenthood when NFP is not an option due to historical, cultural, or contextual variables.

Traditions evolve in their understanding of the good through virtues that sustain an ongoing search for the good; so also do the nature, understanding, and interrelationship between the virtues themselves in this search. There seems to be more of an ongoing dialectic between practice, narrative, and traditions in evolving traditions than MacIntyre allows. Lived narratives, of Gandhi and Martin Luther King, for instance, change traditions and the definition of their good; they also change the definition of the virtues that sustain the practices, narratives, and traditions. Prior to the lived narrative of Martin Luther King, segregation between races was an accepted good in the United States. After his lived narrative, the good in the United States no longer included segregation. King's lived narrative changed the tradition and the definition of the universal good in the United States. It also changed the virtue of justice.

VIRTUE ETHICS

In the Introduction we discussed virtue *theory*, which is concerned neutrally with the nature of virtue in general. In this section, we discuss virtue *ethics*, which is more an advocacy of virtue and virtuous action. In the post-enlightenment period, virtue was distrusted, largely because of anxiety over both the authenticity of virtues humanly acquired through imitation of exemplars or role models and questions of divine and human

[71]Hursthouse, *On Virtue Ethics,* 52–55.

agency.[72] In *After Virtue*, however, Alasdair MacIntyre makes the "disquieting suggestion" that in the contemporary world the language of morality is in a state of disorder. "We possess indeed," he argues, "simulacra of morality; we continue to use many of the key expressions. But we have—very largely, if not entirely—lost our comprehension, both theoretical and practical, of morality."[73] Jennifer Herdt adds that "contemporary revivers of virtue ethics, in contrast [to the distrust of virtue] have enthusiastically embraced the notion that habituation in virtue takes place within the context of a community and its practices."[74] Post-Kantian moral philosophers concentrated their attention on specific acts that are mandated by laws and rules. Post-Tridentine Catholic theological ethicists also concentrated their attention on acts mandated by laws and rules, and they created a taxonomy of *sins* arising from the violation of laws and obligations. Such an approach ignored questions of personal virtue, character, fulfillment, and well-being/doing. It ignored, Louis Janssens argued, "the human *person* integrally and adequately considered."[75]

Janssens developed a personalism rooted in the methodological transformation in the Second Vatican Council's *Gaudium et Spes* from a biological to a rational perception of natural law that we dealt with in Chapter 1. "When there is a question of harmonizing conjugal love with the responsible transmission of life," the Council decreed, "the moral aspect of any procedure . . . must be determined by objective standards. These [are] *based on the nature of the human person* and his acts."[76] At the same time, other philosophers and theologians, not all of them challenged by the Second Vatican Council, were also paying increasing attention to the human person, his/her character, habits, feelings, perceptions, judgments, and perhaps above all goodness and well-being/doing. Virtue ethics was coming, not so much to birth as to *re*birth, for it had already flourished in the Greece of Plato and Aristotle and in the medieval Europe of Thomas Aquinas, not to mention in the Christian New Testament of the first centuries.

Focus on the total human person rather than on his/her isolated acts led to the assertion that virtue ethics focuses on *being* and *character*, the being of a personal subject, and that the deontological ethics of duty or utilitarian ethics of consequences focuses on the subject's *doing* or action. That assertion is true enough, but it is not particularly clarifying of virtue ethics, and, indeed, if it is understood to mean that virtue ethics ignores *doing*, it

[72]See Herdt, *Putting on Virtue*, passim.

[73]MacIntyre, *After Virtue*, 2.

[74]Herdt, *Putting on Virtue*, 350.

[75]Louis Janssens, "Artificial Insemination: Ethical Considerations," *Louvain Studies* 8 (1980): 3–29, at 4, emphasis added.

[76]*Gaudium et Spes*, no. 51, emphasis added (hereafter *GS*).

is untrue, for we expect the virtuous person to *do* virtuously. We expect the character with the virtue of justice to *do* just actions, we expect the character with the virtue of compassion to do compassionate actions, and so on for all the virtues. Contrary to critics who suggest that virtue ethics does not offer ethical directions or rules, it does offer rules. It offers, Hursthouse insists, "v-rules."[77] Sometimes, these v-rules are prescriptive: do justly, do compassionately. Sometimes they are proscriptive: do not do what is mean, unjust, or cruel. Ethical action is action according to some virtue; vicious action is action according to some vice. The ethics of Aristotle and Aquinas was, and contemporary virtue ethics is, an ethics of character and being, but there was and there is always the axiom *agere sequitur esse*, action follows being. It is, in fact, as we argued earlier, the habitual doing of acts of justice, compassion, and so on for all the virtues that first instills and then reinforces the habits that are virtues and the actions to which they are ordered. "Morality," John Mahoney asserts, "is ultimately in this view not about actions but about the acting subject."[78]

Rather than say, then, that virtue ethics focuses on being and character, and deontological ethics focuses on action or doing, we prefer to say that virtue ethics gives precedence to virtue, character, and being over action and doing. Broadly speaking, deontological ethics holds that only judgments about right action are basic in ethics and that virtues, and the virtuous character, are always derivative from right action. In virtue ethics the converse is the case; only judgments about virtue and the virtuous character are basic in ethics, and right action is derivative from virtue and the virtuous character. In virtue ethics, the virtuous agent and his/her character come first, and ethical actions come second. Ethical actions are as important in virtue ethics as in any other ethical system, but the primary judgment in virtue ethics is not about the actions but about the character from which they stem.[79] In virtue ethics, Paul Wadell argues, "the project of the moral life is to become a certain kind of person,"[80] a virtuous person, one who knows how to feel and act in ways appropriate to the circumstances. We believe this approach to, and articulation of, virtue ethics is correct and provides greater insight into and understanding of the nature of virtue ethics than the bald statement that virtue ethics is an ethics of being rather than doing.

Here we must add that persons deemed virtuous may on occasion act

[77]Hursthouse, *On Virtue Ethics*, 36–39.

[78]Mahoney, *The Making of Moral Theology*, 220. See also Darlene Fozard Weaver, *The Acting Person and the Christian Moral Life* (Washington, DC: Georgetown University Press, 2011).

[79]See Daniel Statman, "Introduction to Virtue Ethics," in *Virtue Ethics*, 7; Michael Slote, "Virtue Ethics and Democratic Values," *Journal of Social Philosophy* 24 (1993): 5–37, at 15; Peter Van Inwagen, "Response to Slote," *Social Theory and Practice* 16 (1990): 385–95, at 392.

[80]Paul Wadell, *Friendship and the Moral Life* (Notre Dame, IN: University of Notre Dame Press, 1989), 136.

less than virtuously. As subjects in history, they have not yet finished their journeys to virtue; they may be deemed already virtuous, but they are not yet as authentically or consistently virtuous as they could be. Aristotle recognized this problem and solved it by arguing that a person is not to be judged virtuous except "in a complete life. For one swallow does not make a summer . . . and so too one day, or a short time, does not make a man blessed and happy," or virtuous.[81] Contemporary theologians say that subjects in history, along with their virtues and ethics, are eschatological.

CHRISTIAN VIRTUE ETHICS

We have argued that virtue, virtue ethics, and the learning of both are rooted in some community and culture, and up to this point we have been developing a virtue ethics rooted broadly in human culture. We have been developing what might be called a natural virtue ethics. We turn our attention now briefly to a Christian virtue ethics, one rooted in belief in Jesus Christ as the revelation of God.[82] In the 1970s, some Catholic ethicists were tempted to argue that Christian ethics was not distinctively different from natural ethics,[83] by which they meant that virtuous actions were the same in both natural and Christian ethics. We, and most Christian ethicists today, do not accept their argument. Those earlier ethicists were locked into an ethics that focused on actions as moral or immoral, and they meant that natural ethics and Christian ethics held many of the same actions as moral. We grant that many of the virtues and the actions they demand and enable appear to be the same in natural and Christian ethics, but the community in which Christians learn virtues, the rainbow of exemplars they have for the imitation and habituation of virtuous actions, the proximate and final ends to which their virtuous actions tend, the perspective out of which they are done, all are different in natural and Christian ethics. That, we submit, creates major differences between the two.

The Christian perspective shines out brightly throughout the New Testa-

---

[81]*NE*, I, 7, 1098a, 18–19.

[82]For modern treatments of Christian virtue ethics, see Josef Fuchs, *Personal Responsibility and Christian Morality* (Washington, DC: Georgetown University Press, 1983); Bruno Schüller, *Wholly Human* (Washington, DC: Georgetown University Press, 1985); Joseph J. Kotva, Jr., *The Christian Case for Virtue Ethics* (Washington, DC: Georgetown University Press, 1997); Keenan, "Proposing Cardinal Virtues"; Grabowski, *Sex and Virtue*; William C. Mattison, III, *Introducing Moral Theology: Happiness and the Virtues* (Grand Rapids: Brazos Press, 2008); Martin Rhonheimer, and Gerald Malsbary, *The Perspective of Morality: Philosophical Foundations of Thomistic Virtue Ethics* (Washington, DC: Catholic University of America Press, 2011); Daniel J. Harrington and James F. Keenan, *Paul and Virtue Ethics: Building Bridges between New Testament Studies and Moral Theology* (Lanham, MD: Rowman & Littlefield, 2010).

[83]See Norbert J. Rigali, "On Christian Ethics," *Chicago Studies* 10 (1971): 227–47.

ment, but we call attention to two specific texts, one in the conclusion to the parable of the Good Samaritan, the other in Paul's letter to the Philippians. After offering his Samaritan parable, Jesus asks the lawyer who initiated the discussion, "Which of these do you think proved neighbor to the man who fell among robbers?" The lawyer answered, "the one who showed mercy on him." And Jesus said to him "go and do likewise" (Lk 10:36–37). That "go and do likewise" controls everything moral that Christians are called to do. Paul articulated the same vision, if in different language: "Have this mind among yourselves which is yours in Christ Jesus, who though he was in the form of God did not count equality with God a thing to be grasped, but emptied himself, taking the form of a servant, being born in the likeness of men" (Phil 2:5–7). Self-sacrificing love for God and neighbor and obedience to God's discerned will in imitation of Jesus the Christ: these specifically distinguish the person the Christian is called to be.

Virtue ethics offers an answer to the question, "Who am I to become?" The New Testament invites the followers of Jesus to *become* and *be* like Jesus and, because they *are* like him, to *do* like him. The controlling principle of Christian virtue ethics is *imitatio Christi*: first, *be* like Jesus and, then, *do* like Jesus. The specifically *Christian* virtuous life is in answer to the popular acronym WWJD, what would Jesus do. That principle roots a specifically Christian virtue ethics. It is, as is all virtue ethics, agent centered; who Christians are called to be takes precedence over what they are called to do. The imitation of Christ is not some means external to character that makes being and doing like Christ possible; it is something that is an internal, essential constituent of the specifically Christian character. It is what Karl Rahner called an *existential* of their Christian character, "an ontological modification . . . added indeed to nature by God's grace and therefore 'supernatural,' but in fact never lacking in the real order."[84] Having the mind of Christ as an essential specification of their character, Christians are called to act out of that mind habitually. They act, as the New Testament regularly says, out of their "heart" (Mt 5:8, 28; 6:21; 12:34, 40; 13:15; 15:8, 18, 19; 22:37), in Jewish anthropology the zone of "mind, wisdom, folly, intention, plan, will, affection, love, hate, sight, regard, blindness."[85]

Consideration of the "heart" leads us to the virtue Aquinas calls "the mother and root of all virtues"[86] and "the most excellent of the virtues,"[87]

---

[84]Karl Rahner and Herbert Vorgrimler, *Concise Theological Dictionary*, 2nd ed. (London: Burns & Oates, 1983), 161; Karl Rahner, "The Dignity and Freedom of Man," in *Theological Investigations* (London: Darton, Longman, Todd, 1967), 2:239–40.

[85]Bruce J. Malina, *The New Testament World: Insights from Cultural Anthropology* (Louisville, KY: Westminster/John Knox, 1993), 74.

[86]*ST*, I-II, 62, 4.

[87]*ST*, II-II, 23, 6.

namely, charity or self-sacrificing love. A scribe asked Jesus "which commandment is the first of all?" Jesus answered that the first is "you shall love the Lord your God with all your heart" and "the second is this, you shall love your neighbor as yourself." "There is no other commandment," he added, "greater than these" (Mk 12:29–31). Nor, in the Christian perspective, is there any other virtue greater than charity, for all other virtues are quickened by charity and receive from charity their full complement as virtues. Virtues, we already explained, are both means to, and constituents of, human goodness and well-being/doing. Aquinas argued that man's happiness is twofold. "One is proportionate to human nature, a happiness, to wit, which man can obtain by means of his natural principles. The other is a happiness surpassing man's nature, and which man can obtain by the power of God alone." It is necessary, then, "for man to receive from God some additional principles, whereby he may be directed to supernatural happiness. . . . Such principles are called *theological virtues:* first, because their object is God; secondly, because they are infused in us by God alone."[88] These infused theological virtues are charity, faith, and hope.

"Charity is the theological virtue by which we love God above all things for God's own sake, and our neighbor as ourselves for the love of God."[89] Jesus's greatest commandment invites us to do acts of love toward God and neighbor. "Faith is the theological virtue by which we believe in God and believe all that he has said and revealed to us."[90] Paul insisted on the necessity of theological faith for salvation (Rom 1:16–17, 3:26–30, 5:1; Gal 3:6–9), and that theological tradition flowered on both sides of the Reformation controversies. Martin Luther took his stand on "faith alone" and the Council of Trent taught that faith is "the beginning of human salvation . . . without which it is impossible to please God."[91] Neither doubted that faith must issue in "works," that is, acts in accord with faith. Another notable difference appears here between natural and Christian ethics: the natural man practices virtue according to reason; the Christian practices virtue according to reason quickened by charity and faith. "Hope is the theological virtue by which we desire the kingdom of heaven [or God] and eternal life as our happiness, placing our trust in Christ's promises."[92] Hope, too, must issue in action. There is a critical caveat, however, to which we must attend when we talk of virtues, even God-infused virtues, and their contribution to supernatural goodness, well-being/doing, and happiness.

All virtues, including theological virtues, are qualities, dispositions, and

[88] *ST*, I-II, 62, 1, emphasis added.
[89] *CCC*, no. 1822.
[90] *CCC*, no. 1814.
[91] DS, 1532.
[92] *CCC*, no. 1817.

habits[93] in the human person that are ordered to acts.[94] A virtue is a prerequisite to its corresponding act, but it is not the act nor does it ineluctably lead to the act. Translation from the virtue to the act requires the subject to be attentive, perceptive, understanding, judging, and deciding, and again it is only at the point of judgment, decision, and action that moral action enters in. The Christian traditions hold that the virtues of charity, faith, and hope are infused into the new Christian at baptism. For any of those virtues to become personal acts of love, faith, or hope, they must be translated by the believer into free and moral action. Jean Porter puts it well: infused virtues are "present only potentially in those who lack the use of reason, and . . . present only in a minimal degree even in some of those who possess the use of reason."[95] For a person to be self-responsible and personally moral, "infused virtue must blossom out in a personal act"[96] and, as we have seen, "a habit of virtue cannot be caused by one act, but only by many."[97] Repeated acts of charity, faith, and hope, therefore, on the right occasion, toward the right people, and for the right reasons, habituate the theological virtues in the Christian character, as repeated acts of any virtue habituate acquired virtues in any agent's character. The Christian becomes and does more like Jesus Christ by repeated acts of virtue. Even the theological virtues, infused by God though they are, need to be exercised over and over by the agent to habituate his/her character to Christian excellence and ultimate goodness.

Besides the three God-infused virtues, there are what are called four "cardinal virtues" important to Christians, cardinal because they are hinges around which other human virtues turn. They are prudence, justice, fortitude, and temperance, described by Aquinas as principles of integration of both the agent and his actions.[98] Aristotle argued that prudence is "A true and *reasoned* state of capacity to act with regard to the things that are good or bad for man."[99] Aquinas followed him, arguing that prudence is a special virtue[100] by which "right reason is applied to action."[101] Prudence is an intellectual virtue that discerns and applies universal principles to particular situations and enables subjects to make practical judgments that this is the right thing to do on this occasion, toward this right person, and for this right

[93]*ST*, III, 69, 4.

[94]*ST*, I-II, 49, 3.

[95]Jean Porter, "The Subversion of Virtue: Acquired and Infused Virtues in the *Summa Theologiae*," *Annual of the Society of Christian Ethics* (1992), 19–41, at 30.

[96]Ladislas Orsy, "Faith, Sacrament, Contract, and Christian Marriage: Disputed Questions," *Theological Studies* 43 (1982): 379–98, 383, n. 7. See also Michael G. Lawler, "Faith, Contract, and Sacrament in Christian Marriage: A Theological Approach," *Theological Studies* 52 (1991): 712–31.

[97]*ST*, I-II, 51, 3.

[98]*ST*, I-II, 61, 2 and 3.

[99]*NE*, VI, 5, 1140b, 5, emphasis added.

[100]*ST*, II-II, 47, 5.

[101]*ST*, II-II, 47, 2.

reason. Its ethical importance is evident from the fact that practical judgment is what the Catholic tradition calls "conscience." Prudence is crucially important for both the natural and the Christian agent.

Justice, "the perpetual and constant will to render to each one his right,"[102] is essentially about equality;[103] equality as human and equality as child of God. Since it is about rendering to each person his/her right, it is also essentially about human relationships, for persons must be somehow related to other persons in order to render them their rights. Indeed, in relations between equal agents, Aristotle writes, "justice is often thought to be the greatest of virtues."[104] Aquinas agrees: justice "excels the other moral virtues," and it excels them for two reasons: first, it is "in the more excellent part of the soul, viz. the rational appetite or will;" second, "justice is somewhat the good of another person."[105] Is it because justice excels the other moral virtues that the paradigmatic virtuous man is often called simply the "just man," as is Joseph (Mt 1:19), or "righteous man," as is Noah (Gn 6:9) and Abraham (Gn 15:6)? "Keep justice and do righteousness," preaches Isaiah, "blessed is the man who does this" (56:1). Jesus condemns the scribes and Pharisees who "have neglected the weightier matters of the law, justice and mercy and faith" (Mt 23:23). The virtuous Christian, thus far in our analysis, is the one who *is* prudent and just and *does* prudent and just acts quickened by charity.

The human, Aquinas writes, "is hindered in two ways from following the rectitude of reason. First, by being drawn by some object of pleasure to something other than what the rectitude of reason requires; and this obstacle is removed by the virtue of temperance. Second, through the will being disinclined to follow that which is in accord with reason, on account of some difficulty that presents itself," and this obstacle is removed by the virtue of fortitude.[106] Both fortitude and temperance are cardinal virtues required to overcome difficulties and enable the practice of other moral virtues. "Fortitude is the moral virtue that ensures firmness in difficulties and constancy in the pursuit of the good."[107] It strengthens persons to overcome obstacles that present themselves to the practice of the virtues and the morally good life. It is mental fortitude that enables them to overcome obstacles and clears the way for them to exercise virtues. Acts of charity and compassion hinge on the prior act of mental fortitude; that makes fortitude a cardinal virtue.

---

[102]*ST*, II-II, 58, 1 and 11.

[103]See Paul Ricoeur, "Love and Justice," in *Radical Pluralism and Truth: David Tracy and the Hermeneutics of Religion*, ed. Werner G. Jeanrond and Jennifer L. Rike (New York: Crossroad, 1991), 195. Ricoeur argues that from Aristotle to Rawls justice has always been about equality.

[104]*NE*, V, 1, 1129b, 27.

[105]*ST*, II-II, 58, 12.

[106]*ST*, II-II, 123, 1.

[107]*CCC*, no. 1808.

Aristotle and Aquinas both classify temperance as a virtue, and Aquinas further classifies it as a cardinal virtue.[108] Temperance "is the moral virtue that moderates the attraction of pleasures and provides balance in the use of created goods."[109] Temperance is about balance, the mean between excess and defect that prudence finds to indicate where virtue lies. From the Christian perspective, the behavior of the two clerics on the road to Jericho in Jesus's parable of the Good Samaritan (Lk 10:29–37) is a series of excesses: disdain instead of charity, contempt instead of compassion, injustice instead of justice toward the man they find on the road, an equal child of God. Temperance, quickened by charity and illuminated by prudence, clears the way for the balanced act of charity, compassion, and justice; it is a cardinal virtue. Since it, however, "moderates only the desires and pleasures which affect man himself," it is not as excellent as justice and fortitude, which regard more the common good. "Prudence and the theological virtues are more excellent" than any of the other virtues.[110]

An often-raised objection to the notion of a Christian virtue ethics is the fact that it is *Christian* and, therefore, not universally applicable. It is applicable, so runs the objection, only to Christians and is, therefore, relative. The answer to this objection stretches in a long line from MacIntyre and Lonergan back to Aristotle: meaning systems, including ethical meaning systems, are learned in a specific community and are indeed, therefore, all community relative.[111] A second response to the objection is an empirical one. For all their undoubted perspectivisms, the great ethical systems reach conclusions that are not as different as is supposed. What we have called their perspectives and lenses may be different, but they agree broadly that the good can be defined, on core moral values, norms, and behaviors, as evidenced by their various and uncommonly similar versions of the Golden Rule. For Christians it is, "Whatever you wish that men would do to you do so to them; for this is the law and the prophets" (Mt 7:12); for Jews it is, "What is hateful to you do not do to your fellowman" (Talmud, Shabbat, 3id); for Muslims it is, "No one of you is a believer until he desires for his brother that which he desires for himself" (Sunnah); for Buddhists it is, "Hurt not others in ways that you yourself would find hurtful" (Udana-Varga 5,1); for Hindus, it is "This is the sum of duty; do naught unto others what you would not have them do unto you" (Mahabharata 5, 1517). The saints in these various religious traditions, the virtuous persons to be

---

[108] *ST*, II-II, 141, 7.

[109] *CCC*, no. 1809.

[110] *ST*, II-II, 141, 8.

[111] Lonergan, *Insight*, 344. For a fuller explanation of perspectivism, see Todd A. Salzman and Michael G. Lawler, *Sexual Ethics: A Theological Introduction* (Washington, DC: Georgetown University Press, 2012), xxi–xxiii.

imitated for the habituation of virtue, all endorse and exhibit a common core of behaviors. Since *agere sequitur esse* (that is, action follows being), it is easy to conclude to similar character states and virtues that are shaped and limited, but in no way nullified, because they derive from particular stances or perspectives.

Jesuit James Keenan offers an alternative theory of cardinal virtues based on "rightly realizing the ways we are related."[112] "Our identity," he argues, "is relational in three ways: generally, specifically, and uniquely."[113] From this trinity he derives the cardinal virtues of justice, fidelity, and self-care, and adds to them the virtue of prudence on which all three hinge. For a reason that will become clear, we prefer a different trinity: generally, particularly, and self-ishly. In general, humans are beings in relation to other beings who, as humans, are equals and, as Christian, are equal children of God. This essential human and religious equality demands the virtue of justice as we have explained it above. In specific, we are in relation to particular persons with bonds of family or friendship. Christians are, Augustine enjoins, to love all within their reach;[114] they are, Aquinas specifies, following the Letter to Timothy, which instructs us to have care "especially for family members" (1 Tm 5:8), to love those nearest to us most of all.[115] Justice is about universality and impartiality; fidelity is about legitimate particularity and partiality. John Henry Newman endorses this legitimate partiality when he argues that "the best preparation for loving the world at large, and loving it duly and wisely [under the guidance of prudence], is to cultivate an intimate friendship and affection toward those who are immediately about us."[116] All these relationships demand the virtue of fidelity and its cognates, loyalty and constancy.

Each of us is also in essential relationship to our self; we are in a relationship that we have already termed self-ish and/or self-loving. Everything we said earlier about the Christian legitimacy of self-love recurs here, and this legitimate and moral virtue of self-love demands what Keenan calls the virtue of self-care. Self-care includes self-awareness, self-knowledge, self-acceptance, and self-love. Psychological studies repeatedly indicate that one of the greatest threats to healthy human flourishing is poor self-esteem[117] and, despite Jesus's injunction to "love your neighbor *as yourself*" (Mk 12:31), the Christian tradition has not been a noted promoter of

---

[112]Harrington and Keenan, *Jesus and Virtue Ethics*, 122.

[113]Ibid., 123.

[114]Augustine, *The City of God*, trans. Marcus Dods (New York: Modern Library, 1994), 693.

[115]*ST*, II-II, 26, 6, 7, and 8.

[116]John Henry Newman, *Parochial and Plain Sermons* (San Francisco: Ignatius, 1987) Sermon 5, 258.

[117]See Jack Dominian, "Sexuality and Personal Relationships," in *Embracing Sexuality: Authority and Experience in the Catholic Church*, ed. Joseph Selling (Burlington, VT: Ashgate, 2001), 13.

healthy self-love.[118] Self-care is the virtue that points to healthy self-love and invites reflection on my unique self as a gift of God that summons me to recognize, accept, appreciate, and use that gift in the Christian task of drawing closer in self-sacrificing love to neighbor and to God. The three virtues of justice, fidelity, and self-care, neither of which takes precedence over the others, clear the ground for the practice of other virtues in each relationship. They are, that is, Keenan argues, cardinal virtues. They are, however, all preceded in importance by a fourth cardinal virtue, once again prudence, which discerns and judges which acts qualify as just, faithful, and self-caring, just as it discerns and judges which acts are just, courageous, and temperate for the traditional cardinal virtues. Whether one numbers the cardinal virtues as we explain them or as Keenan explains them, it remains critical that they be habituated by repeated actual exercise in imitation of role models respected in the Christian community of meaning.

CHRISTIAN VIRTUE ETHICS: MARTIN RHONHEIMER

The presentation we have made of the virtues is a standard Catholic theological ethical presentation, and Keenan's approach, we judge, fits within the legitimate parameters of that standard presentation. Catholic philosopher Martin Rhonheimer offers another alternative presentation that we must consider. Rhonheimer's interpretation of natural law emphasizes the role and function of virtue to justify moral absolutes. His unique contribution is to develop an "intimate connection" between virtues and the precepts of the natural law.[119] He seeks to provide an alternative reading of Aquinas's theory of natural law that critiques and diverges from the neo-Scholastic interpretation that grounds natural law in the natural order that contains intrinsic moral meaning, which is read by practical reason to determine moral action. Rhonheimer judges that this interpretation of natural law suffers from the "dualistic fallacy,"[120] a separation between objective nature and subjective reason. He seeks to overcome the dualistic fallacy by developing a "personal structure of practical reason"[121] that integrates nature and reason. This view of practical reason shapes his anthropology and his view of human sexuality.

---

[118]In his "Proposing Cardinal Virtues," Keenan eschews both self-love and self-esteem in favor of self-care (727). We have no problem with the notion of self-love as we have earlier explained it.

[119]Martin Rhonheimer, "The Cognitive Structure of the Natural Law and the Truth of Subjectivity," *Thomist* 67 (2003): 38.

[120]Martin Rhonheimer, *Natural Law and Practical Reason: A Thomist View of Moral Autonomy* (New York: Fordham University Press, 1993), 557; Rhonheimer, "Cognitive Structure."

[121]Jean Porter, *Nature as Reason: A Thomistic Theory of Natural Law* (Grand Rapids: Eerdmans), 188.

The basic tenets of Rhonheimer's personal anthropology and ethics are the following. First, the human person is a "corporeal-spiritual unity;"[122] there is no dualism between body and spirit. The neo-Scholastic interpretation of Aquinas's natural law theory is open to the accusation of physicalism or biologism,[123] and Rhonheimer's theory of corporeal-spiritual unity responds to this accusation. He argues that the subjectivity of the person, specifically subjective reason, is part of the objective nature of the human person. The natural law exists in persons as knowing subjects and in that sense is "subjective." It is also "objective" in that the natural inclinations draw us to the good in its various manifestations as part of the eternal law we know in and through reason. Inclination toward the good emerges out of our corporeal-spiritual unity, which practical reason perceives as a good that must be respected as an aspect of the human person. We know the nature of the person only by first knowing the specifically human good.[124]

The human person possesses "real autonomy," what Rhonheimer calls "participated theonomy," which means that the person "will understand the good known by him not only as a 'good to be done' but also as the will of God."[125] He believes that this autonomy–theonomy distinguishes his theory from the so-called autonomous ethics school of natural law, which claims that natural law essentially means to act reasonably and responsibly according to the principle of proportionate reason, that is, balancing the premoral values and disvalues of particular acts.[126] In his view, autonomy is grounded in the eternal law known through practical reason that guides specific choices and in this way is intimately linked to the virtues. This linkage between natural law and the virtues is a central aspect of Rhonheimer's ethical theory and an important contribution to both virtue theory and virtue ethics.

Rhonheimer notes that the key to understanding Aquinas's theory of natural law, one often overlooked by Aquinas scholars, is Question 94, Article 3, which provides a "conclusive explanation" of the natural law. That article asks, "Is every act of virtue of natural law?" He summarizes Aquinas's response: "insofar as any action can have the character (*ratio*) of moral virtue, so all virtuous actions belong to the natural law; for the natural law constitutes, in a universal way, that which makes a virtuous act virtuous."[127] Virtues "are the fulfillment of the natural law at the level of concrete acting

[122] Rhonheimer, "Cognitive Structure," 4.

[123] From this perspective, natural law's "objective" realm constitutes the "natural order" and its subjective realm constitutes reason or moral knowledge. The subjective "ought" of natural law is deduced from the objective "is" of the natural order, thus committing the naturalistic fallacy (ibid., 1–4).

[124] Ibid., 5.

[125] Ibid., 15.

[126] Rhonheimer, *Natural Law*, 570–74.

[127] Ibid., 581.

since they are the *habitus* of choosing what is good for man at a concrete level."[128] This focus on the connection between the precepts of natural law and moral virtues allows him to argue that theological ethics, even in its absolute normative prescriptions, is focused more on virtue than on law. Artificial contraception, for instance, is intrinsically wrong and absolutely prohibited, not because it is a violation of a prescriptive natural law norm but because it is a violation of virtue, specifically the virtue of chastity.

At the heart of Rhonheimer's natural law theory, then, is the intimate connection between the precepts of the natural law and the moral virtues. In the specific case of the natural law precepts that guide moral sexual behavior, the foundational virtue is chastity, defined as "mastery of one's own sexual drives so as to integrate them into the order of personal love."[129] Conjugal love arises from natural desire or sexual inclination, and the virtue of chastity provides "*habitual* or *virtual* integration of this desire into the order of reason which is the order of human love."[130] A major part of the virtue of chastity, he argues, is what he calls "procreative responsibility," defined as the "virtuous integration of sexual drives into the dominion of reason and will."[131] Acts of procreative responsibility respect the virtue of chastity and the truth of human sexuality, a truth defined in acts of loving union as the unitive and procreative meanings of every such act. In this way, Rhonheimer establishes the connection in natural law between the virtue of chastity, procreative responsibility as part of the virtue of chastity, the inseparability principle, and marital acts of loving union. "Virtues are shaped by and aim at concrete performances of acts and their corresponding choices, and single acts and their corresponding choices are morally specified by their intentional contents which spring from the virtues to which they belong."[132] On the combined basis of the truth of human sexuality and the virtue of chastity, Rhonheimer condemns as objectively immoral all acts that contradict this truth, including nonmarital sexual acts, contraceptive marital acts, and homosexual acts.

Rhonheimer points out that at the foundation of this teaching there is a "philosophically relevant perspective" that represents "an important doctrinal development." This perspective emphasizes "the 'intentionalness of the thing one is doing',"[133] which distinguishes, for instance, periodic abstinence from contraceptive sexual behavior. In periodic abstinence, the couple's intention is to respect both the natural unitive and procreative

[128]Rhonheimer, "Cognitive Structure," 38.
[129]Ibid., 39.
[130]Ibid.
[131]Ibid.
[132]Ibid., 40.
[133]Ibid., 23.

meanings of the conjugal act. Periodic abstinence is a "real conjugal act"[134] that includes both the unitive and procreative meanings of marital love. It is procreative because the intention for practicing periodic abstinence is procreative responsibility; the couple chooses to abstain from possibly fertile intercourse and in so doing "spouses relate to sexual acts, to themselves, and to each other as a possible cause of new life."[135] Periodic abstinence is also unitive because the spouses behave alike; their joint intention is grounded in procreatively responsible continence, which has "a proper *marital* and even *parental* meaning."[136] Contraceptive intercourse, on the other hand, he argues, "is not an expression of *marital* love." It alters the natural, objective meaning of the sexual act by intentionally removing its procreative meaning. "Insofar as the contraceptive choice involves intentionally rejecting procreative responsibility for one's sexual behavior, it also involves an anti-procreative volition"[137] and is an act contrary to chastity.

We agree with Rhonheimer's attempted integration of nature and reason and his understanding of the natural law as nature-as-reason, but we have dialogical questions about his theory concerning the univocal correlation between virtues and acts, the definition of intentionality, and procreative acts. We consider each question in turn. The first question asks whether Rhonheimer can claim a necessary correlation between the act of abstaining from sexual intercourse and the virtue of chastity. Aquinas makes a distinction in referring to acts of virtue. In the first instance, all acts of virtue are of natural law. In the second instance, there are acts which, due to the particularity of individual circumstances, may be virtuous for some people because they are right and proper and vicious to others because they are wrong and improper.[138] This distinction raises questions about the univocal correlation between specific acts and specific virtues. Germain Grisez asserts that "virtues are not concerned with specific kinds of acts"[139] and we agree with that assertion. The continuum mean of a virtue we explained earlier permits, we would argue, a plurality of acts that are all acts of the virtue. While abstaining from sexual intercourse *may* incarnate the virtue of procreative responsibility and chastity, it may also, if done with a contraceptive intention, as Rhonheimer himself admits,[140] violate the virtue of chastity. This would seem to indicate that there is no necessary correlation between

---

[134]Ibid.

[135]Ibid., 42.

[136]Ibid.

[137]Ibid., 44, emphasis in original.

[138]*ST*, I-II, 94, 3.

[139]Germain Grisez, *The Way of the Lord Jesus, Vol. 1. Christian Moral Principles* (Chicago: Franciscan Herald Press, 1983), 192.

[140]Martin Rhonheimer, "Contraception, Sexual Behavior and Natural Law," *Linacre Quarterly* 56, (1989): 44.

a virtue and a specific act and that the moral meaning of the act, and the virtue to which it is or is not an expression, cannot be determined without, as Aquinas and we would require, a consideration of the circumstances in which the act takes place and intention of the act.

The *Catechism of the Catholic Church* faithfully articulates the Catholic tradition with respect to circumstances when it teaches that "imputability and responsibility for an action can be *diminished and even nullified* by ignorance, inadvertence, duress, fear" and that "affective immaturity, force of acquired habit, conditions of anxiety or other psychological or social factors *lessen or even extenuate* moral culpability" and therefore grave sin.[141] We underscore the terms *nullified* and *extenuated* in that teaching of the *Catechism* and point out that Pope Francis stands firmly in that long-established Catholic tradition and adds to it the nullifying and extenuating circumstances of "dire poverty and great limitations," drug use, and family and societal violence, for instance.[142] Circumstances impact the assessment of moral culpability and the meaning of the act for relationships. As Pope Francis correctly points out, "it is reductive simply to consider whether or not an individual's actions correspond to a general law or rule" or, we add, virtue. He cites affirmatively Aquinas's teaching: "Although there is necessity in the general principles, the more we descend to matters of detail [and circumstances], the more frequently we encounter defects. . . . In matters of action, truth or practical rectitude is not the same for all, as to matters of detail [and circumstances], but only as to general principles; and where there is the same rectitude in matters of detail, it is not equally known to all. . . . The principle will be found to fail, according as we descend further into detail.[143] Rather than indicating a necessary correlation between a virtue and a specific act, then, we would argue that circumstances and the agent's intention indicate only its relationship with virtue. Might it be possible, then, to recognize the virtue of procreative responsibility also in artificial contraceptive acts?

Just as it is possible that the intention of a married couple practicing periodic abstinence can be associated with the vice of a contraceptive mentality,[144] so too it is possible that the intention of a married couple prac-

---

[141]*CCC*, nos. 1735 and 2352, emphases added.

[142]*AL*, nos. 50 and 51.

[143]*AL*, no. 304, citing *ST*, I-II, q. 94, a. 4.

[144]See Ronald Lawler et al., *Catholic Sexual Ethics: A Summary, Explanation, and Defense* (Huntington, IN: Our Sunday Visitor, 2011), 304, n. 72. They admit it is possible for couples to use NFP for selfish reasons, in which case NFP would be wrong, but they argue that "it is not wrong because it is contraceptive." We argue that the selfishness involved in using NFP is a "contraceptive mentality," and the intentionality for abstaining at this time is to engage in sexual intercourse at a later time when procreation is not possible. At the heart of the difference between the two positions is how one defines the human act. For a similar critique, see Lisa Sowle Cahill, "Catholic Sexual Ethics and the Dignity

ticing artificial birth control can be associated with the virtue of procreative responsibility. Rhonheimer would respond, we believe, that in the case of periodic abstinence, the couple's intention is to respect the procreative meaning of sexual intercourse and, in the most extreme cases of contraceptive sterilization, the procreative dimension of marital love "is entirely 'off'."[145] How is it, we ask, that couples who practice periodic abstinence during the wife's fertile period and couples who are infertile, all of whom know that procreation is "entirely 'off,'" can intentionally realize the procreative dimension of sexual intercourse? Rhonheimer answers that "the intentional relation to naturally given and voluntarily produced sterility is different." Naturally given sterility "does not imply a choice of rendering needless the modification of sexual behavior," whereas voluntarily produced sterility does imply such a choice. It is the intentionality of the choice "which specifies and shapes further actions."[146] Intention here is the essential link between virtue and moral action.

The second question asks about Rhonheimer's notion of intention. In periodic abstinence, he insists, the intention of the couple is to modify their sexual behavior, which objectively situates their sexual intercourse in the chastity-related virtue of procreative responsibility.[147] In artificially contraceptive behavior, on the other hand, the intention of the couples is to reject any procreative responsibility for their sexual behavior.[148] Two different intentions yield two different moral acts: periodic abstinence and contraceptive behavior. The two intentions are formulated thus: first, to abstain from sexual intercourse to respect the procreative meaning of the act; second, to engage in sexual intercourse while eliminating the procreative meaning of the act. Rhonheimer argues that in the case of periodic abstinence, there are "two different, although closely correlated actions of 'sexual behavior' . . . both the performance of engaging in intercourse and the performance of abstinence."[149] What correlates these sexual actions is the intention that undergirds them.

The intention to abstain from an act of sexual intercourse in periodic abstinence, we would argue, is only a partial description of the total intention involved, for there is also the intention to engage in intercourse at a later time when the procreative meaning of the act cannot be actualized, though the unitive meaning can. It is this fuller description of intention that, at least in part, we argue, specifies the intention of abstaining from an act of conjugal

---

of the Person: A Double Message," *Theological Studies* 50 (1989): 136–37.

[145]Rhonheimer, "Contraception," 44.

[146]Ibid., 56, n. 34.

[147]Ibid., 42–43.

[148]Ibid., 44.

[149]Ibid., 41.

intercourse at this particular time.[150] The act of periodic abstinence and the act of artificial contraception are linked by the same intention, namely, to engage in sexual intercourse while eliminating the procreative meaning of the act. To avoid this logical conclusion, Rhonheimer has to argue that the procreative and unitive meanings of intercourse are broken "on the level of single acts of contraceptive intercourse."[151] This argument reveals, we respond, a classicist worldview of an intention willed and an act performed at a specific and definitive time and place. A historically conscious view of the same intention and act recognizes its relational meaning as a progressive reality, to which we refer elsewhere as the relational, progressive, holistic understanding of the act as a human act adequately considered.[152] The human act adequately considered acknowledges the complexity of the act, including the fact that the intention of an act can carry over and define another act directly and intrinsically related to it. Rhonheimer himself allows for such a historically conscious, holistic interpretation of the human act in certain act descriptions.

A third question asks whether Rhonheimer expands the definition of the conjugal act in some situations and narrows it in others, depending on the point he is arguing. He asserts, for example, that the conjugal act includes both the act of engaging in and the act of abstaining from sexual intercourse.[153] Periodic abstinence has "a fully procreative meaning" since "[i]t actually is, by its very intentional content and thus objectively, an act of [the virtue of] procreative responsibility."[154] This claim warrants comment. If the procreative meaning of the act of sexual intercourse, we ask, does not have some *intrinsic* relationship to *actual* procreation, then how is it to be distinguished from the unitive meaning of the act? If there is no distinction between the procreative and unitive meanings of an act of sexual intercourse, there would seem to be also no clear moral distinction between periodic abstinence and artificial contraception, both of which lead to fully realized union between the spouses.

Rhonheimer notes that "the conjugal act is perfectly licit even if it is performed *only* for the reason of expressing mutual love."[155] Following the Catholic tradition's longtime teaching on the ends of *marriage*,[156] rather than

[150]A similar point is made by Gareth Moore, *The Body in Context: Sex and Catholicism*, *Contemporary Christian Insights* (New York: Continuum, 2001), 163–65.

[151]Rhonheimer, "Contraception," 44.

[152]See Todd A. Salzman, "The Human Act and Its Moral Evaluation in the *Catechism of the Catholic Church*: A Critical Analysis," in *Ethics and the Catechism of the Catholic Church*, ed. Michael E. Allsopp (Scranton, PA: University of Scranton Press, 1999), 68–71.

[153]Rhonheimer, "Contraception," 41–42.

[154]Ibid.

[155]Ibid., 41, emphasis added.

[156]See *GS*, nos. 48–50; *Code of Canon Law,* can. 1055; Michael G. Lawler, *Marriage in the Catholic*

the novel teaching introduced by Paul VI's encyclical *Humanae Vitae* on the ends of each and every *act of sexual intercourse* within marriage, frees Catholic theological ethicists to argue for the use of artificial birth control to responsibly regulate fertility. If the intention of periodic abstinence is to not procreate and that intention can be considered an act of chastity, we ask, why cannot artificial contraception, which has the same intention, not also be considered an act of chastity? Both methods of responsibly regulating conception, we would argue, can be "performed for reasons of procreative responsibility."[157]

We acknowledge the importance of Rhonheimer's attempt to develop a comprehensive and comprehensible explanation of the interrelationship between action theory and virtue ethics to explain and defend Catholic sexual teaching, but we are not convinced by it. His claim for the necessary correlation between the virtue of chastity and *specific* sexual acts is not proven, his theory of intentionality is inadequate, and his definition of the conjugal act is inconsistent. That we are unconvinced by his arguments, however, is not a cause for dismissing his theory altogether. Neither is it a cause for an intractable and polarizing divide between us. Rather, it is a cause for acknowledging the legitimate plurality of Catholic theological positions recommended by the International Theological Commission and for the charitable dialogue recommended by Popes John Paul II and Francis. John Paul teaches that dialogue is rooted in the nature and dignity of the human person and "is an indispensable step toward human self-realization, the self-realization of *each individual* and *every human community*,"[158] including therefore the Catholic theological community. Francis exhorts humans with differing ideas and opinions not to "get bogged down in your own limited ideas and opinions, but to be prepared to change or expand them. The combination of two different ways of thinking can lead to a synthesis that enriches both."[159] We accept this exhortation to charitable dialogue, not only on this occasion with Martin Rhonheimer but also with every other theological ethicist who holds a different perspective on ethics and virtue than we do. After all, as we acknowledged in our discussion of perspectivism, we are human beings metaphorically looking out a third-story window and wondering what we would see if we would move up to a twentieth-story window.

Church: Disputed Questions (Collegeville, MN: Liturgical Press, 2002), 27–42.

[157]Rhonheimer, "Contraception," 41–42.

[158]*Sollicitudo Rei Socialis*, no. 3.

[159]*AL*, no. 139.

3

Virtuous Perspective and Ethical Method

SOURCES FOR A RECONSTRUCTED ETHICAL METHOD

In this chapter, we address two questions. The first is the question of the sources of moral knowledge, the second the related question of the selection, interpretation, prioritization, and integration (or SIPI) of those sources from a virtuous perspective. Perspectivism, we have argued, is an epistemology that accounts for plural partial definitions of human dignity and the formulation and justification of principles and norms for its attainment. A well-formed conscience gives ethical authority to those definitions, and an ethical method provides a justification for them by proposing sources of evidence and a normative pattern for the SIPI of evidence to define human dignity and to formulate and justify norms to facilitate its attainment. By common theological and ecumenical agreement, this evidence is mined from what is called the Wesleyan Quadrilateral, four established sources of moral knowledge in the various Christian perspectives, namely, scripture, tradition, reason/science, and human experience. The Second Vatican Council called for the renewal of Catholic theological ethics. As noted in our Introduction, we use the Wesleyan Quadrilateral to respond to this call and to propose a Catholic virtuous-perspective method for the twenty-first century.

We employ the Quadrilateral for four reasons. First, it includes the sources of moral knowledge we judge essential for doing Christian ethics, sources highlighted in various ways throughout Christian tradition. Second, these four sources are essential to every Catholic ethical method, though particular methods select, interpret, prioritize, and integrate them differently. Third, there is a growing appreciation for, and specific reference to, these sources in the Catholic ethical literature from divergent normative perspectives,[1]

[1]Lisa Sowle Cahill, *Between the Sexes: Foundations for a Christian Ethics of Sexuality* (Cincinnati, OH: Fortress Press, 1985), 4–7; Charles E. Curran, *The Catholic Moral Tradition Today: A Synthesis* (Washington, DC: Georgetown University Press, 1999), 47–55; Todd A. Salzman, *What Are They Saying*

though there remains the need for methodological discussion to investigate how the sources are to be selected, interpreted, prioritized, and integrated. This discussion will clarify the sources and their use and integration and account for pluralist perspectives. Fourth, use of these four sources may encourage ecumenical methodological considerations that should inform Catholic ethics and aid in the formation of a well-formed conscience.[2]

Scripture

The Second Vatican Council's *Decree on Priestly Formation* prescribes that the scientific exposition of moral theology "should be more thoroughly nourished by scriptural teaching," since scripture is the "very soul of sacred theology."[3] Consequently, any Catholic ethical method must integrate scripture and demonstrate how scripture functions in its method. When using scripture, we suggest, two things need to be kept in mind. First, when investigating the role of scripture in a particular method, it is important to recognize that contemporary readers of scripture bring certain lenses, perspectives, preunderstandings, and presuppositions to the text. A crucial part of any investigation of Catholic ethics is to bring these presuppositions to the fore in order to comprehend a particular method more fully.[4] Second, the attempt to incorporate scripture into an ethical method is akin to coherently integrating the full mystery of the divine reality to which scripture attests. As both Augustine and Aquinas remind us, this cannot be comprehensively and definitively done. "*Si comprehendis non est Deus*," if you understand, it is not God, Augustine judges.[5] Sacred scripture, a collection of diverse books from diverse times and cultures, seeks to reveal the mystery of God, but this mystery is so incomprehensibly rich that it can never be grasped in a single citation or perspective.

The fullness of revelation, Christians believe, is not contained in a scriptural book. It is contained, they believe, in a person, the person of Jesus Christ, who even after his revelation in human form remains a mystery. The project of developing an ethical method cannot be content to live with

---

about Catholic Ethical Method? (Mahwah, NJ: Paulist Press, 2003).

[2]See James Gustafson, "Charles Curran: Ecumenical Moral Theologian Par Excellence," in *A Call to Fidelity: On the Moral Theology of Charles E. Curran*, ed. James J. Walter et al. (Washington, DC: Georgetown University Press, 2002), 211–34.

[3]*Dei Verbum*, no. 24 (hereafter *DV*).

[4]See William C. Spohn, *Go and Do Likewise: Jesus and Ethics* (New York: Continuum, 2007); Daniel J. Harrington, and James F. Keenan, *Jesus and Virtue Ethics: Building Bridges between New Testament Studies and Moral Theology* (Lanham, MD: Sheed & Ward, 2002); and Daniel J. Harrington, and James F. Keenan, *Paul and Virtue Ethics: Building Bridges between New Testament Studies and Moral Theology* (Lanham, MD: Rowman & Littlefield, 2010).

[5]Augustine, *Sermon* 117, *PL* 38, 360.

mystery and, as a result, there is a fundamental tension between the truths contained in scripture and how those truths are used in Christian ethics. Christian ethics will never contain the fullness of revelation, no more than does scripture, though it can reflect certain parts of that revelation that, while no doubt important and foundational, do not tell the whole story. The use of scripture in Christian ethics is similar to the viewers at fourth-story, thirteenth-story, and twenty-first-story windows of the Empire State Building; each gets a different, but no less partial, view of the total panorama that unfolds outside the building. The richness of scripture and of the mystery to which it attests defy full human comprehension, though there are methodological guidelines from magisterial documents for properly interpreting scripture.

In his encyclical *Divino Afflante Spiritu*, Pope Pius XII laid the foundation for the methodological integration of scripture into ethical method by endorsing the historical–critical method for its interpretation. This method was reaffirmed by the Second Vatican Council's *Dei Verbum*, which prescribes that scriptural texts are to be read in the "literary forms" of the writer's "time and culture."[6] The Pontifical Biblical Commission's *The Interpretation of the Bible in the Church* continues in this line, teaching that "Holy Scripture, in as much as it is 'the word of God in human language,' has been composed by human authors in all its various parts and in all the sources that lie behind them. Because of this, its proper understanding not only admits the use of [the historical-critical] method but actually requires it."[7] The Commission insists that "the scientific study of the Bible requires as exact a knowledge as possible of the social conditions distinctive of the various milieus in which the Traditions recorded in the Bible took shape."[8] The Catholic approach to reading biblical texts is clear: it is to be done using an historical–critical methodology. We accept that instruction as mandatory, and our ethical method seeks to follow it.

Of particular relevance to this book is the Commission's application of its principles for biblical exegesis to Catholic theological ethics. Though the Bible is God's word to the church, "this does not mean that God has given the historical conditioning of the message a value which is absolute. It is open both to interpretation and being brought up to date." It follows, therefore, that it is not sufficient for moral judgment that the scripture "should indicate a certain ethical moral position [the practice of slavery, or divorce, or the prohibition of homosexual acts, for example] for this

[6]*DV*, no. 12; Pius XII, *Divino afflante spiritu*, *AAS* 35 (1943): 297–325.

[7]Pontifical Biblical Commission, "Interpretation of the Bible in the Church," *Origins* 24 (January 6, 1994): 500.

[8]Ibid., 506.

position to continue to have validity. One has to undertake a process of understanding the text in its socio-historical contexts and of discerning its contemporary relevance in the light of the progress in moral understanding and sensitivity that has occurred over the years."[9] It is for these reasons that Josef Fuchs can assert correctly that what Augustine, Jerome, Aquinas, and Trent said about ethical behavior cannot exclusively control what theological ethicists say today.[10] One must understand, judge, and apply scripture according to the "signs of the times," in dialogue with the other sources of moral knowledge, all in a particular historical–cultural context and from a particular virtuous perspective.

Discovering what scripture says about ethics, therefore, is never as straightforward as simply reading a text. The reader must get behind the text to understand how the church and its theologians interpret it and apply it to contemporary ethical issues. The Second Vatican Council issued instruction on how the scriptures of both Testaments are to be read. Those who search out the intentions of the sacred writers, it teaches, must, among other things have regard for "literary forms." For truth is proposed and expressed in a variety of ways, depending on whether a text is history of one kind or another, or whether its form is that of prophecy, poetry, or some other type of speech. Poetry and parable are to be read and interpreted differently from history. The interpreter must investigate what meaning the sacred writer *intended to express and actually expressed* in particular circumstances as he used contemporary literary forms in accordance with the situation of his own time and culture.[11] It is never enough simply to read a scriptural text to find out what it says about Christian ethics. Its original sociohistorical context must first be clarified, and then the text can be translated, interpreted, and applied in a contemporary context.[12]

Tradition

The second source of moral knowledge is tradition, and it is intrinsically related to scripture. Scripture and tradition, indeed, are but one source of divine revelation since the New Testament is itself the tradition of the earliest Christian communities. Scripture was written in a particular time and place for a particular people, and may be said to be secondary revelation as the early Christian community's written interpretations of the primary

---

[9]Ibid., 519.

[10]Josef Fuchs, *Moral Demands and Personal Obligations* (Washington, DC: Georgetown University Press, 1993), 36.

[11]*DV*, no. 12, emphasis added.

[12]Daniel J. Harrington and James F. Keenan do this in their *Jesus and Virtue Ethics* and in their *Paul and Virtue Ethics*.

revelation, God's self-revelation in the person of Jesus Christ. The word *tradition* is used with two meanings. It can mean both handing on the church's continuing interpretation of the primary revelation in Jesus and the secondary revelation in scripture and the content that is handed on. There are fundamental truths contained in tradition, Trinity and Incarnation for example, but our *understanding* of even these truths develops gradually in light of contemporary advances in history, culture, knowledge, and experience. This evolution takes place not only in dogmatic truths but also in ethical truth and praxis, which also gradually evolve and develop in light of advances in ethical questions and challenges. Under the guidance of the Holy Spirit, tradition interprets and applies the primary revelation in Jesus and the secondary revelation in scripture in ever new and contextually appropriate ways.

Since the impact of tradition on theological ethics is extensive and warrants far greater treatment than we can provide here, we narrow our investigation to what Sandra Schneiders presents as three meanings of tradition: foundational gift, content, and mode.[13] *Foundational gift* is the unfolding experience of the church throughout history under the guidance of "the Holy Spirit who is the presence of the risen Jesus making the Church the Body of Christ."[14] All Catholic ethical methods accept tradition as foundational gift. They disagree, however, on who in the body of Christ is *gifted* to discern and interpret that gift and the criteria for determining that *giftedness*, often referred to as charism.[15] Richard McCormick invites attention to the fact that there are unresolved theological tensions in the documents of the Second Vatican Council,[16] tensions that are evident in different passages within the same document describing who are the gifted for discerning ethical truth. *Lumen Gentium,* for instance, teaches the following: "Bishops who teach in communion with the Roman Pontiff are to be revered by all as witnesses of divine and Catholic truth; the faithful, for their part, are obliged to submit to their Bishops' decision, made in the name of Christ, in matters of faith and morals, and to adhere to it with a ready and respectful allegiance of mind."[17] In this passage, those who are gifted to teach are bishops in communion with the pope; the faithful are gifted to adhere to episcopal teaching.

Lumen Gentium also teaches that the entire People of God, bishops and laity alike, are gifted to discern both dogmatic and ethical truth. "The

[13]Sandra Schneiders, *The Revelatory Text: Interpreting the New Testament as Sacred Scripture* (Collegeville, MN: Liturgical Press, 1999), 72.

[14]Ibid.

[15]See Todd A. Salzman and Michael G. Lawler, "Theologians and the Magisterium: A Proposal for a Complementarity of Charisms through Dialogue," *Horizons* 36, no. 1 (2009): 7–31.

[16]Richard A. McCormick, *Critical Calling: Reflections on Moral Dilemmas since Vatican II* (Washington, DC: Georgetown University Press, 1999), 103.

[17]*Lumen Gentium*, no. 25 (hereafter *LG*).

whole body of the faithful who have an anointing that comes from the holy one . . . cannot err in matters of belief. This characteristic is shown in the supernatural appreciation of the faith (*sensus fidei*) of the *whole* people, when, 'from the Bishops to the last of the faithful' they manifest a universal consent in matters of faith and morals."[18] This gifting of the "whole people" is further affirmed in *Gaudium et Spes* and other Council documents on the nature and authority of conscience. A 2014 document from the International Theological Commission teaches that *sensus fidei* is "a sort of spiritual instinct that enables the believer to judge spontaneously whether a particular teaching or practice is or is not in conformity with the Gospel and with apostolic faith,"[19] that is, with tradition. That instinct enables all believers "to recognize and endorse authentic Christian doctrine and practice and to reject what is false," and "to fulfill their prophetic calling."[20] The document repeats *Lumen Gentium*'s teaching that through this spiritual instinct "the holy People of God shares in Christ's prophetic office," and that "the body of the faithful as a whole, anointed as they are by the Holy One (cf. Jn 2:20, 27), cannot err in matters of belief."

Discerning who are gifted in the church has implications for Schneiders's second meaning of tradition, namely, *content*. Content is "the sum total of appropriated and transmitted Christian experience, out of which Christians throughout history select the material for renewed syntheses of faith."[21] The content of tradition is drawn from scripture, church fathers, councils, encyclicals and official teachings of the Magisterium, and the ongoing theological reflection within the church in dialogue with culture, science, experience, and *sensus fidei*. The content from these sources must be critically selected, understood, and interpreted for its continuing truth and usefulness for the ethical life of the church in the present day, using the same historical–critical method that is used for understanding and interpreting scripture. If found not useful for advancing Catholic ethical life, traditional content may be renewed, as was the traditional content related to the denial of the right to religious freedom at the Second Vatican Council, or it may be discarded, as was the traditional content related to slavery.

Judging who are the gifted in the People of God, who has the authority to discern, interpret, and transmit the content of ethical truth, and the content that is transmitted, are all intrinsically linked to Schneiders's third meaning of tradition. The third meaning is *mode*, "by which that content is made available to successive generations of believers, the way in which

---

[18]Ibid. 12, emphasis added.

[19]International Theological Commission, Sensus Fidei *in the Life of the Church* 49 (2014), www.vatican.va/roman_curia/congregations/cfaith/cti_documents/rc_cti_20140610_sensus-fidei_en.html.

[20]Ibid., 2.

[21]Schneiders, *The Revelatory Text*, 72.

the traditioning of the faith is carried on throughout history."[22] Mode is congruous with tradition, the infrastructure and process for handing on lived faith. The point is frequently made that how one understands the role of the teaching authority within the church is intimately linked with one's ecclesiology or how one understands the nature of church.[23] One's ecclesiology is central to how one understands tradition as mode, especially the role and function of the Magisterium in relation to the rest of the People of God, theologians and faithful.

Since the Second Vatican Council, Catholic theologians have generally adhered to one of two fundamentally different ecclesiological models. The model that predominated in the second millennium is a hierarchical model, according to which the content of revelation and tradition flows downward from the Magisterium to the faithful. Pope Pius X's encyclical, *Vehementer Nos*, fully endorsed this model.[24] The role and function of theologians in this model is to make clear to the faithful the teaching of the Magisterium, but not to question or challenge that teaching.[25] Both experience and *sensus fidei* are sources of moral knowledge, but it is for the Magisterium to determine how those sources are to be interpreted and incorporated into its teaching. In cases where there is a disparity between *sensus fidelium* and magisterial teaching, as is now the case with norms prohibiting contraception and homosexual activity, for instance, the Magisterium gives the definitive interpretation of the meaning of human experience for human dignity, and the formulation and justification of norms that facilitate or frustrate its attainment. If we think of this hierarchical model as a pyramid, the Magisterium is at the pinnacle of the pyramid and is the hermeneutical key for discerning, understanding, and interpreting all other sources of moral knowledge.

The Second Vatican Council introduced a renewed model of church and, by implication, a renewed model of ethical epistemology, namely, a People of-God-in-Communion model.[26] In this model, the church is People-of-God-in-Communion,[27] and moral knowledge is discerned, understood, and interpreted by the People of God in communion, Magisterium, theolo-

---

[22]Ibid., 72.

[23]See, for example, McCormick, *Critical Calling*, 19–21, 34–45, 54–55, 163–69; Richard McCormick, "Some Early Reactions to *Veritatis Splendor*," in *Readings in Moral Theology No. 10: John Paul II and Moral Theology*, ed. Charles Curran and Richard McCormick (New York: Paulist Press, 1998), 28–30.

[24]*Vehementer Nos*, no. 8.

[25]This model is clearly reflected in Pius XII's *Humani generis* (see, for example, DS, 2313–14) and more recently in Congregation for the Doctrine of the Faith (CDF), *Donum Veritatis*.

[26]For the explanation of Church as communion, see Gustave Martelet, *Les idées maitresses de Vatican II* (Paris: Desclée, 1966); J. M. R. Tillard, *Church of Churches: The Ecclesiology of Church as Communion* (Collegeville, MN: Liturgical Press, 1992); Michael G. Lawler and Thomas J. Shanahan, *Church: A Spirited Communion* (Collegeville, MN: Liturgical Press, 1995).

[27]*LG*, nos. 8–17; see especially *LG*, no. 12. For a full development of this teaching, see Lawler and Shanahan, *Church: A Spirited Communion*, 22–27.

gians, and faithful together. There is a trialogue among these three groups guided by the Holy Spirit, with scripture, tradition, secular disciplines of knowledge, and human experience at the center. It is this ongoing trialogue, always conducted in mutual charity and desire to deepen the People of God's understanding of God's and the church's truth about ethical action, which moves the pilgrim church forward in history toward a fuller knowledge, understanding, and judgment of that truth. The Magisterium maintains its authority in this model, and there is a presumption of the truth of its teaching, but its authority is qualified by its role as learner as well as teacher. The faithful in general, and theologians in particular, can facilitate, contribute to, and sometimes even challenge noninfallible magisterial teachings in this learning–teaching process. Yves Congar, the greatest Catholic ecclesiologist of the twentieth century, points out that obedience to church authority is required when the church is conceived on the hierarchical model, and dialogue and consensus is required when it is conceived on the People-of-God-in-Communion model. He adds the historical note that "it is certain that this second conception was the one that prevailed effectively during the first thousand years of Christianity, whereas the other one dominated in the West between the eleventh-century reformation and Vatican II."[28]

Human Experience

We agree with theological ethicist Servais Pinckaers that human experience has "a very important function in moral theology."[29] *Gaudium et Spes* emphasizes the relevance of human experience for theological reflection. Theologically interpreted human experience, of both past and present, helps to construct a definition of human dignity and to formulate and justify norms to facilitate its attainment; experience serves as a window onto the ethically true and normative. To deny the ethical relevance of human experience for assisting in the definition of human dignity reflects a reductionist methodology where the only legitimate human experience is that which conforms to, and confirms, established norms. It was such a methodology, in large part, which allowed the Magisterium's approbation of slavery until Pope Leo XIII's rejection of it in 1890 and the denial of religious freedom until the Second Vatican Council's approbation of it in 1965. John Noonan comments with respect to the Magisterium's late condemnation of slavery:

[28]Yves Congar, "Reception as an Ecclesiological Reality," in *Election and Consensus in the Church, Concilium Church History Vol. 77*, ed. Giuseppe Alberigo and Anton Weiler (Freiburg: Herder and Herder, 1972), 62.

[29]Servais Pinckaers, *The Sources of Christian Ethics* (Washington, DC: Catholic University of America Press, 1995), 91.

"it was the *experience* of unfreedom, in the gospel's light, that made the contrary shine clear."[30]

A legitimate question at this point is whose experience is to be used in the formulation of a definition of human dignity and the formulation and justification of norms that facilitate its attainment? We emphasize that human experience is only one part of the Wesleyan Quadrilateral and never a stand-alone source of ethical theory. Though a crucial part of my experience is my self-experience, "my experience" alone is never a source at all. Ethical authority is granted in the People of God only to "our experience," to *communal* experience, and only in constructive conversation with the three other sources—scripture, tradition, and science—as well as with the theological reality called *sensus fidei*, the sense of the faithful and their lived experience. An ethical truth is true when it adequately resonates with the People of God's common experience. We now clarify what we mean by experience.

There is little to be gained from simply encountering the world in which we live; many people have many such encounters and learn little from them. In the Wesleyan Quadrilateral, experience means "the human capacity to encounter the surrounding world consciously, to observe it, be affected by it, and to learn from it."[31] It is of the essence of such experience that it is never raw, neutral encounter with the world. It is always encounter perceived and interpreted as socially constructed by both communities and individuals in specific sociohistorical contexts. It is, therefore, also dialectical, differently construed, perhaps, by "me," by "you," by "us," by "them." For genuine human experience as we have defined it, the dialectic is necessarily a "dialectic of reason *and* experience" and never a dialectic controlled by either reason or experience alone. It is also a dialectic that results not in an absolutist ethical code but in what Edward Vacek, in historically conscious mode, calls "various revisable rules."[32] In a church that is the People-of-God-in-Communion the resolution of different construals of experience to arrive at ethical truth requires the respectful and charitable dialogue lauded and rhetorically embraced by Pope John Paul II.[33] Charitable dialogue must occur internally, among the communion of believers, some of whom are laity, some of whom are theologians, and some of whom are bishops including the Bishop of Rome,[34] all of whom acquire knowledge through

[30] John T. Noonan, "Development in Moral Doctrine," *Theological Studies* 54 (1993): 662–77, at 674–75.

[31] Neil Brown, "Experience and Development in Catholic Moral Theology," *Pacifica* 14 (2001): 300.

[32] Edward Collins Vacek, "Catholic 'Natural Law' and Reproductive Ethics," *Journal of Medicine and Philosophy* 17 (1992): 342–43.

[33] *Ut Unum Sint*, nos. 28–39. See Salzman and Lawler, "Theologians and the Magisterium."

[34] We shall use this tripartite division of believers throughout for purposes that will become apparent

practice or action,[35] that is, through experience. Importantly, dialogue must take place also externally, among all people of good will. In the formation of conscience, people are tasked to discern what human experience confirms or challenges their definition of human dignity and, correspondingly, to formulate and justify norms that facilitate its attainment.

Sciences

The sciences aid in illuminating, analyzing, and evaluating human reality and experience and are essential methodological sources of moral knowledge for a well-formed conscience. Pope John Paul II states that "the Church values sociological and statistical research when it proves helpful in understanding the historical context in which pastoral action has to be developed and when it leads to a better understanding of the truth."[36] He highlights, as we noted in the Introduction, the need for intense dialogue between science and theology.[37] Theology and science must enter into a "common interactive relationship" whereby, while maintaining its own integrity, each discipline is "open to the discoveries and insights of the other." Physicist Ian Barbour proposes a fourfold typology of the relationship between theology and science: conflict, independence, dialogue, and integration.[38] Particularly germane to our topic are the dialogue and integration typologies. Ethicist Neil Messer proposes a similar dialogue between theological ethicists and neuroethicists, seeking to persuade both "to move from mutual neglect to serious and careful engagement with each other—engagement which could prove creative, rewarding and productive for both sides."[39]

The *dialogue* typology explores methodological parallels, content, and boundary questions. Methodological parallels are similarities and dissimilarities between the methods of science and theology that may complement or serve the method of the other. Boundary questions delimit the capabilities of each discipline and stipulate how far each may go in explaining reality. The *integration* typology encompasses natural theology and a systematic synthesis of science and religion. For natural theology, the empirical world is the point of departure and the proximate goal is

---

as we proceed.

[35]Richard Bernstein, *Beyond Objectivism and Relativism* (Philadelphia: University of Pennsylvania Press, 1985), 74.

[36]*Familiaris Consortio*, no. 5 (hereafter *FC*).

[37]John Paul II, "The Relationship of Science and Theology: A Letter to Jesuit Father George Coyne," in *Origins* 18 (November 17, 1988): 375–78.

[38]Ian G. Barbour, *Nature, Human Nature, and God* (Minneapolis: Fortress Press, 2002), 1–2.

[39]Neil Messer, *Theological Neuroethics: Christian Ethics Meets the Science of the Human Brain* (Bloomsbury T&T Clark, 2017), 181.

to deepen theological understanding of the world and the peoples who live in it; the ultimate goal is to integrate the two into a single system.[40] Barbour's dialogue and integration typologies parallel Pope John Paul II's proposal for a "community of interchange" between theology and science to expand the partial perspectives of each and "form a new unified vision." In this process boundaries must be respected. Theology should steadfastly remain true to itself and not seek to become science, and science should steadfastly remain true to itself and not seek to become theology in terms of either method or content. "Unity always presupposes the diversity and the integrity of its elements."[41] Neither science nor theology should become less itself but, rather, more itself in a dynamic interchange. Each discipline retains its own autonomy and language and yet draws knowledge and insight from the other.[42]

VIRTUOUS PERSPECTIVES AND THE SELECTION, INTERPRETATION, PRIORITIZATION, AND INTEGRATION (SIPI) OF THE SOURCES OF ETHICAL KNOWLEDGE

Before discussing plural Catholic virtue ethical methods, it will be helpful to emphasize the common ground between them. Most basically, Catholic virtue ethical methods attempt to articulate the shared Catholic ethical tradition, as this is related to and guided by virtue and virtuous practice. Those methods recognize the impact of Christian perspectives on individual and communal virtuous perspectives on reality and the acts that follow from, and shape, those perspectives. They recognize an objectivist metaethic; the good can be defined universally. They agree that the good is defined as human dignity, human fulfillment, or some similar cognate. They agree that principles and norms are important to formulate and justify the attainment of the good. They recognize that acts in imitation of Christ, over time, shape who Christians are and can become as believing members of a People-of-God-in-Communion.[43] They generally accept historical consciousness as a vital tool in a virtuous ethical perspective. Our proposed ethical method

---

[40]Ibid. See also Robert John Russell and Kirk Wegter-McNelly, "Science and Theology: Mutual Interaction," in *Bridging Science and Religion*, ed. Ted Peters and Gaymon Bennett (Minneapolis: Fortress Press, 2003), 19–34.

[41]John Paul II, "The Relationship of Science and Theology," 377.

[42]Ibid. See also Michael J. Buckley, "Religion and Science: Paul Davies and John Paul II," *Theological Studies* 51 (1990): 310–24.

[43]See Darlene Fozard Weaver, *The Acting Person and Christian Ethical Life* (Washington, DC: Georgetown University Press, 2011).

aligns with all those points. Even with these fundamental agreements, however, the virtuous perspectives of different ethical methods indicate fundamental methodological, anthropological, and normative differences. What accounts for these fundamental differences?

Since the Second Vatican Council's call in *Optatum Totius* for a renewal of Catholic theological ethics, ethical method has been a central focus of this renewal. Plural ethical methods have emerged in Catholic ethics, but for clarity throughout the book we isolate only two general methods. We have already characterized the two major ones as *conservative* and *progressive*. The conservative method strictly prioritizes tradition as guarded and interpreted by the Magisterium among the four sources of moral knowledge. Tradition is accorded absolute priority and authority, and conservative ethicists in general follow and defend the Magisterium's interpretations of tradition. The progressive method has a dialectical approach to the selection, interpretation, prioritization, and integration of the sources of moral knowledge. The sources inform, critically analyze, and complement one another in the discernment of a definition of human dignity and the formulation and justification of principles and norms that facilitate its attainment, but no interpretation is understood as absolute. Forewarned by the notorious errors of some traditional teachings in the past, progressive ethicists submit magisterial teaching to scholarly critique so that, if need be, it may be refined and progress into the future more attuned to the realities of which it speaks, including, in this book, ethical realities. These two different approaches have led to a great polarizing divide over ethics in the church to which we have already referred. We align ourselves and our book with the progressive method.

That both conservative and progressive ethicists embrace historical consciousness is suggested by the fact that each recognizes an "epistemological crisis" in the justification for the absolute prohibition of artificial contraception in *Humanae Vitae.* An epistemological crisis occurs when the conceptual perspective or lens through which we view reality is no longer adequate to present reality. To resolve the crisis, we need a new perspective and a new narrative, one that adjusts criteria of truth and understanding to interpret present reality correctly. The epistemological crisis created by *Humanae Vitae* was exposed by critically analyzing the justification for its teaching, which was grounded in the physical structure of the sexual act and did not adequately account for the relational and virtuous dimensions of the tradition that may or may not justify its norm. Both conservative and progressive ethicists have attempted to respond to the crisis. The conservatives have attempted to do so by reshaping the narrative to defend the teaching from a virtuous perspective. John Paul II developed a "theology of the body" grounded in his phenomenology and the virtues to defend the teaching;[44] Martin Rhonheimer developed an "integral/personal anthropology" that is grounded in ethical virtue;[45] and John Grabowski proposes a sexual ethic grounded in the scriptural covenant, personalism, and virtue.[46] The progressives have attempted to respond to the crisis by revising the arguments of justification and, in so doing, challenging the teaching itself from a virtuous perspective. When attempting to resolve any epistemological crisis from any perspective, we must always keep in mind MacIntyre's warning: "We are never in a position to claim that now we possess the truth or now we are fully rational. The most that we can claim is that this is the best account which anyone has been able to give so far, and that our beliefs about what the marks of 'a best account so far' are will themselves change in what are at present unpredictable ways."[47] We seek to uncover in this book "a best account so far" by presenting and critically analyzing both conservative and progressive perspectives.

Our investigation of the two virtuous perspectives begins in the common ground between them we have sought to clarify in this section. Bernard Lonergan writes of historical consciousness, which the two perspectives accept, that "there are, then, new perspectives that arise in history by the passage of time. . . . The New Testament throws a backward light upon the Old Testament." It is the same with Aristotle and Aquinas; Aquinas throws a backward light on Aristotle. The Second Vatican Council similarly throws a backward light on the Catholic tradition that controlled Catholic ethics before the Council. "There is in the course of time," Robert Doran advises, "an opening up of new perspectives on the past." These new perspectives may be either a type of relativism or skepticism or they may be perspectivism and historical objectivism, all of which we discussed in Chapter 1. We embrace a perspectivism that "acknowledges the truth of many, that conceives history as no more in possession of its ideal goal than is any other science, that affirms the possibility of many perspectives being joined together into a single fuller view [of truth]."[48] Perspectivism, historical objectivism, an evolving knowledge of the good and the normative, and the anthropological and ethical implications of that understanding reflect the evolving understanding of the objectivism of the natural law found in all Catholic ethicists.

[44]Pope John Paul II, *The Theology of the Body: Human Love in the Divine Plan* (Boston, MA: Pauline Books & Media, 1997).

[45]Martin Rhonheimer, *Natural Law and Practical Reason: A Thomist View of Moral Autonomy*, trans. G. Malsbary (New York: Fordham University Press, 2000), 117.

[46]John Grabowski, *Sex and Virtue: An Introduction to Sexual Ethics* (Washington, DC: Catholic University of America Press, 2003).

[47]Alasdair MacIntyre, "Historicism and Epistemology," *The Monist* 60, no. 4 (1977): 455.

[48]Robert M. Doran and Robert C. Croken, eds. *Collected Works of Bernard Lonergan: Early Works on Theological Method I* (Toronto: University of Toronto Press, 2010), 248.

Pope John Paul II and Veritatis Splendor

Pope John Paul II's encyclical on ethical method, *Veritatis Splendor*,[49] recognized the great divide in Catholic theological ethics, sparked in large part by theological disagreements over the teaching against artificial birth control in *Humanae Vitae*, and sought to address it. In doing so, it both implicitly recognized and confirmed this divide, but by no means resolved it. It recognized the divide by addressing a contemporary approach to theological ethics known as proportionalism.[50] Though it clearly condemned this approach to theological ethics as mistaken, it did not settle the debate among Catholic ethicists. What it did do was to emphasize the need for a clear conceptual understanding of the two predominant interpretations of natural law ethical theory within the Catholic Church. It begins by stating grave concern over dissent on sexual and biomedical ethical issues that is no longer "limited and occasional" but is "overall and systematic."[51]

The encyclical is divided into three chapters. The first chapter introduces the scriptural source of Catholic ethics, specifically Jesus's dialogue with a rich young man (Mt 19:16–21). The man poses the question, "What good must I do to inherit eternal life?" Jesus responds "keep the commandments" and "Come follow me" (Mt 19:21). There follows a meditative reflection on discipleship and the invitation to enter into a deep and profound virtuous relationship with Christ[52] that is a prime source of both Catholic virtue ethics and our virtue ethics. The second chapter is radically different in style and content. It shifts from a scriptural foundation for a virtue-type ethic, grounded in the human person in a loving and serving relationship with neighbor, to a philosophical reflection on anthropological and ethical presuppositions. The anthropological presupposition separates freedom from objective and universal truth, and serves as the genesis of relativism. The ethical presuppositions that have created and fostered relativism are labeled "teleologism" (sic) and include "consequentialism" and "proportionalism." The ethical flaw in these methods "for discovering the ethical moral norm"[53] is that they "deny the existence of negative ethical norms regarding specific kinds of behavior, norms which are valid without exception."[54] John Paul asserts that proportionalism holds that one can justify a morally wrong act by a good intention. Such a method is unacceptable since it denies the ex-

[49] *Veritatis Splendor* (hereafter *VS*).

[50] *VS*, no. 75.

[51] *VS*, no. 4.

[52] See Livio Melina, *Sharing in Christ's Virtues: For the Renewal of Moral Theology in Light of* Veritatis Splendor, trans. William E. May (Washington, DC: Catholic University Press of America, 2001).

[53] *VS*, no. 75.

[54] *VS*, no. 90.

istence of intrinsically evil acts that are designated according to the object of the act.[55]

The third chapter draws out the logical implications of the first two chapters and includes a warning to the bishops that is revealing of the encyclical's method. "We have the duty, as Bishops," John Paul writes, "to *be vigilant that the word of God is faithfully taught.* My Brothers in the Episcopate, it is part of our pastoral ministry to see to it that this moral teaching is faithfully handed down and to have recourse to appropriate measures to ensure that the faithful are guarded from every doctrine and theory contrary to it."[56] Later he adds that "This truth of the moral law . . . unfolds down the centuries: the norms expressing that truth remain valid in their substance, but must be specified and determined *'eodem sensu eademque sententia'* in the light of historical circumstances *by the Church's Magisterium*."[57] This imperative establishes the hierarchical methodology for the SIPI of the sources of moral knowledge. *Veritatis Splendor* and virtually all magisterial documents have recourse to all the sources of moral knowledge, but there is a strict hierarchy in the sources. Tradition, interpreted by the Magisterium, is the primary lens for the SIPI of the sources of moral knowledge, especially in its teaching of absolute proscriptive norms, for instance, in sexual and biomedical ethics.

Catholic Ethicists and the SIPI of the Sources of Ethical Knowledge

Though he is neither a theological nor a virtue ethicist, philosopher Germain Grisez sums up well the methodology of many Catholic scholars for the SIPI of the sources of moral knowledge. "For her members the Catholic Church is the supreme moral authority under God. Catholics ought to *conform* their consciences to her teaching in every question, every detail, every respect. If they are faithful, they will."[58] This methodology is also advanced by Michel Therrien who is a virtue ethicist: "I believe the necessity of practice [of responsible parenthood] . . . demonstrates perfectly why the virtue of obedience is so critical to this practice. It is precisely when we conform ourselves to the 'objective moral order,' which the Christian tradition puts before us as the 'standard of excellence' for responsible parenthood, that we are able 'through an upright conscience' to identify the goods which the practice of responsible parenthood is to achieve."[59] In his

[55] *VS*, no. 80.

[56] *VS*, no. 116.

[57] *VS*, no. 53, emphasis added.

[58] Germain Grisez, *Christian Moral Principles: The Way of the Lord Jesus, Volume One* (Quincy, IL: Franciscan Press, 1983), 566, emphasis added.

[59] Michel Therrien, "The Practice of Responsible Parenthood, NFP, and the Covenantal Unity of

essay, responsible parenthood is limited to natural family planning. John Grabowski stands in the same line, judging that "Apostolic Tradition and the Church's teaching office provide a baseline for authentic readings of the biblical text."[60] He does evidence historical consciousness, however, stating that "the understanding of the biblical text can develop and deepen over time" and citing John Noonan's work to substantiate this development.

Historically, however, we would point out, it has often not been the case that the apostolic tradition and the church's teaching office have provided an accurate baseline for authentic readings of biblical or church teaching. On issues of usury, torture, slavery, and religious freedom in history, the church has been gravely mistaken and has admitted that it has been wrong by reversing its judgments on those issues.[61] It is through other sources of knowledge, especially human experience and the work of theologians, that those mistakes have been exposed and corrected, and change in church teaching has taken place. But despite these historical mistakes, some theologians continue to insist that the Magisterium is the ultimate source of moral knowledge. For Grisez, Therrien, Grabowski, and many other Catholic theological ethicists looking through the same theological lens, there is a strict hierarchy in the sources of moral knowledge that grounds their method in ethics. Tradition, guarded and interpreted by the Magisterium, is the primary hermeneutical lens for the SIPI of the sources of moral knowledge and the primary virtue is obedience. William Spohn articulates this attitude thus: "The virtue of obedience . . . displaces prudence in applying negative moral precepts because norms prohibiting certain concrete actions or kinds of behavior as intrinsically evil do not allow for any legitimate exception."[62]

Other Catholic theologians, we among them, also accept the four sources of moral knowledge, scripture, tradition, science, and human experience, but acknowledge none of them as either the primary or the stand-alone source for the definition of human dignity and the determination of principles and norms for its attainment. For a full analysis, they argue, all the sources must be considered when defining human dignity and formulating and justifying principles and norms for its attainment. Theologians in this perspective must address, James Gustafson stipulates, the following questions about the sources: "(a) which sources are valid and relevant; (b) which sources are to be decisive when they conflict, and why; (c) what specific 'content'

Spouses," in *Leaving and Coming Home: New Wineskins for Catholic Sexual Ethics*, ed. David Cloutier (Eugene, OR: Cascade Books, 2010), 182.

[60]Grabowski, *Sex and Virtue*, 28.

[61]See Noonan, "Development in Moral Doctrine," 662–77; John T. Noonan, *A Church That Can and Cannot Change: The Development of Catholic Moral Teaching* (Notre Dame, IN: University of Notre Dame Press, 2005); Charles E. Curran, ed., *Change in Official Catholic Moral Teachings: Readings in Moral Theology No. 13* (New York: Paulist Press, 2003).

[62]Spohn, *Go and Do Likewise*, 101.

is to be taken and what to be ignored from these sources, and why; and (d) how this 'content' is to be interpreted and why it is interpreted as it is."[63] There are other methodological considerations to be taken into account when attempting to respond to these questions. These considerations will impact differently in the different ethical methods, the theological anthropology and definition of human dignity they construct, and the formulation and justification of norms that facilitate its attainment.

One of the major developments in contemporary Catholic ethical method has been the emphasis on doing theological ethics in context. Stephen Bevans defines contextual theology as "a way of doing theology in which one takes into account the spirit and message of the gospel; the Tradition of the church; the culture in which one is theologizing; and social change within that culture."[64] The science of ethnography, which illuminates contextual situations, offers a very useful tool for theologizing in real contextual situations. Christian Scharen and Aana Vigen define ethnography as "a process of attentive study of, and learning from, people—their words, practices, traditions, experiences, memories, insights—in particular times and places in order to understand how they make meaning (cultural, religious, ethical) and what they can teach us about reality, truth, beauty, moral responsibility, relationships, and the divine."[65] We would add also what they can teach us about virtue and how it is practiced. Ethnography requires "empathetic listening."[66] Researchers immerse themselves in the life story of a social community and, by living with "the smell of the sheep"[67] and getting their shoes "soiled with the mud of the street"[68] in the community, learn from that story a human narrative in which dignity is either supported, empowered, and fulfilled or opposed, disenfranchised, and denigrated. Virtue ethicists need to engage enthnography more in depth in the church to learn how it promotes virtue in its members, what virtues it promotes, and what are its institutional biases or impediments that impact the definition and application of the virtues.[69] Gloria Albrecht has conducted such a study[70] that highlights unacknowledged power structures in community that shape definitions of

[63]James Gustafson, *Protestant and Roman Catholic Ethics* (Chicago: University of Chicago Press, 1978), 142.

[64]Stephen Bevans, *Models of Contextual Theology* (New York: Orbis Books, 2002), 1.

[65]Christian Scharen and Aana Marie Vigen, "What Is Ethnography," in *Ethnography as Christian Theology and Ethics*, ed. Christian Scharen and Aana Marie Vigen (New York: Continuum, 2011), 16.

[66]See Emily Reimer-Barry, "The Listening Church: How Ethnography Can Transform Catholic Ethics," in *Ethnography* as *Christian Theology and Ethics*, 97–117.

[67]*Evangelii Gaudium*, no. 24.

[68]*Amoris Laetitia*, nos. 45, 308 (hereafter *AL*).

[69]Peter R. Gathje, "The Cost of Virtue: What Power in the Open Door Community Might Speak to Virtue Ethics," in *Ethnography* as *Christian Theology and Ethics*, 209.

[70]Gloria Albrecht, *The Character of Our Communities: Toward an Ethic of Liberation for the Church* (Nashville, TN: Abingdon, 1995).

virtues like justice. She argues that a primary concern of Christian ethicists should be to learn "how to use the power of the dominant for the purpose of liberating others from oppression and ourselves from domination."[71] Investigating and exposing power structures might invite conversion from one perspective to another and might even require a reformulation of the definition of virtues that sustain practices, narratives, and traditions, and perhaps also a reformulation of the practices, narratives, and traditions themselves. We leave readers to conclude for themselves what such an ethnographic study in the Catholic Church would reveal.

No theological ethicist has done more to recognize and promote contextual theological ethics and ethnography than James Keenan who organized major global ethics conferences in Padua (2006), Trent (2010), and Sarajevo (2018).[72] Padua and Trent brought together four hundred and six hundred theological ethicists from sixty-three and seventy-five countries, respectively, and provided a rare opportunity for contextual and intercontinental dialogue.[73] The fruits of this endeavor are still in their early stages, but it is already reshaping the method for doing theological ethics, the theological anthropologies that evolve out of contextual dialogue, the reflection on and interpretation of what constitutes human dignity, and the formulation and justification of principles that facilitate its attainment. Such intercultural dialogue in no way implies cultural relativism. It reflects, rather, objectivism shaped by virtuous perspectivism. Bryan Massingale argues that, "the only way to universal insights is through particular perspectives,"[74] and we and theological ethicists like us fully agree.

The focus of contextual theology on particularity highlights two other methodological considerations, deductive and inductive reasoning and classicist and historically conscious perspectives, both of which apply to the dimensions of virtue. Deductive reasoning, which characterized Catholic theological ethics prior to the Second Vatican Council, starts with an abstract and accepted definition of human dignity and universal principles and norms that facilitate or frustrate its attainment, and deductively judges intentions and acts as ethical or unethical in light of this accepted definition. Inductive reasoning, which is a central part of our method, begins with concrete cultural, social, and contextual definitions of human dignity, and inductively formulates, justifies, and applies principles and norms that facilitate or

---

[71]Ibid., 169.

[72]See James F. Keenan, "Notes on Moral Theology: What Happened at Trento 2010?" *Theological Studies* 72 (2011): 131–49; Agnes M. Brazal et al., *Transformative Theological Ethics: East Asian Contexts* (Quezon City, Philippines: Ateneo de Manila University, 2010).

[73]Keenan, "What Happened at Trento 2010."

[74]Massingale, "Beyond Revisionism," 258.

frustrate its attainment. It begins with concrete particular perspectives in order to attain realistic universal insights.[75]

A classicist perspective sees knowledge, understanding, and truth as fixed realities; there is but one objective knowledge, one possible understanding, and one truth. A classicist perspective asserts that reality is static, necessary, fixed, and universal. The method utilized, anthropology formulated, and principles and norms taught in this perspective are timeless, universal, and immutable, and the acts condemned by those principles and norms are always so condemned without exception. A historically conscious perspective, which is also central to our method, sees knowledge, understanding, and truth as unfolding realities within the dialectic of the human person integrally and adequately considered, sociohistorical experience, and historical relationships. There is a plurality of definitions of human dignity, of theologies that respond to it, and of principles and norms that promote its attainment because there is a plurality of cultural perspectives on the human person, knowledge, understanding, and truth, and they are all gradually evolving in history. In a historically conscious perspective, reality is dynamic, evolving, changing, and particular. The method utilized, anthropology formulated, and principles and norms justified in this perspective are contingent, particular, and changeable, and the acts condemned by those norms are ethically evaluated in terms of an evolving virtuous perspective on human reality, knowledge, and understanding. Up to the Second Vatican Council in the mid-twentieth century, Catholic theological ethics was characterized by a classicist approach. Since the Council, it has been largely characterized by a historically conscious approach in social ethics but a still classicist approach in sexual ethics.[76]

Pope Francis's Methodology

In his recent apostolic exhortation on marriage and the family, *Amoris Laetitia*, Pope Francis has introduced a Copernican revolution in the church's pastoral practice of marital and sexual ethics. First, he challenges a strictly law–approach to marriage and family.[77] Historically, church teaching on marriage and sexuality has been largely law-oriented, act-focused, static, and deductive. It began with absolute laws, no use of artificial contracep-

[75]See Richard B. Miller, *Casuistry and Modern Ethics: A Poetics of Practical Reasoning* (Chicago: University of Chicago Press, 1996).

[76]See Todd A. Salzman and Michael G. Lawler, "*Amoris Laetitia*: Towards a Methodological and Anthropological Integration of Catholic Social and Sexual Ethics," *Theological Studies* (forthcoming, 2018).

[77]*AL*, no. 35.

tion within a marital relationship, for instance, and applied the law in a one-size-fits-all approach to all people, everywhere, without regard for historical, cultural, relational, or developmental considerations. As Francis notes, "If we consider the immense variety of concrete situations . . . it is understandable that neither the Synod nor this Exhortation could be expected to provide a new set of general rules, canonical [legal] in nature and applicable to all cases."[78] He cites with approval Aquinas's teaching that the more we descend into the details of irregular situations, the more universal principles will be found to fail.[79] "It would be quite simplistic to think," he writes, "that ethical principles present themselves purely in the abstract, detached from any context."[80] The same applies to rules; rules are important, but they are also secondary to values and, we add, virtues.[81] In educating young people, the power of witness and virtuous living is more effective in shaping virtuous character than using authority and rules to compel obedience.[82]

Second, Francis rejects an authoritarian approach to rules[83] and calls for the presentation of reasons and motivations grounded in virtues and values, for choosing marriage, for instance. These reasons and motivations "help men and women better to respond to the grace that God offers them."[84] Francis's method is a radical departure from the method of his immediate predecessors for whom virtues serve deductively to reinforce absolute magisterial norms. It is a virtue-oriented, relational, dynamic, developmental, ethnographic, and inductive method focusing on the particular contextual realities of couples throughout the world. Francis's focus is not on rules to be obeyed and the acts they prescribe but on virtuous ways of being in the world. The members of the church are invited to live a life like Christ in the service of God, spouse, family, neighbor, and society, and to realize that God's mercy is infinite if and when we fall short of this invitation. Chapter Four of *Amoris Laetitia*, "Love in Marriage," is a beautiful reflection on St. Paul's passage on the nature of true love (1 Cor 13:4–7) and the virtues associated with it. The virtue of chastity, so central historically to Catholic ethics on sexuality and marriage, is mentioned only once in the entire document, and that to insist that it proves "invaluable for the genuine growth of love between persons."[85]

Third, and central to Francis's method, is the idea of a gradual, life-long

---

[78]*AL*, no. 300.
[79]*AL*, no. 304.
[80]*Laudato Si'*, no. 199 (hereafter *LS*).
[81]*AL*, no. 201.
[82]*AL*, no. 288.
[83]*AL*, no. 35.
[84]Ibid.
[85]*AL*, no. 206.

growth in virtue that he learned from John Paul II. John Paul proposed his *law of gradualness* because, he argued, the human being "knows, loves, and accomplishes moral good by different stages of growth."[86] Francis argues that the canon law of the church with specific respect to marriage, and we would argue with respect to ethical life in general, has laid upon "persons tremendous burden."[87] He changes the church's ethical approach from law to virtue and teaches that marriage is a life-long challenge, "which advances gradually with the progressive integration of the gifts of God."[88] We would say the same thing about the ethical life in general, which advances gradually with the virtues of love, justice, commitment, fidelity, mercy, compassion, patience,[89] tenderness,[90] and Jesus's "own gentleness in speaking to one another."[91] Rather than reiterating old rules or offering new ones, Francis seeks to highlight the kind of virtuous character Christians are called to *be* so that they may *do* what is necessary to be like Jesus. He makes no change in *doctrine* in *Amoris Laetitia*, but he prescribes a methodological shift in *pastoral practice*, away from obedience to law to a gradual growth in the many virtues we explained in Chapter 2.

CHRISTIAN ETHICAL PERSPECTIVES

We clearly specified our proposed virtue ethical method in our Introduction to this text, including the five mysteries that shape the Christian ethical perspective. We now apply it by way of example to two pressing ethical issues in the contemporary world, the human treatment of the environment and of sexuality. Before doing so, however, we note the following regarding conservative and progressive Christian ethical perspectives. In general, both perspectives accept the fivefold Christian mysteries that we discussed in the Introduction. In addition, they accept the sources of moral knowledge, though they disagree on the SIPI of the sources, depending on the ethical issue being addressed. On the issue of environment, since there is general consensus on magisterial teaching on the moral imperative to care for the environment and the science that defends that teaching, one could reasonably argue that conservatives and progressives agree on the SIPI of the sources of moral knowledge. Where there is a fundamental disagreement on the SIPI of the sources of moral knowledge between conservatives and progressives

[86]*FC*, no. 34.
[87]*FC*, no. 122.
[88]Ibid.
[89]*FC*, no. 2.
[90]*FC*, no. 3.
[91]*FC*, no. 6; see also *FC*, no. 8.

is on sexual and biomedical ethical issues. Whereas conservatives prioritize tradition, narrowly defined as magisterial teaching, and use this source as the hermeneutical lens for selecting, interpreting, and integrating the other sources of moral knowledge, progressives take a more dialectic approach between the sources of moral knowledge, and often critique magisterial teaching based on the selection, interpretation, and integration of those sources. We discuss environmental and sexual ethical issues in turn.

Environmental Ethics

When addressing environmental ethics, a Christian perspective must attempt to define humans' relationship to the mystery of creation and formulate and justify norms that protect and preserve, and do not denigrate, creation. The definition of this mystery focuses on the goodness of God's creation, humans' responsibility to protect and preserve it, and their ability to do so. This mystery must be integrated with, and tempered by, the mystery of sin and the limitations this imposes on the ability to realize responsible stewardship and to repair a damaged ecosystem. Ethical method selects, interprets, prioritizes, and integrates the Christian mysteries that shape their perspectives. This perspective, in turn, shapes the SIPI of the sources of moral knowledge and other considerations to aid in the construction of a theological anthropology. When addressing environmental ethics generally, and climate change specifically, ethical method may select all four sources of moral knowledge and prioritize them in the following order, secular disciplines of knowledge, experience, tradition, and scripture, to define human dignity in relation to the environment and to formulate and justify norms that facilitate its attainment. The prioritization of these sources is not a ranking of the general importance of the sources of moral knowledge, but a ranking of specific importance for the particular issue of environmental ethics.

First, ethical method must consult the natural sciences to gain a scientifically informed perspective on the actual and projected threat of climate change. There is indisputable scientific evidence[92] that climate change is occurring, that human activity significantly contributes to it, and that the consequences for humanity, especially for the poor in developing countries, will be catastrophic in terms of famine, displacement, violence, and extreme weather patterns, if nothing is done to address it. Second, human experience confirms the scientific evidence: widespread drought, famine, and starva-

[92]See James Hansen, "Global Warming Twenty Years Later: Tipping Points Near" (June 23, 2008), www.columbia.edu/~jeh1/2008/TwentyYearsLater_20080623.pdf; Peter T. Doran and Maggie Kendall Zimmerman, "Examining the Scientific Consensus on Climate Change," *EOS, Transaction American Geophysical Union* 90, no. 3 (2009): 22–23.

tion throughout Africa; drought, an increase in the number and severity of both wildfires and hurricanes in North America; more severe flooding in Asia. All of these events point to at least a correlation, if not specifically a cause, between climate change, its impact on local ecosystems, and its devastating impact on millions of people.[93] Pope Francis notes correctly that science alone cannot provide a complete explanation of life; it must be complemented with other sources of moral knowledge.[94] Tradition in the form of recent Catholic teaching, relying on the findings of the sciences and experience, asserts that climate change or global warming is a reality and calls for the international community, especially wealthier countries who are in an economic situation to effect a substantial reduction of greenhouse gas emissions, which are the primary cause of climate change, to work toward reducing these emissions. A report from the Pontifical Academy of Sciences states the following on global warming:

> We call on all people and nations to recognize the serious and potentially irreversible impacts of global warming caused by the anthropogenic emissions of greenhouse gases and other pollutants, and by changes in forests, wetlands, grasslands, and other land uses. We appeal to all nations to develop and implement, without delay, effective and fair policies to reduce the causes and impacts of climate change on communities and ecosystems. By acting now, in the spirit of common but differentiated responsibility, we accept our duty to one another and to the stewardship of a planet blessed with the gift of life.[95]

Pope Francis and the US bishops recognize the scientific claims on climate change and the virtue of stewardship, which the bishops describe as a way of *being* a disciple that "has the power to shape and mold our understanding of our lives and the way in which we live," to respond to this crisis.[96]

It is through the SIPI of science, human experience, and tradition that scripture, the fourth Christian source of moral knowledge, must be selected and interpreted to define human dignity in relation to the environment and

[93]There is debate among scientists on whether we have scientific evidence to determine a correlation or a causation between global warming and severe weather patterns. See "Forum: Is Extreme Weather Linked to Global Warming?" (June 2, 2011), e360.yale.edu/feature/forum_is_extreme_weather_linked_to_global_warming/2411/.

[94]*LS*, no. 199.

[95]"Fate of Mountain Glaciers in the Anthropocene" (May 11, 2011), www.pas.va/content/dam/accademia/pdf/glaciers.pdf.

[96]*LS*, nos. 116, 236; United States Conference of Catholic Bishops (USCCB), "To Be a Christian Steward: A Summary of the U.S. Bishops' Pastoral Letter on Stewardship," www.usccb.org/beliefs-and-teachings/what-we-believe/stewardship/index.cfm; see also *Faithful Stewards of God's Creation: A Catholic Resource for Environmental Justice and Climate Change* (USCCB, 2007).

to formulate and justify norms that facilitate attaining human dignity. In a prophetic article, Lynn White recognizes the ecological crisis and explores the biblical justification in Genesis's creation story that has led, at least in part, to this crisis.[97] In the later, priestly account of creation (Gn 1:1–2:4), God creates human beings on the sixth day and gives them "dominion [*radah*] over the fish of the sea, the birds of the air, and all the living things that crawl on earth" (Gn 1:28). The Hebrew verb *radah* can be interpreted in a strong sense as "subdue, rule over," or in a softer sense as "govern." The strong sense of *radah* allows humans' dominion over creation and justifies exploitation and disregard for it;[98] we see the consequences of dominion in the current ecological crisis. The soft sense of *radah* emphasizes humans' stewardship over creation and justifies and demands responsible care for it. Scientific evidence that proves the damage humans have done to the environment justifies the soft over the strong interpretation of *radah* when reading Genesis 1:26, 28. An integrated and dialectical hermeneutic of the SIPI of the sources of moral knowledge has anthropological implications for defining human dignity and normative implications for humans' relationship with the environment.[99] Human dignity is facilitated to the extent that we respond positively to the environmental crisis; it is frustrated to the extent that we do not respond. [100]

In the discernment of climate change and virtuous environmental ethics in response to it, the inductive approach used in our ethical method underscores the importance of the natural sciences that provide a factual assessment of the situation. This factual assessment serves as the point of departure for any theological–ethical reflection on the crisis, its implications for human dignity, and the formulation of a positive and normative ethical response to it. The contributions of the sciences to understanding the present environmental crisis are crucial to any ethical reflection seeking to address the challenges that the sciences uncover. Historical consciousness, also part of our method, contributes the information that there is a gradual growth in knowledge and understanding in all four sources of moral knowledge. Contextual theology highlights the cultural, historical, and specific socioeconomic challenges that confront attempts to respond

[97]Lynn White, "The Historical Roots of Our Ecological Crisis," *Science* 155, no. 3767 (March 10, 1967): 1203–7.

[98]Harrington and Keenan, *Jesus and Virtue Ethics*, 185.

[99]Such an integrated methodological approach is reflected in Pope Francis's *Laudato Si'*.

[100]For theological reflections on environmental ethics, see Richard W. Miller, ed., *God, Creation, and Climate Change: A Catholic Response to the Environmental Crisis* (Maryknoll, NY: Orbis, 2010); William C. French, "Natural Law and Ecological Responsibility: Drawing on the Natural Law Tradition," *University of St. Thomas Law Journal* 5/1 (2008): 12–36; William C. French, "With Radical Amazement: Ecology and the Recovery of Creation," in *Without Nature? A New Condition for Theology*, ed. David Albertson and Cabell King (New York: Fordham University Press, 2010), 54–79.

to the crisis. The virtue of required stewardship and the norms that follow from it will have very different specific implications, for example, in the United States, which has the financial and technological resources to affect climate change nationally and internationally, and in Sudan, which has very limited financial and technological resources. The ability to respond to particular ethical issues is always very much context dependent. Again, "the only way to universal insights is through particular perspectives." Universal insight defines the good as that which facilitates human dignity; particular perspectives dialogue with the cultural, historical, contextual, and socioeconomic realities to formulate and justify the appropriate norms for attaining human dignity in any particular situation. On social ethics, like climate change, there is considerable anthropological, methodological, and normative agreement among virtue ethicists of different methodological persuasions. It is different in sexual ethics, to which we now turn.

Sexual Ethics

In sexual ethics in general, and homosexuality and chastity in particular, we demonstrate some fundamental tensions between plural Christian perspectives.

Chastity: A Conservative Christian Perspective

The central virtue in the Christian tradition guiding questions of human sexuality is undoubtedly chastity. The *Catechism of the Catholic Church* provides a succinct definition: chastity is "the successful integration of sexuality within the person and thus the inner unity of [the hu]man in his [and her] bodily and spiritual being. Sexuality, in which [the hu]man's belonging to the bodily and biological world is expressed, becomes personal and truly human when it is integrated into the relationship of one person to another in the complete and lifelong mutual gift of *a man and a woman*."[101] This definition of chastity, informed by other magisterial teachings, suggests a perspective on the selection, interpretation, prioritization, and integration of four Christian mysteries, creation, incarnation, redemption, and sin, and asserts two claims, one anthropological and the other normative. Anthropologically, the mystery of creation recognizes the fundamental goodness of God's creation generally and of human sexuality specifically. Normatively, according to the phrase we have italicized in the *Catechism's* definition of chastity, human sexuality can be fulfilled ethically only in a

[101] *Catechism of the Catholic Church*, no. 2337 (hereafter *CCC*), emphasis added. We have corrected the *Catechism's* language to be gender inclusive. The gender exclusive language of the *Catechism* and most magisterial documents is a revealing indicator of perspective.

permanent relationship between a man and a woman. Creation's design for human sexuality is referred to as sexual complementarity between a man and a woman whereby a man and a woman, though fundamentally equal and complete in themselves,[102] are complete as a couple.[103] Sexual complementarity in marriage completes the couple by bringing the male and female physiological and psychological elements together in a unified whole. Creation is designed to complete man and woman as a couple in lifelong mutual self-gift. The mystery of the incarnation affirms the unity of body and soul, mind and spirit in human sexuality; there is no dualism. The mystery of redemption recognizes the possibility of the successful integration "into the relationship of one person to another in the complete and lifelong mutual gift of a man and a woman."

In the Christian perspective, however, original sin has damaged the fundamental goodness of creation, including the goodness of human persons and their sexuality. The Christian tradition has always been suspicious of sexuality and has regarded human sexuality in general as "objectively disordered" as a consequence of original sin.[104] This suspicious view of human sexuality is gradually being corrected in the tradition with the help of the human sciences. Heterosexual orientation is said to be objectively ordered; marital sexuality is fully affirmed as good; and heterosexual marital reproductive sexual acts are morally good. Creation, incarnation, and redemption fully affirm the goodness of heterosexual, marital sexuality and the virtue of chastity, as defined in the *Catechism*, specifies how this good is to be realized. Original sin, however, continues to damage the goodness of human sexuality in both the ontological and ethical orders. Homosexual orientation is said to be one instance of this ontological damage, and some ethicists continue to follow the Magisterium in describing it as an "objective disorder."

Mark Jordan makes an important association between original sin and homosexual orientation that is evident in a subtle revision, approved by the Vatican, to the US bishops' *Always Our Children*.[105] In the original letter, sexual orientation is described as a "fundamental dimension" of human beings; in the revised version, it is a "deep-seated dimension." "Fundamental" might suggest that sexual orientation is an essential element of the human being from creation; "deep-seated" implies only that sexual orientation

---

[102]John Paul II, "Authentic Concept of Conjugal Love," *Origins* 28 (March 4, 1999): 655.

[103]John Paul II, "Letter to Women," *Origins* 25 (July 27, 1995): 141.

[104]Mark Jordan, *The Silence of Sodom: Homosexuality in Modern Catholicism* (Chicago: University of Chicago Press, 2000), 34.

[105]USCCB, "Always Our Children: A Pastoral Message to Parents of Homosexual Children and Suggestions for Pastoral Ministers," www.usccb.org/issues-and-action/human-life-and-dignity/homosexuality/always-our-children.cfm.

is stubborn. Humanity is fundamental, original sin is deep-seated, and homosexuality is more like original sin than like humanity.[106] According to the Congregation for the Doctrine of the Faith (CDF), a homosexual orientation "is a more or less strong tendency ordered toward an intrinsic moral evil."[107] If acted upon, this orientation leads to intrinsic evil in the ethical order. The *Catechism's* definition of chastity and its suggested SIPI of the Christian mysteries contain both an anthropological and a normative claim. The former is that creation justifies only heterosexual orientation and heterosexual mutual self-gift as natural, and prescribes that mutual self-gift can be realized only between a man and a woman in marriage. The mystery of sin demonstrates homosexual orientation and homosexual mutual self-gift as "objectively disordered" and unnatural. The latter claim is that only reproductive-type sexual acts, or at least sexual acts open to reproduction[108] within a heterosexual marriage, are moral; all nonreproductive-type sexual acts—heterosexual, homosexual, or bisexual—are immoral. This magisterial perspective on chastity, we argue, derives from a too narrow focus on *biological* animal nature that ignores the specific difference of human nature as not only biological but also, indeed above all, *rational*. It can be countered by a focus on this rational human nature, to which we now proceed.

Chastity: A Progressive Catholic Perspective

An alternative Catholic perspective agrees with the *Catechism's* suggested selection of four Christian mysteries to define chastity. Further, it accepts the *Catechism's* definition on the authentic integration of a person's sexuality into human relationship and the practical living out of that relationship in fidelity and commitment to another person. An alternative perspective, however, discards the final clause that limits this integration to heterosexual relationships and extends it to homosexual and bisexual relationships. Discarding and extending the final clause is contingent on the relationship of the mystery of sin to sexual orientation and has implications also for the mysteries of creation and redemption.

Relying on secular disciplines of knowledge, some Catholic ethicists disagree with the conservative stance on the mystery of sin that justifies the claim that homosexual orientation is "objectively disordered." Credible science finds that homosexual orientation is a not-infrequent reality in creation. Peer-reviewed scientific literature has documented that human

[106]Jordan, *The Silence of Sodom*, 47.

[107]CDF, "Letter to the Bishops of the Catholic Church on the Pastoral Care of Homosexual Persons," *Origins* 16 (November 13, 1986): 379, n. 3.

[108]See John Finnis, "Law, Morality, and Sexual Orientation," *Notre Dame Law Review* 69 (1994): 1067.

sexual practice has been incredibly varied across time and cultures,[109] and has identified same-sex practice in over three hundred species of vertebrates as a natural component of the social system.[110] Based on such studies, James Alison challenges the claim that a homosexual orientation is objectively disordered. "There is no longer any reputable scientific evidence of any sort: psychological, biological, genetic, medical, neurological," he argues, "to back up the claim."[111] In fact, there is substantial scientific evidence to the contrary. In addition, it is accepted in contemporary scientific and theological literature, including the *Catechism*[112] and other magisterial documents,[113] that people do not choose their sexual orientation. Sexual orientation, "the sustained erotic attraction to members of one's own gender, the opposite gender, or both—homosexual, heterosexual, or bisexual respectively,"[114] is given and not chosen. It is a result of a mix of genetic, neurological, and psychological "loading."[115] Such evidence leads evolutionary biologist Joan Roughgarden to assert the following: "To the extent that information about nature can inform theological discourse on human and biological diversity, the message for full and proper inclusion of gay, lesbian, and transgender persons is clear and unequivocal."[116]

Based on the evidence of the contemporary sciences, some Catholic ethicists argue that the mystery of sin does not justify the claim that homosexual orientation is objectively disordered. This theological claim, according to the CDF, is contingent on whether homosexual acts are intrinsically unethical: "Although the particular inclination of the homosexual person is not a sin, it is a more or less strong tendency ordered toward an intrinsic moral evil; *and thus* the inclination itself must be seen as an objective disorder."[117] The central reason why homosexual orientation is labeled as objectively disordered is because it has a "strong tendency ordered toward an intrinsic moral evil." If it can be established that homosexual acts are not intrinsically

[109]Michel Foucault, *The History of Sexuality*, trans. Robert Hurley, 3 vols. (New York: Vintage Books, 1988–90).

[110]See Bruce Bagemihl, *Biological Exuberance: Animal Homosexuality and Natural Diversity* (New York: St. Martin's Press, 1999).

[111]James Alison, "The Fulcrum of Discovery Or: How the 'Gay Thing' Is Good News for the Catholic Church," unpublished essay, 8.

[112]*CCC*, no. 2358.

[113]USCCB, *Always Our Children*, 5.

[114]Richard C. Pillard and J. Michael Bailey, "A Biological Perspective on Sexual Orientation," *Clinical Sexuality* 18 (1995): 1.

[115]This terminology articulates our position that homosexual orientation as we know it is neither exclusively genetic nor exclusively social in origin. See John E. Perito, *Contemporary Catholic Sexuality: What Is Taught and What Is Practiced* (New York: Crossroad, 2003), 96.

[116]Joan Roughgarden, "Evolutionary Biology and Sexual Diversity," in *God, Science, Sex, and Gender: An Interdisciplinary Approach to Christian Ethics*, ed. Patricia Beattie Jung et al. (Champaign: University of Illinois Press, 2010), 103.

[117]CDF, "Letter to the Bishops of the Catholic Church," at 379, n. 3, emphasis added.

evil, then the understanding of the mystery of sin that justifies the claim that homosexual orientation is objectively disordered must be reconsidered.

Scientific and theological arguments have much to tell us about the ethics of homosexual acts between homosexual couples. Regarding the judgment that homosexual acts are intrinsically disordered and therefore violate chastity and frustrate human dignity, peer-reviewed and credible social-scientific studies indicate that this is not the case. Lawrence Kurdek, who has carried out extensive social-scientific research on gay and lesbian couples for many years, reports that they experience similar levels of relationship satisfaction to heterosexual couples.[118] A growing body of peer-reviewed, social-scientific data demonstrates that committed, stable, and justly loving gay and lesbian unions are as personally complementary and fulfilling as heterosexual ones. Gay and lesbian acts of making just love are as unitive as heterosexual acts of making just love. An equally impressive body of social-scientific data shows that, contrary to magisterial claims with no supporting evidence, partnered gays and lesbians raise children to be every bit as healthily developed and heterosexual as the children of heterosexuals.[119]

Following the demands of their rational nature, some Catholic ethicists reject the Magisterium's normative claim that homosexual acts are intrinsically disordered, but they disagree on how to describe these acts. Richard McCormick, for instance, labels homosexual acts as premorally evil. Such acts are "'pre-moral evils' in that their sheer presence does not *necessarily* make the total act or relation of which they are a part 'morally evil or sinful.'"[120] For McCormick, homosexual acts can be considered premorally evil because "homogenital acts always depart from the ideal or the normative."[121] Other Catholic ethicists reject this judgment because of its implicit anthropological and normative implications. These disagreements must be sorted out to substantiate our claims to redefine the mysteries and the implications these redefinitions have for the virtue of chastity. The claim that homosexual acts depart from the ideal or normative can be made only

[118]Lawrence A. Kurdek, "What Do We Know about Gay and Lesbian Couples?" *Current Directions in Psychological Science* 14 (2005): 251–54; Lawrence A. Kurdek, "Differences between Partners from Heterosexual, Gay, and Lesbian Cohabiting Couples," *Journal of Marriage and Family* 68 (2006): 509–28; Lawrence A. Kurdek, "Lesbian and Gay Couples," in *Lesbian, Gay and Bisexual Identities over the Lifespan*, ed. Anthony R. D'Augelli and Charlotte J. Patterson (New York: Oxford University, 1995), 243–61; Lawrence A. Kurdek, "Are Gay and Lesbian Cohabiting Couples *Really* Different from Heterosexual Married Couples?" *Journal of Marriage and Family* 66 (2004): 880–900.

[119]See Todd A. Salzman and Michael G. Lawler, *Sexual Ethics: A Theological Introduction* (Washington, DC: Georgetown University Press, 2012), 173.

[120]Richard A. McCormick, *Notes on Moral Theology, 1981 through 1984* (Lanham, MD: University Press of America, 1984), 11, citing Lisa Sowle Cahill, "Moral Methodology: A Case Study," in *A Challenge to Love: Gay and Lesbian Catholics in the Church*, ed. Robert Nugent (New York: Crossroad, 1983), 91, emphasis added.

[121]McCormick, *Critical Calling*, 312.

if there is a definition of the normative, and the present definition of the normative is skewed because it is justified by an exclusive heterosexual anthropological norm. According to this anthropology, heterosexual orientation is the norm and anything that departs from this norm is "objectively disordered."[122] There is tension in McCormick's thought here. On the one hand, he resists labeling homosexual orientation an objective disorder. On the other hand, by labeling homosexual acts premorally evil, he implies not only that these acts are nonnormative but also that there is something normative in human nature that makes such acts nonnormative. Exploration of this tension will provide us with an essential anthropological and normative insight that warrants a revision of the conservative definition of the mystery of sin in relation to homosexual orientation.

McCormick presents and critiques the CDF's 1975 Declaration *Persona Humana*, regarding human sexuality, homosexual orientation, and its ethical correlation with homosexual acts. Regarding human sexuality, the CDF states the following:

> The human person, present-day scientists maintain, is so profoundly affected by sexuality that it must be considered one of the principal formative influences of a man or woman. In fact, sex is the source of the biological, psychological and spiritual characteristics which make a person male or female and which thus considerably influence each individual's progress towards maturity and membership of society.[123]

McCormick notes the problematic between claiming, on the one hand, that one's sexuality as reflected in one's sexual orientation is "one of the principal formative influences in the person" and, on the other hand, that for persons with a homosexual orientation, this principal influence is disordered. Such a statement means, quite simply, "the person is disordered."[124] McCormick responds to this by claiming that the CDF has drawn too close an association between the immorality of homosexual acts and the objective disorder of homosexual orientation, such that the orientation itself becomes ethically decisive. In effect, McCormick is resisting the CDF's method of moving from an established definition of homosexual acts as intrinsically evil to an anthropological claim that homosexual orientation is disordered. The latter claim has moral implications from the former for, so runs the argument, while a homosexual inclination is not a sin, it is a more or less strong tendency toward sin. McCormick resists this move to draw a moral

[122]CDF, "Vatican List of Catechism Changes," *Origins* 27 (September 25, 1997): 257.

[123]*Persona Humana*, no. 1 (hereafter *PH*).

[124]McCormick, *Critical Calling*, 310.

correlation between homosexual acts and homosexual persons, and asks "what is achieved by designating homosexual orientation as a 'disorder'?"[125]

We believe there is a similar correlation in McCormick's own thought, not between homosexual acts as *intrinsically* evil and homosexual orientation but between homosexual acts as *premorally* evil and homosexual orientation. We pose to him his own question: what is achieved by designating homosexual acts as premoral evils? Is not this label already a negative judgment on homosexual orientation, aligning it with a definition of the mystery of sin that justifies the claim that homosexual orientation is an objective disorder similar to that advanced by the CDF? Is not a "premoral evil," precisely as "evil," a "disordered" value? It seems to us that one could draw a similar conclusion on the disorderedness of the person's orientation from McCormick's statement that homosexual acts are a premoral disvalue and from the CDF's statement that homosexual acts are "intrinsically disordered."[126] Both take their stance on the unproven anthropological assertion that heterosexual orientation is the norm of sexual morality for humans and that homosexual orientation, therefore, must be objectively disordered. We believe that labeling heterosexual acts as normative, and acts that depart from this ideal as premorally evil, does not give the human sexual person integrally and adequately considered due consideration.

By claiming that heterosexual acts are normative, one has already made a judgment about sexual anthropology and implicitly affirmed the Magisterium's position that heterosexual orientation is, in the words of Jordan, a "fundamental" normative dimension of humanity as a "divine creation" and that a homosexual orientation is "deep-seated" and "stubborn," "more like original sin than like humanity." Any sexual expression that deviates from that norm is, therefore, by definition, at least premorally evil. McCormick and other ethicists, however, leave room for the possibility that some homosexual acts, while they may be premorally evil, are not morally evil and may, indeed, be morally good. McCormick's resistance to labeling sexual orientation disordered, and his further assertion that some homosexual acts can be morally good,[127] would seem to imply that homosexual acts are not premoral evils. What may be at the root of this dilemma, and a way out of it, is how we define sexual orientation in relation to sexual anthropology and determine premoral disvalue in light of this anthropology.

Whether judged intrinsically or premorally evil, homosexual acts are being measured against an accepted perspective that includes a sexual anthropology that posits *heterosexual* orientation, rather than simply *sexual*

[125]Ibid., 311.
[126]*PH*, no. 8.
[127]McCormick, *Critical Calling*, 309.

orientation, as normative for human beings. This is a classicist and deductive approach to anthropology, and it betrays fundamental methodological commitments. It is classicist, because it accepts from the past that heterosexual orientation is the absolute and unchanging anthropological norm. While this may be true statistically, as the Magisterium realizes,[128] there are people with a permanent homosexual orientation who do not choose that orientation; for them, a homosexual orientation *is* normative. The approach is deductive, because it first defines heterosexual orientation as normative and then deduces from that principle that all homosexual activity is morally evil. Catholic ethicists who oppose this perspective utilize a historically conscious and inductive method, which looks at human beings in their particularity and draws out anthropological generalizations that reflect this particularity.

Historical consciousness recognizes both that sexual orientation is natural and that, therefore, there is a need to incorporate it in a sexual anthropology. An ethical method that assesses sexual behavior must be founded on that anthropology and must formulate its values and norms for assessing sexual persons and sexual acts in light of it. A Christian perspective, in turn, must allow the Christian mysteries to be informed by that accurate anthropology. If the scientific data and our revision of Catholic ethical arguments are correct, then homosexual acts are not intrinsically evil and, when holistically complementary, just and loving,[129] can be morally good. If homosexual acts are not intrinsically evil, the CDF's central reason for labeling a homosexual orientation objectively disordered is corrected. The mystery of sin does not justify the claim that homosexual orientation is "objectively disordered;" it is more like humans as created rather than like original sin. The mystery of creation justifies sexual orientation, and heterosexual, homosexual, and bisexual mutual self-gifts are objectively ordered for heterosexual, homosexual, and bisexual persons, respectively. It further justifies that holistic complementarity, that is, *an integrated orientation, biological, and personal complementarity* can be realized between a man and a woman, a man and a man, and a woman and a woman, depending on the person's sexual orientation. The mystery of incarnation affirms the "inner unity" of body and soul, mind and spirit in all humans, heterosexual, homosexual, and bisexual; there is no dualism. The mystery of redemption justifies that the integration of one person and another can occur in the total, loving, and lifelong mutual self-gift of a man and a woman, a man and a man, and a woman and a woman. This approach provides a hermeneutical lens that

[128]*PH*, no. 8; USCCB, "Always Our Children," 6.

[129]For a full explanation of these criteria for sexual morality, see Todd A. Salzman and Michael G. Lawler, "*Quaestio Disputata*. Catholic Sexual Ethics: Complementarity and the Truly Human," *Theological Studies* 67 (2006): 625–52; Salzman and Lawler,*The Sexual Person*, 156–61; Salzman and Lawler, *Sexual Ethics*, 60–86.

justifies both a definition of human dignity that includes sexual orientation as an objective, intrinsic dimension of the sexual person, and a definition of chastity, integrated with the virtues of justice and love, as "the successful integration of [heterosexual, homosexual, or bisexual orientation] within the person and thus the inner unity of [the hu]man in his [and her] bodily and spiritual being."

Looking to the Future

Recognizing the centrality of a virtuous Christian perspective, historical consciousness, evolution, and development in Christian ethical method, we conclude this chapter with two considerations as we look to the future. First, as the theological disciplines develop in both method and content, our methodological criteria for the SIPI of the sources of moral knowledge will evolve and develop, and the additional methodological criteria will be expanded and nuanced. As humans climb higher in the metaphorical Empire State Building or as stories are added to it, perspectives will change. Our proposal can accommodate that development and serve to guide dialogue between a plurality of perspectives and methods.

Second, we concur with William Spohn that whatever these sources and considerations offer "must be tested against the basic norm of Christian identity, the canonical scriptures," which fundamentally define Christians' imagination and virtuous perspective. "This process of testing is synthetic," he continues, "involving a good deal of cross-checking among the various sources. The precise weight given to each source varies with the problem at hand: no formula can be specified in the abstract."[130] That epistemology, virtuous perspective, the sources of moral knowledge, and additional methodological considerations are relevant to Christian ethical method is self-evident. The specific problem at hand, in large part, will influence how these dimensions are integrated and justified and how they account for a plurality of methods and particularities in defining human dignity, and the formulation and justification of norms that facilitate its attainment. Authority without justification, whether it be the Magisterium's authority or ours, equates to no justification, as Catholic theological history so richly shows.

[130]Spohn, *Go and Do Likewise*, 63.

4

Human Dignity

Defining the Good

In the previous chapter we saw how a person's virtuous perspective impacts the selection, interpretation, prioritization, and integration (SIPI) of the various sources of ethical knowledge. In this chapter, we investigate dimensions of the person to provide a framework for defining the good as human dignity. As the most vibrant and divisive debate about human dignity in the contemporary world is the debate about sexual human dignity, we will exemplify and specify our discussion of human dignity by focusing on sexual human dignity, believing with *Gaudium et Spes* that anything learned specifically about sexual human dignity will apply in general to the entire realm of human dignity and the norms to achieve its full attainment.

DIMENSIONS OF HUMAN DIGNITY

Gaudium et Spes indicates how to define human dignity. In its section on marriage and the family, it notes that the ethical aspect of any procedure to harmonize conjugal love with the transmission of life "must be determined by objective standards. These, *based on the nature of the human person and his acts*, preserve the full sense of mutual self-giving and human procreation in the context of true love."[1] The official commentary on *Gaudium et Spes* explains that this principle is applicable not only to marriage and sexuality but also to the entire realm of human activity and is formulated as a general principle: "human activity must be judged insofar as it refers

[1]*Gaudium et Spes*, no. 51, emphasis added (hereafter *GS*).

to the human person integrally and adequately considered."[2] Drawing from *Gaudium et Spes*, as we saw in the Introduction, Louis Janssens specifies the commentary's personalist principle and constructs a theological anthropology explaining the dimensions of the human person. The human person is a subject; in corporeality; in relationship to the material world, to others, to social groups, and, we add, to self; created in the image and likeness of God; a historical being; and fundamentally unique but equal to all other persons.[3] Edward Schillebeeckx develops a similar list of "anthropological constants" constitutive of humanity.[4] We have already considered Janssens's dimensions of the human in the Introduction, and we refer the reader to that consideration before moving on.

We use the term *dimensions* of human dignity, intending by it that the dimensions and their understanding are gradually evolving as the nature of knowledge itself is gradually evolving. As human knowledge gradually evolves and changes, so too will the definition of human dignity evolve and change. One movement that presents a fundamental challenge to theological anthropology, to the definition of human dignity, and to claims to objective truth in ethics is postmodernism, with its emphasis on "fragmentation and plurality." What is called the postmodern movement is difficult to define, but a clear emphasis of the movement is on the particular of the present rather than the universal of the past and present that continues into the future. Paul Lakeland notes that there is "interplay between the given and the novel,"[5] and this interplay allows for positing Janssens's "dimensions" of the human person or Schillebeeckx's "anthropological constants" as constitutive components of the human while, at the same time, revising and refining those dimensions or constants in light of gradually evolving human experience and knowledge, including theological experience and knowledge.

In the dialectic between the universal and the particular, it is inevitable there will be different perspectives and that these different perspectives will all define human dignity in dialogue with history and culture, drawing from the past, in the present, and going forward into the future. Plural perspectives lead to disagreements on both the definition of human dignity and the norms that facilitate its attainment. In the case of such disagreements, the first step is to value the conscience decisions of those with whom we disagree. The next step, to repeat what we have stated several times already, demands a dialogue about the disagreement in which, heeding

---

[2] *Schema constitutionis pastoralis de ecclesia in mundo huius temporis: Textus recognitus et relationes*, pars 11 (Vatican City: Vatican Press, 1965), 9.

[3] Louis Janssens, "Artificial Insemination: Ethical Considerations," *Louvain Studies* 8 (1980): 3–29.

[4] Edward Schillebeeckx, *Christ: The Experience of Jesus as Lord* (New York: Seabury, 1980), 734–43.

[5] Paul Lakeland, *Postmodernity: Christian Identity in a Fragmented Age* (Minneapolis: Augsburg Fortress, 1997), 1.

John Paul II's advice, the participants "explain to one another the truth they have discovered, or think they have discovered, in order thus to assist one another in the quest for [more universal] truth."[6] The final outcome of this dialogue is the judgment about which of the conflicting positions is better informed; more integrally considers the human person; and is, therefore, to be followed. Mutual disrespect, name-calling, ecclesial sanctions, and excommunication are not Christian strategies in such a free, equal, and open dialogue. An essential prerequisite before entry into such a dialogue is the judgment that what is good or right facilitates both the various dimensions of the human person and ultimately human dignity itself. We now explore the historical evolution of Catholic definitions of human sexual dignity, and from this exploration, we will draw insights to construct and explain our own preferred definition of human dignity in general.

CATHOLIC TRADITION AND THE EVOLVING DEFINITION OF HUMAN AND SEXUAL DIGNITY

Historically there has been a single definition of human dignity in Catholic sexual ethics, one that prioritizes the corporeal over the relational dimensions of the human person. First, sexual human dignity is grounded in the biological complementarity of male/female genitalia. The point of departure for any consideration of the sexual human person in a sexual relationship, in other words, is male and female genitalia. If these biological organs are not present in a sexual relationship then, by definition, sexual human dignity is frustrated, regardless of the spiritual and relational meanings of the sexual relationship for the persons involved. Second, sexual human dignity is ultimately and primarily realized through procreation, which was the primary end of marriage up to the Second Vatican Council. These emphases on the biological over the spiritual and relational dimensions of the human person reflect what we label a *biological-procreative* definition of sexual human dignity. This definition emphasizes procreation within marriage and shaped much of the theological reflection on marriage, human sexuality, and sexual human dignity up to the twentieth century. Although infertile marriages were recognized as valuable and even sacramental in this definition, since the primary end of marriage was not realized, such relationships were at least ontologically, though not sacramentally, deficient in comparison to fertile marriages. There is now evidence of a gradual evolving understanding of this definition, integrating into it the relational dimensions of human persons.

With the Second Vatican Council and its elimination of the language of

[6] *Ut Unum Sint*, no. 18 (hereafter *UUS*).

the hierarchy of the ends of marriage, there has been a gradual evolution to a *procreative-relational union* definition of sexual human dignity, which emphasizes persons-in-relationship and the communion of life between them. This personalist and unitive shift reflects a greater appreciation of the relational dimensions of the human person integrally and adequately considered. Though the male/female biological genitalia remain the *sine qua non* for any moral sexual relationship, the so-called unitive or relational and procreative ends of marriage are, in theory, equally and adequately considered. A historical study of the evolution of sexual human dignity in the Catholic tradition is crucial to understanding the past, present, and possible future of Catholic sexual theology in light of the evolving understanding of sexual human persons and definitions of their sexual dignity.

The Biological-Procreative Definition of Human and Sexual Dignity

One definition of sexual human dignity dominated the Catholic theological tradition from the second to the twentieth century. Traditional Catholic sexual morality is essentially *marital* morality; sexual activity was carefully confined in marriage. Michel Foucault's comment on the Stoic tradition accurately describes the Catholic sexual tradition as well. "The conjugal family took custody of [sexuality] and absorbed it into the serious function of reproduction."[7] Sexual intercourse in this tradition is exclusively for marriage and procreation and, in the Catholic ethical tradition, every intentional genital act outside of marriage is seriously sinful.[8] The tradition defined sexual human dignity as a *procreative* dignity, a stable structure of meanings in which a man and a woman become husband and wife to procreate and rear children. That definition has its origin in the Genesis command to "be fruitful and multiply" (Gn 1:22), overly strictly interpreted, and it was solidified in the early Christian struggle to legitimate marriage as something good against Greek dualist theories, which viewed reproduction negatively.

This legitimation found its most thorough argument in the thirteenth century in the writings of Thomas Aquinas. "Marriage has its principal end in the procreation and education of offspring." It has also "a secondary end in man alone, the sharing of tasks which are necessary in life, and from this point of view husband and wife owe each other faithfulness. . . . The first end is found in marriage in so far as man is animal, the second in so far as he is

[7]Michel Foucault, *The History of Sexuality*, vol. I, translated by Robert Hurley (New York: Pantheon Books, 1978), 3.

[8]For a brief conspectus of the history of sexuality in Catholicism, see James F. Keenan, "Catholicism, History of," in *Sex from Plato to Paglia: A Philosophical Encyclopedia*, ed. Alan Soble (Westport, CT: Greenwood Press, 2006), 143–52; Christine E. Gudorf, "Catholicism, Twentieth- and Twenty-First Century," in Soble, *Sex from Plato to Paglia*, 153–63.

man."[9] This is a tightly reasoned argument, as is customary in Aquinas, and his *primary end-secondary end* terminology came to dominate the definition of sexual human dignity and the discussion of the ends of marriage in Roman Catholic manuals for the next seven hundred years. We note, however, that it is a curious argument, for it makes the claim that the primary end of specifically *human* marriage is dictated by the human's generically *animal* nature; the corporeal, biological dimension of the human person shared with animals is prioritized over the rational, relational dimension that is unique to humans. It was this curious argument that would be challenged in the twentieth century, leading to a more personalist definition of sexual human dignity and approach to the morality of sexual activity within marriage. The Catholic Church did not abandon this *primary end–secondary end* language until the Second Vatican Council in the 1960s.

Before it was abandoned, however, it had been enshrined for the first time in an official Catholic document in the *Code of Canon Law* in 1917.[10] "The primary end of *marriage* is the procreation and nurture of children; its secondary end is mutual help and the remedying of concupiscence" (Can 1013, 1). Note here something that is generally overlooked: in Aquinas and the *Code* procreation is the primary end of *marriage*, not of *sexual intercourse*, as it would become in Pope Paul VI's encyclical *Humane Vitae* and in subsequent Catholic debate. This theological fact will be important in a later context. The procreative institution is the result of a contract in which, the 1917 *Code* asserts, "each party gives and accepts a perpetual and exclusive right over the body for acts which are of themselves suitable for the generation of children" (Can 1081, 2). Notice that the marital contract was about *bodies* and their *acts*, and the procreative institution was only secondarily and reluctantly about persons and their mutual relationship and love. There was a gradual evolution in the Catholic definition of sexual human dignity toward a greater recognition and acknowledgment of the relational dimension of human sexuality equal to its biological, procreative dimension. The catalyst for this evolution was spawned, in large part, by historical realities and philosophical movements.

Evolution toward a Procreative-Relational Union Definition of Human and Sexual Dignity

The unprecedented horrors of the First World War transformed the context of human affairs in Europe, where the horrors were localized. This period

[9] Thomas Aquinas, *Summa Theologiae*, 3 (Suppl.), 65, 1c.

[10] See Urban Navarette, "Structura Juridica Matrimonii Secundum Concilium Vaticanum II," *Periodica* 56 (1967): 366.

of "bereavement" and "national trauma"[11] gave birth to a variety of philosophical movements, including the movement that came to be known as personalism. This personalism gradually affected theology and made its first, tentative appearance in an official Catholic document in December 1930, in Pope Pius XI's encyclical *Casti connubii*, his response to the Anglican Lambeth Conference's approval of the ethics of artificial contraception. That encyclical initiated the expansion of the biological-procreative definition of sexual human dignity into a more relational definition of conjugal love and intimacy. *Casti connubii* began timidly to give way to an *interpersonal-relational union* definition, in which procreation remained an important facet of *marriage* but did not exhaust all that marriage is. Pius insisted that marriage had as its primary end procreation but that the mutual love and life of the spouses was also an important end. Both the relational dimension of sexual human dignity and of human relationality in general grew in prominence from this perspective.

Mutual spousal love expressed by just and loving acts, Pius taught, has "as its primary purpose that husband and wife help each other day by day in forming and perfecting themselves in the interior life . . . and above all that they may grow in true love toward God and their neighbor." So important is the mutual love and life of the spouses, he argued, that "it can, in a very real sense, be said to be *the chief reason and purpose of marriage*, if marriage be looked at not in the restricted sense as instituted for the proper conception and education of the child but more widely as the blending of life as a whole and the mutual interchange and sharing thereof."[12] In other words, Pius taught, if we do not focus exclusively on a procreation perspective but broaden the perspective to embrace also the marital life and love of the spouses, then that life and love is the primary reason for marriage. With this authoritative teaching, Pius introduced a new, transitional definition of sexual human dignity, a *procreative-relational union* definition, which gave greater emphasis to the personal, relational dimension between husband and wife. After thirty-five years of growing pains, this revised definition eventually blossomed into an entirely new and previously unheard of Catholic definition of sexual human dignity, a definition that attempts to fully integrate the concept of *interpersonal-relational union* into the primarily biological-procreative definition of sexual human dignity. This attempt was essentially realized in *Gaudium et Spes* by eliminating the language of the hierarchy of the ends of marriage, though not without resistance.

Pius XI suggested there is more to marriage than the procreative,

[11]The words are from Stephen Schloesser, *Jazz Age Catholicism: Mystic Modernism in Postwar Paris* (Toronto: University of Toronto Press, 2005), an insightful look into this period.

[12]*Acta Apostolicae Sedis*, 22 (1930): 548–49, emphasis added (hereafter *AAS*).

biologically rooted, act-focused definition of sexual human dignity can explain. He suggested a personal procreative-relational union definition, a suggestion that was taken up by European theologians. In marriage, they taught, spouses enter an interpersonal relationship in which they confront one another as unique "I" and "Thou" and initiate a mysterious union of their very beings into a conjoined "We." This interpersonal union of their very beings, and not merely the physical union of their bodies, is what the oft-quoted "one body" of Genesis 2:24 intends. The bodily union achieved in sexual intercourse both signifies and enhances this interpersonal union, and intercourse achieves its primary end when it actually does enhance this interpersonal union, when it actually does "make love." "Every marriage," wrote Dietrich Von Hildebrand, "in which conjugal love is thus realized bears spiritual fruit, becomes *fruitful*—even though there are no children."[13] So, too, does every human relationship become personally fruitful when it is just and loving. The resonance of this interpersonal description of marriage, human relationship, and mutual love with the lived experience of modern married couples soon became clear, and it enhanced in their minds not only their sexual dignity but also their human dignity.

Some theologians argue the logical, theological, and ethical implications of this interpersonal union definition of sexual human dignity. The primary end of *marriage* is the creation and enhancement of the union of love between the spouses, and this primary end is achieved in every just and loving act of intercourse, sexual or otherwise, in and through which the spouses actually enter into intimate communion. In this definition, there is an inversion in the ends of marriage and relationship and, therefore, also in the definition of sexual and human dignity. The relational dimension becomes primary; the biological, procreative dimension becomes secondary. Even in childless marriages, marriage and sexual intercourse achieve their primary end in the blossoming of the loving union of the spouses. "The immediate purpose of *marriage* is the realization of its meaning, the conjugal two-in-oneness. . . . This two-in-oneness of husband and wife is a living reality, and the immediate object of the marriage ceremony and their legal union." The union and love of the spouses tends naturally to the creation of a new person, their child, who fulfills both parents individually and as a two-in-oneness. "Society is more interested in the child than in the natural fulfillment of the parents, and it is this which gives the child primacy among the natural results of marriage."[14] Contemporary social scientific data, however, demonstrate the fallacy in assigning primacy to

[13]Dietrich Von Hildebrand, *Marriage* (London: Longman's, 1939), 25, emphasis in original.

[14]Heribert Doms, *The Meaning of Marriage* (London: Sheed and Ward, 1939), 94–95, emphasis added.

the child, for the relational well-being of the parents is demonstrated to be the key to the well-being of their child.[15]

The Catholic Church's reaction to these new ideas was, as so often in theological history, a blanket condemnation that made no effort to sift truth from error. In 1944, the Holy Office (now the Congregation for the Doctrine of the Faith) condemned "the opinion of some more recent authors, who either deny that the primary end of marriage is the generation and nurture of children, or teach that the secondary ends are not essentially subordinate to the primary end, but are equally primary and independent."[16] In 1951, after yet another world war of even greater horror, as personalism gained more adherents, Pope Pius XII felt obliged again to intervene. "Marriage," he taught, "as a natural institution in virtue of the will of the creator, does not have as a primary and intimate end the personal perfection of the spouses, but the procreation and nurture of new life. The other ends, in as much as they are intended by nature, are not on the same level as the primary end, and still less are they superior to it, but they are essentially subordinate to it."[17] The terms of the question of the ends of marriage and its implications for the definition of human and sexual dignity could not have been made more precise.

Gaudium et Spes *and Human and Sexual Dignity*

Though the Second Vatican Council did not deal in detail with marriage, its document *Gaudium et Spes* did provide material intimately related to our present discussion. Marriage, it taught, is a "*communion of love* . . . an intimate partnership of life and love."[18] In spite of insistent demands from a small Vatican minority to repeat the centuries-old classicist tradition of marriage as procreative institution, thus consigning the relational union dimension of spousal love to its traditional secondary place, the Council declared the mutual love of the spouses to be of the very essence of marriage, founded in "a conjugal covenant of irrevocable personal consent."[19] Covenant is a biblical word, saturated with overtones of divine, steadfast love, characteristics that are now applied to the marriage between a man and a woman. The description of the object of the marital covenant places

[15]See Ronald J. Angel and Jacqueline L. Angel, *Painful Inheritance: Health and the New Generation of Fatherless Families* (Madison: University of Wisconsin, 1993); David Blankenhorn, *Fatherlessness in America: Confronting Our Most Urgent Social Problem* (New York: Basic Books, 1995); David Popenoe, *Life without Father* (New York: Free Press, 1996); Judith Wallerstein et al., *The Unexpected Legacy of Divorce: A 25 Year Landmark Study* (New York: Hyperion, 2000).

[16]*AAS* 36 (1944): 103.

[17]*AAS* 43 (1951): 848–49.

[18]*GS,* no. 47–48.

[19]*GS,* no. 48.

the relational character of marriage beyond doubt. The spouses, the Council teaches, "mutually *gift and accept one another*;"[20] the focus on animal bodies and their acts is replaced by a focus on persons. In their marital covenant, spouses create, not a procreative institution, but a loving interpersonal union that, since covenanted love is steadfast, is to last as long as life lasts, and may or not be procreative.[21] This shift in focus from procreation as the primary end of marriage to persons-in-relationship as the focus is a fundamental anthropological shift in defining sexual human dignity, though its normative implications have yet to be fully realized in magisterial teaching.

The intense, and well-documented, debate that took place in the Council makes it impossible to claim, as Germain Grisez wishes to claim,[22] that the refusal to sustain the received marital tradition was the result of a simple avoidance of the language. It was the result of deliberate and hotly deliberated choice, a choice replicated and given canonical formulation twenty years later in the revised *Code of Canon Law* in 1983, often called the Second Vatican Council's final document. Marriage "is ordered to the well-being of the spouses and to the procreation and upbringing of children,"[23] with no suggestion that either end is superior to the other. Notice that, once again, it is *marriage* and not *sexual intercourse* that is ordered to procreation. Marriage is "brought into being by the lawfully manifested consent of persons who are legally capable,"[24] and that consent "is an act of the will by which a man and a woman by irrevocable covenant mutually give and accept *one another* for the purpose of establishing a marriage."[25] It would be naïve and would demonstrate a complete ignorance of past conciliar history to assume that the debate over marriage and procreation ended with the Council. It continued most vociferously in the deliberations of the Pontifical Birth Control Commission and the promulgation of Pope Paul VI's encyclical *Humanae Vitae*.

The thinking about the relational union that is marriage throughout the late twentieth century gradually extended to relational unions other than marriage and what was concluded about the marital union was gradually concluded also about nonmarital unions that are now known as *cohabitation*. In 2015, Pope Francis convoked a Synod on Marriage and Family and, when the preparatory document for discussion at the Synod was distributed,

---

[20]Ibid.

[21]For an extended analysis of covenant, see Michael G. Lawler, "Marriage as Covenant in the Catholic Tradition," in *Covenant Marriage in Comparative Perspective*, ed. John Witte, Jr. and Eliza Ellison (Grand Rapids: Eerdmans, 2005), 70–91.

[22]Germain Grisez, *The Way of the Lord Jesus, Volume Two: Living a Christian Life* (Quincy, IL: Franciscan Herald Press, 1993), 565, n. 35.

[23]*Code of Canon Law* Can 1055, 1.

[24]*Code of Canon Law* Can 1057, 1.

[25]*Code of Canon Law* Can 1057, 2.

Marriage Care, the group charged with the marriage preparation of Catholics in England, responded that nearly every couple attending their courses was already cohabiting. Couples seeking to be married in the church and not already living together were a rarity, not only in England but throughout the Western world. The sharp increase in cohabitation is one of the most fundamental social changes in Western countries today. Over half of all first marriages in the United States are preceded by cohabitation.[26] Studies find a similar trend in Europe,[27] Great Britain,[28] Norway,[29] Sweden,[30] the Netherlands,[31] France,[32] Belgium and Germany,[33] Ireland,[34] Canada,[35] and Australia.[36] A 2013 report from the Centers for Disease Control in the United States further documented that prevalence: 48 percent of women interviewed in 2006–2010 cohabited as a first union compared with 34 percent of women in 1995; 40 percent of those cohabitations transitioned to marriage within three years.[37] Cohabitation is an ever-increasing phenomenon in our human experience, and human experience is a long-established ground for Catho-

---

[26]Larry L. Bumpass, *The Declining Significance of Marriage: Changing Family Life in the United States* (Madison: University of Wisconsin-Madison: Center for Demography and Ecology, 1995), 8; L. Bumpass and Hsien-Hen Lu, *Trends in Cohabitation and Implications for Children's Family Contexts* (Madison: University of Wisconsin-Madison: Center for Demography and Ecology, 1998), 7; Center for Marriage and Family, *Time, Sex, and Money: The First Five Years of Marriage* (Omaha, NE: Creighton University: Center for Marriage and Family, 2000).

[27]John Haskey, "Patterns of Marriage, Divorce, and Cohabitation in the Different Countries of Europe," *Population Trends* 69 (1992): 27–36; François Hopflinger, "The Future of Household and Family Structures in Europe," *Proceedings of the Seminar on Present Demographic Trends and Lifestyles in Europe* (Strasbourg, France: Council of Europe, 1991), 291–338.

[28]John Haskey, "Pre-marital Cohabitation and the Probability of Subsequent Divorce: Analyses Using the New Data from the General Household Survey," *Population Trends* 68 (1992): 10–19.

[29]Oystein Kravdal, "Does Marriage Require a Stronger Economic Underpinning than Informal Cohabitation?," *Population Studies* 53 (1999): 63–80.

[30]Neil G. Bennett et al., "Commitment and the Modern Union: Assessing the Link between Premarital Cohabitation and Subsequent Marital Stability," *American Sociological Review* 53 (1988): 127–38; Ann-Zofie E. Duvander, "The Transition from Cohabitation to Marriage: A Longitudinal Study of the Propensity to Marry in Sweden in the Early 1990s," *Journal of Family Issues* 20 (1999): 698–717.

[31]Aart C. Liefbroer, "The Choice between a Married or Unmarried First Union by Young Adults," *European Journal of Population* 7 (1991): 273–98.

[32]Henri Leridon, "Cohabitation, Marriage, Separation: An Analysis of Life Histories of French Cohorts from 1968 to 1985," *Population Studies* 44 (1990): 127–44.

[33]R. Lesthaeghe et al., "Living Arrangements and Values among Young Adults in the Netherlands, Belgium, France and Germany, 1990," Paper presented at the annual meetings of the Population Association of America, Cincinnati (April 1–3, 1993), www.vub.ac.be/demography/wp-content/uploads/2016/02/WP-IPD-1992–3.pdf.

[34]John Mee, "Cohabitation Law Reform in Ireland," *Child and Family Law Quarterly* 23 (2011): 323–43.

[35]Charles Hobart and Frank Grigel, "Cohabitation among Canadian Students at the End of the Eighties," *Journal of Comparative Family Studies* 23 (1992): 311–37.

[36]Michael Bracher et al., "Marriage Dissolution in Australia: Models and Explanations," *Population Studies* 47 (1993): 403–25.

[37]Casey E. Copen et al., "First Premarital Cohabitation in the United States: 2006–2010 National Survey of Family Growth," *National Health Statistics Report* 64 (April 4, 2013), https://www.ncbi.nlm.nih.gov/pubmed/24988817.

lic moral reflection and judgment.[38] Inspired by Pope Francis's apostolic exhortation, *Amoris Laetitia*, we reflect on that phenomenon and seek to make faith sense of it, that is, we come to the experience of cohabitation with a faith nourished in the Catholic tradition and attempt to allow that faith to enter into dialogue with the experience of cohabitation and the effect it has on the Christian lives of cohabiting couples. Francis's exhortation, we believe, marks a clear turning point in the magisterial approach to cohabitation, after which the ethical situation of what we will call nuptial cohabitation has changed.[39]

We introduce here an important distinction, for not all cohabitors and not all cohabitations are alike. Ten years ago, we introduced a twofold typology of cohabitors and their cohabitations: there are cohabitors who intend to marry one another and are even engaged and cohabitors who have no intention of marrying one another. The former we named *nuptial cohabitation*, the latter *nonnuptial cohabitation*.[40] In *Amoris Laetitia*, Pope Francis embraces our distinction, if not our terminology. He makes a distinction between "cohabitation which totally excludes any intention to marry," our nonnuptial cohabitation, and cohabitation dictated by "cultural and contingent situations,"[41] which can lead to marriage when circumstances permit it, our nuptial cohabitation. He instructs that "these [nuptial] couples need to be welcomed and guided patiently and discreetly" to the point that their nuptial cohabitation gradually grows into "the full reality of marriage and family in conformity with the gospel."[42] Fully aware of the Catholic ethical tradition that every sexual act outside of marriage is *objectively* wrong, he is aware also that the tradition teaches the freedom and inviolability of individual conscience and the mitigating influence of circumstances, and he refuses to classify all cohabitation as *subjectively* sinful. Instead, borrowing from Jesus's treatment of the Samaritan woman (Jn 4:1–26) and John Paul II's law of gradualness already mentioned, he values nuptial cohabitation "in the knowledge that the human being knows, loves, and accomplishes moral good by different stages of growth."[43] Instead of condemning nuptial cohabitors, Francis urges that the church must accompany them "with mercy and patience" and await "the eventual stages of personal growth as these progressively [and gradually] appear."[44] He cites not a law that condemns

[38]See Michael G. Lawler and Todd A. Salzman, "Human Experience and Catholic Moral Theology," *Irish Theological Quarterly* 76 (2011): 35–56.

[39]See Stephan Goertz and Caroline Witting, Amoris Laetitia*: Wendpunkt für die Moraltheologie* (Freiburg: Herder Verlag, 2016).

[40]Michael G. Lawler and Gail S. Risch, "A Betrothal Proposal," *U.S. Catholic* (June 2007): 18–22.

[41]*Amoris Laetitia*, nos. 53, 294 (hereafter *AL*).

[42]*AL*, no. 294.

[43]*AL*, no. 295.

[44]*AL*, no. 308.

but a law of virtue that grows in love, mercy, patience, accompaniment, and encouragement, acknowledging the Catholic position on the authority and inviolability of conscience that, in turn, acknowledge human dignity of men and women fully and adequately considered.

There is a well-known social scientific fact about cohabitation that is still cited by some Catholic ethicists. It is that premarital cohabitation tends to be associated with a heightened risk of divorce,[45] a fact on which there was consensus from a large variety of early researchers, samples, and measures. This fact became beloved of Catholic commentators on cohabitation and its implications for subsequent marriage,[46] which leaves both them and their pastoral responses to cohabitors at risk of being uninformed and outdated. More recent studies on more recent cohorts report more nuanced data about the relationship of cohabitation and marital instability. As early as 1992, Robert Schoen showed that the inverse relationship between premarital cohabitation and subsequent marital instability was minimal for recent birth cohorts, a result that he linked to the growing prevalence of cohabitation. "As the prevalence of cohabitation rises sharply, the instability of marriages preceded by cohabitation drops markedly."[47] In 1997, Susan McRae demonstrated the common negative association between premarital cohabitation and marital instability when she analyzed her British sample *in toto*. When, however, she analyzed her sample by age cohort, her findings supported Schoen: "younger generations do not show the same link between pre-marital cohabitation and marriage dissolution." She agreed with Schoen's conclusion that "as cohabitation becomes the majority pattern before marriage, this link will become progressively weaker."[48] That majority pattern, as already noted, has now arrived. When they analyzed their data *in toto*, Lakeesha Woods and Robert Emery uncovered much the same result as McRae: "premarital cohabitation had a small but significant predictive effect on divorce." When they controlled for age of the cohabitors, however, premarital cohabitation had no predictive effect on divorce.[49]

---

[45]Larry L, Bumpass et al., "The Changing Character of Stepfamilies: Implications of Cohabitation and Nonmarital Childbearing," *Demography 32* (1995): 425–36; Robert Schoen, "First Unions and the Stability of First Marriages," *Journal of Marriage and Family* 54 (1992): 281–84; David R. Hall and John Z. Zhao, "Cohabitation and Divorce in Canada: Testing the Selectivity Hypothesis," *Journal of Marriage and Family* 57 (1997): 421–27.

[46]See, as an example replicated in diocesan policies across the United States, National Conference of Bishops, Committee on Marriage and Family, *Marriage Preparation and Cohabiting Couples* (Washington, DC: USCC, 1999), 10. See also Pontifical Council for the Family, *Marriage, Family, and De Facto Unions* (Rome: Typis Polyglottis Vaticanis, 2000), 4.

[47]Schoen, "First Unions and the Stability of First Marriages," 283.

[48]Susan McRae, "Cohabitation: A Trial Run for Marriage?," *Sexual and Marital Therapy* 12 (1997): 259–73, at 259.

[49]Lakeesha N. Woods and Robert E. Emery, "The Cohabitation Effect on Divorce: Causation or Selection," *Journal of Divorce and Remarriage* 37 (2002): 101–21.

In a sophisticated study of an Australian sample that controlled for age at union formation, educational level, and importance of religion in the relationship, David De Vaus and his colleagues found the same result, the link between cohabitation and marital instability was apparent only for earlier cohorts.[50] Jay Teachman replicated that result in 2002, showing that when a woman has cohabited only with her husband, nuptial cohabitation is not associated with increased likelihood of divorce.[51] Sheri Stritof reported the same finding from Europe in 2017.[52]

Humanae Vitae *and Challenges to the Procreative Definition of Human and Sexual Dignity*

The debate on contraception, which greatly impacted the evolving definition of human and sexual dignity in the Catholic tradition, was tightly focused in 1968 with the publication of Pope Paul VI's encyclical *Humanae Vitae*. This document emerged from the long-established procreative definition of marriage and sexual human dignity and prescribed that "each and every marriage act must remain open to the transmission of life."[53] Notice the difference from the previous tradition. Paul VI argued not that *marriage* but that each and every *marriage act* must remain open to procreation. The pope who convoked the Second Vatican Council, John XXIII, had established a commission to study the issue of birth control, and the final vote in the commission was in response to three questions. In answer to a first question, "Is contraception intrinsically evil?" nine bishops responded "No," three responded "Yes," and three abstained. In answer to a second question, "Is contraception, as defined by the Majority Report, in basic continuity with tradition and the declarations of the Magisterium?" nine bishops responded "Yes," five responded "No," and one abstained. In answer to a third question, "Should the Magisterium speak on this question as soon as possible?"

[50]David de Vaus et al., "Does Pre-Marital Cohabitation Affect the Chances of Marriage Lasting?" Paper Presented at the Eighth Australian Institute of Family Studies Conference, Melbourne, February 2003, www.aifs.org.au

[51]Jay Teachman, "Premarital Sex, Premarital Cohabitation, and the Risk of Subsequent Marital Dissolution among Women," *Journal of Marriage and the Family* 65 (2002): 444–55.

[52]Sheri Stritof, "Cohabitation Facts and Statistics You Need to Know," https://www.thespruce.com/cohabitation-facts-and-statistics-2302236

[53]*Humanae Vitae*, no. 11 (hereafter HV). The encyclical was written in Italian, probably because its main editor was the Franciscan Ermenegildo Lio, who made such sustained efforts to reintroduce Ottaviani's rejected schema, *De Castitate, Virginitate, Matrimonio, Familia,* into Schema XIII, which became *Gaudium et Spes*. Janet Smith references several English translations and offers her own translation "based on the Latin, though on a few occasions, when the Latin seemed irrecoverably obscure, recourse was made to the Italian" (Janet Smith, *Humanae Vitae: A Generation Later* [Washington, DC: Catholic University of America Press, 1991], 269). When compared to the official Latin text and official English translation, the translation she offers is rather idiosyncratic.

fourteen responded "Yes," and one responded "No."[54] A preliminary vote of the theologian advisors to the commission, in answer to the question "Is artificial contraception an intrinsically evil violation of the natural law?" resulted in a count of fifteen "No" and four "Yes" votes.[55] Both an official majority and an unofficial minority report were then submitted to Paul VI who, professing himself unconvinced by the arguments of the majority and sharing the concern of the minority that the church could not repudiate its long-standing teaching on contraception without undergoing a serious blow to its overall ethical authority, approved the minority report in his encyclical letter *Humanae Vitae*.[56] The fundamental difference between the two groups is easily categorized.

The minority report argued that "each and every *marriage act* . . . must remain open to the transmission of life." The majority report argued that *marriage* itself, not "each and every *marriage act*," is to be open to the transmission of life. It asserted that "human intervention in the process of the marriage act *for reasons drawn from the end of marriage itself* should not always be excluded, provided that the criteria of morality are always safeguarded."[57] The fundamental difference in the two positions was caused by adherence to two different definitions of marriage and of human sexual dignity. The minority report was based on the traditional biological-procreative definition that focused on the "natural" meaning of the *act* of sexual intercourse. The majority report was based on the new interpersonal-relational definition that emerged from the Council and that focused, first, on the total meaning of *marriage* and, only second, on the meaning of sexual intercourse within marriage. Richard McCormick's judgment that "the documents of the Papal Commission represent a rather full summary of two points of view . . . the majority report, particularly the analysis of its rebuttal, strikes this reader as much the more satisfactory statement,"[58] continues to be the judgment of the majority of Catholic theologians and Catholic couples, because they adhere to the same relational definition of human and sexual dignity on which the majority report was based.

The judgment of the majority on the papal commission continues to be the judgment of the majority of Catholic couples worldwide.[59] They do not

[54]See Robert McClory, *Turning Point: The Inside Story of the Papal Birth Control Commission and How Humanae Vitae Changed the Life of Patty Crowley and the Future of the Church* (New York: Crossroad, 1997), 127.

[55]Ibid., 99.

[56]For detail on this, see Smith, *Humanae Vitae*, 11–33.

[57]Cited in Clifford Longley, *The Worlock Archive* (London: Chapman, 2000), 233, emphasis added.

[58]Richard McCormick, *Notes on Moral Theology* 1965–1980 (Lanham, MD: University of America Press, 1981), 164.

[59]See the statistics in Julie Clague, "Catholics, Families, and the Synod of Bishops: Views from the Pews," *Heythrop Journal* 55 (2014): 994.

accept the prescription that every *act* of sexual intercourse must be open to new life, because they do not accept the biological-procreative definition of sexual human dignity and marriage on which it is based. Rather, they embrace the interpersonal-relational definition on which the majority report was based. The sociologically documented overwhelming nonreception of *Humanae Vitae* and the nuanced reception of the interpersonal-relational model of marriage, among both those expert in marriage and those expert in theology, suggest a contemporary example of a fundamental revision in the definition of human and sexual dignity in line with the fundamental revision indicated by the development in doctrines on usury, slavery, religious freedom, and membership in the body of Christ.[60] Sociological research suggests that dramatic development is now well under way. It shows that the assertion, "the Church believes that each and every marriage act must be open to the transmission of new life" is not true today for the majority of Catholics who make up the People-of-God-in-communion on whom the Second Vatican Council placed such emphasis.[61] At the very least, the social scientific data suggest a development that the whole church, "from the Bishops to the last of the faithful,"[62] is called to discern in order to judge whether it is or is not an authentic example of rereception of the apostolic truth toward which the Spirit of truth constantly impels the church.

The Unitive Definition of Human and Sexual Dignity

The Second Vatican Council substantially contributed to a revised definition of theological anthropology and, therefore, of human dignity. These revisions marked a fundamental development in the Catholic definition of human dignity, but the Magisterium has not yet fully incorporated them into its definition of human dignity or into its formulation and justification of sexual norms. The emphasis in official church pronouncements, greatly influenced by Pope John Paul II, continues to be on the *nature* of sexual intercourse rather than on the *nature* of marriage and the *meaning* of sexual intercourse within marriage for free and rational human persons. There is another meaning in specifically *Christian* marriages that is frequently forgotten, namely, its requirement to live a virtuous marital life in imitation of Jesus whom spouses confess as the Christ. Though unmarried and childless, Jesus was enormously fruitful, generating and nurturing all those called by his name, *Christians*. He nurtured them to call upon God as *Abba*,

[60]See John T. Noonan, Jr., *A Church That Can and Cannot Change* (Notre Dame, IN: University of Notre Dame Press, 2005); Michael G. Lawler, *What Is and What Ought to Be: The Dialectic of Experience, Theology, and Church* (New York: Continuum, 2005), 119–42.

[61]*Lumen Gentium*, no. 37 (hereafter *LG*).

[62]Augustine, *De Praed. Sanct.*, 14, 27, *PL* 44, 980. See also *LG*, no. 12.

Father (Mk 14:36) and, therefore, to look upon all the children of God as equal brothers and sisters and friends. This reality as sons and daughters of the same God is a major dimension of Christian, and therefore also, human dignity. For a relationship to be genuinely Christian, it must generate and nurture *Christian* virtuous life and communion, not only between the persons in relationship but also within the human community in which they live. The end of relationship sought by Jesus is a neighbor-love both inside and outside the relationship. In this way, Christians fulfill the injunction of the Letter to Timothy to "provide for his relations and especially for his own family" (1 Tm 5:8).

The Procreative Meaning of Human and Sexual Dignity

As indicated, up until the Second Vatican Council, the Catholic Church taught that procreation was the primary end of marriage. *Gaudium et Spes* eliminated that teaching, explicitly emphasizing the unitive meaning of marriage and implicitly de-emphasizing the procreative meaning. This de-emphasis was the culmination of a process that began with Pius XI. For twenty years after Pius XI's encyclical *Casti Connubii*, the church struggled with a paradox. On the basis of its reading of natural law whose author is believed to be God, the primary end of sexual intercourse in marriage is procreation and, therefore, every act of intercourse should be open to procreation. But an ethical question arose. Is it ethical for a couple to practice periodic continence with the *explicit intention* of avoiding conception; or, to put the question bluntly, is it ethical for a couple intentionally to limit their sexual intercourse to the wife's monthly period of infertility? This question raged unanswered for twenty years until Pius XII ruled in 1951 that such action was ethical as long as there were "serious reasons" of a "medical, eugenic, economic, or social kind,"[63] with no specification of what such serious reasons might be. The obligation to procreate, the pope argued, rests not on individual couples but on the entire human race. An individual couple can be excused from adhering to this obligation, even for the lifetime of their marriage, if they have sufficient reason.

This ruling, later validated by Paul VI in *Humanae Vitae*, introduced a strange paradox into Catholic teaching about human and sexual dignity. On the one hand, God, the author of natural law, determined that the end of each and every act of sexual intercourse is procreation. On the other hand, the Catholic Church determined that a couple endowed with the human dignity of reason, freedom, and inviolable conscience may be sexually active and *intentionally* preclude this end if they have sufficient reason.

---

[63] *AAS* 43 (1951): 846.

Joseph Selling's comment is apposite: "Although it has never been admitted by the Magisterium, with the teaching on periodic continence the natural law approach to sexual morality had reached a cul-de-sac."[64] We agree and add that the Magisterium's definition of human and sexual dignity is inconsistent and incomprehensible and had also reached a cul-de-sac. The ethical legitimacy of periodic abstinence to avoid procreation, even for the duration of a marriage, calls into question the ethical relevance of the procreative meaning of the marital act for those who use periodic abstinence and, in doing so, are not open to the *biological* transmission of life in any ethically meaningful sense. The Second Vatican Council, as we have shown, would attempt to resolve this and other paradoxes in church doctrine about human and sexual dignity by abandoning the natural law model in which this papal argument is based.

To procreate literally means "to produce or bring into existence." We reasonably inquire what infertile women, or fertile women on their majority infertile days of the month, produce or bring into existence? This question became all the more pressing with *Humanae Vitae*'s shift from the unitive-procreative ends of *marriage* to the unitive-procreative meanings of *each and every sexual act*. In the infertile sexual acts to which we have referred what a woman, or better a couple, is producing or bringing into existence in just and loving sexual acts is a deepening of their union. Human sexuality is a gift from the Creator God that draws an individual toward union with another person, an intrinsic dimension of human dignity that draws an individual out of herself/himself and toward another person. As the US Catholic bishops teach, "sexuality is a dimension of one's restless heart, which continually yearns for interpersonal communion, glimpsed and experienced to varying degrees in this life, ultimately finding full oneness only in God, here and hereafter."[65] In and through sexual relationship, Christian women and men seek to become whole, holy, and virtuous. The mutual self-gift that is at the heart of just and loving sexual intercourse is at the heart also of the definition of human and sexual dignity. It allows men and women to enter into communion with one another and, through one another, with their neighbors and their God.

To summarize, then, developments in the Catholic tradition with respect to human sexuality have led to a revision of both its anthropology and its definition of human and sexual dignity. First, elimination of the *primary end–secondary end* terminology with its implied hierarchy of the ends of

---

[64]Joseph A. Selling, "Marriage and Sexuality in the Catholic Church," in *Embracing Sexuality: Authority and Experience in the Catholic Church*, ed. Joseph A. Selling (Burlington, VT: Ashgate, 2001), 185.

[65]United States Conference of Catholic Bishops (hereafter USCCB), *Human Sexuality*, 9.

marriage has put greater emphasis on the unitive, relational meaning of marriage and sexual intercourse. Second, not only did the Second Vatican Council emphasize the unitive meaning of marriage and sexual intercourse but it also de-emphasized the biological-procreative meaning of marriage and sexual intercourse. Third, this de-emphasis is further confirmed by the statements of Pius XII and Paul VI that a married couple can choose abstinence and nonprocreation for serious reasons, even for the duration of a marriage. Fourth, despite its emphasis on the unitive-relational meaning of relationship and sexual intercourse and the de-emphasis of the biological-procreative meaning of intercourse, the church continues to ignore rational and free human dignity by continuing to teach that only reproductive heterosexual acts can facilitate human dignity. Fifth, the concept of complementarity has been constructed to reinforce this claim, though it fundamentally grounds sexual anthropology exclusively in heterosexual complementarity and prioritizes, as in the past, the biological corporeal over the relational.[66] Sixth and most recently, Pope Francis in *Amoris Laetitia* has moved away from a strictly law-based approach to marriage and sexuality and, instead, has embraced a virtue approach.[67] There has been an attempt by both conservative and progressive Catholic philosophers and theologians to integrate the personalist anthropological insights of *Gaudium et Spes* into contemporary definitions of human and sexual dignity. We consider those definitions.

CONSERVATIVE AND PROGRESSIVE ETHICISTS AND HUMAN AND SEXUAL DIGNITY

Conservative Ethicists and Human and Sexual Dignity

Remember that *conservative* is the general label we give to Catholic ethicists who aim to conserve and defend tradition as taught by the Magisterium, including the absolute and exceptionless norms prohibiting certain types of sexual acts such as premarital sex, artificial birth control, artificial reproductive technologies, masturbation, and homosexual acts. We contrast them with *progressive* Catholic ethicists, which is the general label we give to theological ethicists who accept tradition but question, not its truth, but rather that its truth is absolute and exceptionless. These two groups disagree on specific sexual norms because they disagree, more fundamentally, on

---

[66]See Todd A. Salzman and Michael G. Lawler, "Catholic Sexual Ethics: Complementarity and the Truly Human," *Theological Studies* 67 (2006): 625–52.

[67]See especially *AL*, chap. 4.

a contemporary Catholic understanding of church, of ethical method, and of human and sexual human dignity. We consider some exemplars of each and their definitions of human and sexual dignity.

New Natural Law Theory (NNLT) and the Basic Goods of Human and Sexual Dignity

NNLT, developed by Catholic philosophers Germain Grisez, John Finnis, Joseph Boyle, et al.,[68] asserts that the human person is essentially *homo rationalis*, a rational agent whose choices are to actualize basic goods. NNLT's definition of sexual human dignity rests on the basic good of heterosexual marriage and its fulfillment through parenthood. Its argument for marriage as a basic good and the absolute norms that follow from that basic good develops in three steps. The first step defines heterosexual marriage as a basic good; the second defines marital, reproductive-type sexual acts in terms of that basic marital good; the third judges all nonreproductive-type sexual acts to be nonmarital and, therefore, unnatural, unreasonable, immoral, and, therefore, contrary to human dignity.

The definition of human and sexual dignity that arises from NNLT's understanding of basic goods can be summarized as follows. Basic goods are aspects of human dignity, and some are aspects of specifically sexual human dignity. Marriage, defined as a communion of life requiring free consent and sexual consummation, is such a basic good, actualized through marital sexual intercourse that has two intrinsic meanings: parenthood and friendship. There is a strict hierarchy between parenthood and friendship, between the biological and the personal meanings of marital sexual intercourse, which reflects the traditional biological-procreative definition of sexual human dignity. The biological aspect is the *sine qua non* for the personal meaning of the sexual act. Marital acts of a reproductive kind, Finnis claims, are "biologically *and thus* personally one."[69] All nonmarital sexual acts, including nonreproductive-type acts within marriage, are merely acts of personal gratification and are unnatural, unreasonable, unethical, and therefore contrary to human and sexual dignity.[70] NNLT argues that the absolute norms of the Magisterium condemning artificial contraception, homosexual sex, masturbation, and reproductive technologies are grounded

[68]The sources for the new natural law are extensive. See, for example, Grisez, *The Way of the Lord Jesus, Volume One*; Germain Griesez, *The Way of the Lord Jesus, Volume Two: Living a Christian Life* (Quincy, IL: Franciscan Herald Press, 1993); John Finnis, *Natural Law and Natural Rights: Fundamentals of Ethics* (Washington, DC: Georgetown University Press, 1983). For a good synthesis of NNLT, see Jean Porter, "The Natural Law and the Specificity of Christian Morality: A Survey of Recent Work and an Agenda for Future Research," in *Method and Catholic Moral Theology: The Ongoing Reconstruction*, ed. Todd A. Salzman (Omaha, NE: Creighton University Press, 1999), 209–29.

[69]Finnis, "Law, Morality, and 'Sexual Orientation'," 1067, emphasis added.

[70]See ibid., 1066–67.

in the basic good of marriage. These norms are absolute, even infallible,[71] and cannot be changed.

Martin Rhonheimer and the Heterosexuality of Virtue

Rhonheimer's unique contribution to a conservative definition of human and sexual dignity is his development of an "intimate connection" between ethical virtue and the precepts of the natural law.[72] His "integral/personal anthropology" is grounded in virtue.[73] He defines the "truth of human sexuality" as married love, "a free, mutual self-giving of indissoluble permanence between two persons of the opposite sex."[74] At the core of human and sexual dignity is autonomy in the nature of the human being to be drawn to the good of marriage. The truth of human sexuality lies necessarily between male and female, and this truth is dependent, not on physical or natural functions but on the personal function of autonomous human beings in relation to one another.

Rhonheimer argues that sexual acts that stand outside this truth contradict it and are objectively unethical, not because they are unnatural "but because they contradict the (practical) truth of the natural, as it appears on the horizon of apprehension and regulation by the reason."[75] We know human nature, he argues, by the inclination toward the good through practical reason. Humans are inclined toward the good of married love, and it is this inclination that reveals their true nature and the truth of human and sexual dignity. This objective truth is specified by the inseparability of the unitive and procreative meanings of sexual intercourse, and is affirmed by the virtue of chastity or "mastery of one's own sexual drives so as to integrate them into the order of personal love."[76] Rhonheimer's virtue-based anthropology and definition of sexual human dignity condemns as objectively unethical and contrary to human and sexual dignity all acts that contradict this truth, including homosexual acts, nonmarital sexual acts, and contraceptive acts.

---

[71]In their "Contraception and the Infallibility of the Ordinary Magisterium," *Theological Studies* 39 (1978): 258–312, Germain Grisez and John Ford claim that the Magisterium's teaching against artificial contraception is infallible. See also Germain Grisez, "*Quaestio Disputata*: The Ordinary Magisterium's Infallibility: A Reply to Some New Arguments," *Theological Studies* 55 (1994): 720–32, 737–38.

[72]Martin Rhonheimer, "The Cognitive Structure of the Natural Law and the Truth of Subjectivity," *Thomist* 67 (2003): 38.

[73]Martin Rhonheimer, *Natural Law and Practical Reason: A Thomist View of Moral Autonomy*, trans. G. Malsbary (New York: Fordham University Press, 2000), 117. See also John Grabowski, *Sex and Virtue: An Introduction to Sexual Ethics* (Washington DC: Catholic University of America Press, 2003).

[74]Rhonheimer, *Natural Law*, 569.

[75]Ibid., 569–70.

[76]Martin Rhonheimer, "Contraception, Sexual Behavior, and Natural Law: Philosophical Foundation of the Norm of '*Humanae Vitae*,'" *Linacre Quarterly* 56, no. 2 (1989): 39.

Pope John Paul II and Ontological Complementarity

John Paul II attempted to move the Catholic tradition beyond a biological-procreative definition of sexual human dignity and to develop its unitive personal-relational dimension by more fully integrating his personalist insights into its definition. For John Paul, "sexuality, by means of which man and woman give themselves to one another through the acts which are proper and exclusive to spouses, is by no means something purely biological, but concerns the innermost being of the human person as such." This is said to be a sign of "a total personal self-giving."[77] The pope develops his philosophical personalism in conjunction with an idiosyncratic reading of scripture to construct a definition of sexual human dignity, which others have called a theology of the body.[78] This theology is grounded in a theological anthropology, developed from Genesis, of the communion between man and woman.[79] Masculinity and femininity are "two 'incarnations' of the same metaphysical solitude before God and the world." These two ways of " 'being a body' . . . complete each other" and are "two complementary ways of being conscious of the meaning of the body."[80] It is through the complementarity of male and female that a "communion of persons" can exist and that the two can "become one flesh."[81]

John Paul's concept of complementarity has become a foundational concept in both his definition of human and sexual dignity and magisterial teaching on human sexuality. It intends that certain realities naturally belong together and produce a whole that neither can produce alone. We note the following characteristics of this complementarity. First, it is nearly always classified along masculine and feminine lines.[82] Second, it is often formulated as a "nuptial hermeneutics" in terms of bridegroom and bride.[83] Third, in his definition of human and sexual dignity John Paul posits an "ontological complementarity" whereby men and women, though fundamentally equal

---

[77]*FC*, no. 11.

[78]Pope John Paul II developed this position in a series of general audience talks he gave from 1979 to 1981. These talks are published in a single volume, *The Theology of the Body: Human Love in the Divine Plan* with a Foreword by John S. Grabowski (Boston: Pauline Books and Media, 1997).

[79]John Paul II, *Theology of the Body*, 48.

[80]Ibid.

[81]Ibid., 49.

[82]It is important to note that the distinction between biological sex (male/female) and socially constructed gender (masculine/feminine) is frequently absent in magisterial discussions of complementarity. See Susan A. Ross, "The Bridegroom and the Bride: The Theological Anthropology of John Paul II and Its Relation to the Bible and Homosexuality," in *Sexual Diversity and Catholicism: Toward the Development of Moral Theology*, ed. Patricia Beattie Jung with Joseph A. Coray (Collegeville, MN: Liturgical, 2001), 56 n. 5.

[83]Ibid.; David M. McCarthy, "The Relationship of Bodies: A Nuptial Hermeneutics of Same-sex Unions," in *Theology and Sexuality: Classic and Contemporary Readings*, ed. Eugene F. Rogers (Oxford: Blackwell, 2002), 206–10.

and complete in themselves,[84] are incomplete as a couple.[85] Sexual complementarity completes the couple in marriage and reproductive-type sexual acts by bringing the biological and psychological elements of femininity and masculinity together in a unified whole. All nonreproductive-type sexual acts damage this complementarity and human dignity and are unethical.

Servais Pinckaers and Dynamic Interiority[86]

Another conservative Catholic ethicist who has been influential in the renewal of Catholic moral theology from a virtuous perspective, especially in Europe, is the Belgian Dominican, Servais Pinckaers. He is an important figure in the virtue ethics methodological divide between conservative and progressive ethicists and, in a sense, bridges that divide. First, in the wake of *Humanae Vitae* and the crisis in moral theology it provoked, there was a little-known attempt by the Congregation for the Doctrine of the Faith to facilitate a dialogue in March 1981 between "innovative moralists," whom we call progressives, and "classical moralists," whom we call conservatives. Among the participants was Pinckaers, who attempted to promote mutual dialogue and discernment between the two schools,[87] an attempt that, unfortunately, met with failure. Pinckaers, however, was established as an important figure in the post–Vatican II attempt to renew Catholic moral theology and was later "intimately involved in shaping" *Veritatis Splendor* and the *Catechism*.[88] Second, Pinckaers's virtue ethics is thoroughly personalist and Christian. Third, both conservatives and progressives are suspicious of some theoretical aspects of his method and its practical implications, though for different reasons. Conservatives worry that his focus on virtue and character minimizes and displaces commitment to laws, absolute norms, and obligations.[89] Progressives worry that his commitment to preserve unchangeable universal norms, to defend the existence of intrinsically evil acts,[90] to endorse and defend *Veritatis Splendor* as pointing

---

[84]John Paul II, "Authentic Concept of Conjugal Love," *Origins* 28 (March 4, 1999): 655.

[85]John Paul II, "Letter to Women," *Origins* 25 (July 27, 1995): 141.

[86]We address Pinckaers's perspective here in greater detail than the other conservatives we list. The reason is that we have detailed their perspectives in elsewhere. See Todd A, Salzman and Michael G. Lawler, *The Sexual Person: Toward a Renewed Catholic Anthropology* (Washington, DC: Georgetown University Press, 2008), chap. 2.

[87]Servais Pinckaers, "The Return of the New Law to Moral Theology (1999)," in *The Pinckaers Reader: Renewing Thomistic Moral Theory*, trans. Sr. Mary Thomas Noble, O.P., et al., ed. John Berkman and Craig Steven Titus (Washington, DC: Catholic University of American Press, 2005), 376–77.

[88]See Craig Steven Titus, "Servais Pinckaers and the Renewal of Catholic Moral Theology," *Journal of Moral Theology* 1 (2012): 57–58, n. 74.

[89]See Janet E. Smith, "*The Pinckaers Reader: Renewing Thomistic Moral Theology*," *American Catholic Philosophical Quarterly* 80 (2006): 638–41.

[90]Pinckaers, "A Historical Perspective on Intrinsically Evil Acts (1986)," in *The Pinckaers Reader*, 185–235, and "Revisionist Understandings of Actions in the Wake of Vatican II (1982)," ibid., 236–70.

the way for the future direction of a renewed Catholic theological ethics,[91] and his call for fidelity to the Magisterium[92] are all signs that the old wine of a rigid, manualist focus on law and obedience is simply dressed up in the new wineskin of virtue theory. From both conservative and progressive perspectives, however, there is much in his virtue theory to recommend. Both schools appreciate Pinckaers's commitment to *ressourcement*, reuniting morality and spirituality, and emphasizing relationship with Christ as the seat of the good and source of all virtue.

Focusing especially on scripture and Aquinas, Pinckaers emphasizes *ressourcement* in his method. Through *ressourcement* he seeks to provide a thoroughly Christian anthropology and perspective and to address the fundamental polarization and impasse in contemporary theological debates, especially as these debates play out over the proportionalist method that was addressed in *Veritatis Splendor*.[93] Consequently, some of the critiques that progressives raise against *Veritatis Splendor*, especially on absolute norms and the meaning and nature of the moral object that specifies the act, apply to Pinckaers as well. To explain Pinckaers's dynamic interiority, we focus on the dignity of the person, marriage directed toward virtue, and virtuous acts that facilitate attaining personal dignity. We consider each in turn.

Dignity of the Person. Pinckaers's foundation for his renewal of Catholic morality is grounded in the "dignity of the person." This dignity draws theologically from the personhood of the Trinitarian God, the personal relationship between God and humans, the personhood of Christ's human and divine natures, and the dignity of the human person that shares in both the dignity and mystery of Christ's human nature created in the image and likeness of God.[94] A challenge with the scriptural foundation for Pinckaers is that it does not use the term *person*. Fortunately, tradition draws from Thomas Aquinas who notes and addresses this lacuna. What is clear from scripture is the sacred dignity of the person created in the image of God. In Aquinas, the term *dignity* is used in its fullest sense in relation to the person; " 'dignity' is a part of the very definition of person as a quality proper to a rational nature."[95] Dignity flows from the rational human person being made in the image of God, and this resemblance is developed through virtue and acts conforming to reason and grace, particularly when their object is God himself and the divine Persons."[96]

---

[91]Servais Pinckaers, "An Encyclical for the Future: *Veritatis Splendor*," in *Veritatis Splendor and the Renewal of Moral Theology: Studies by Ten Outstanding Scholars*, ed. J. A. DiNoia and R. Cessario (Princeton, NJ: Scepter Publications, 1999), 11–71.

[92]Ibid., 60–67.

[93]See Titus, "Servais Pinckaers and the Renewal of Catholic Moral Theology," 43–68.

[94]Pinckaers, "Aquinas on the Dignity of the Human Person (1987)," in *The Pinckaers Reader*, 144–63.

[95]Ibid., 162.

[96]Ibid.

For Pinckaers, the person has intrinsic dignity *qua* person. Through knowledge and love of Christ and the gift of grace, we grow in our resemblance to God in three stages. First and foundationally, we resemble God through the gift of our rational nature, which defines us as person, can never be lost even through sin, and is the source for our knowing and loving God. Our rational nature provides inclinations to truth, goodness, and social life. Second, through conformity to God by the gift of grace, virtuous actions, guided principally by faith, hope, and charity, enable us to pursue those inclinations, which is the goal of the moral life. The third stage in this resemblance is perfect love and knowledge of God, which the just can approach but never fully realize in this life. An essential understanding of both Aquinas and Pinckaers on the dignity of the person is that this dignity is evolving, not static. Growth in the resemblance of God is attained through virtuous acts, and resemblance is most developed "when our acts of knowledge and love focus directly upon God and the divine Persons."[97]

Marriage: School of Virtue. The dignity of the human person is realized for Pinckaers in a most profound way, in and through marriage. He explains his theology of marriage focusing on Aquinas's "new point of view" based on natural inclinations and God's created order, which posits human sexuality as essentially good and "a source of moral excellence" gradually attained through the virtues, "the end and perfection of the inclinations"[98] of temperance, chastity, justice, and charity[99] directed to the good of marriage. He uses the language of complementarity to justify his claim that male and female, bonded in Christ, fulfill one another in marriage through a profound biological, psychological, and spiritual unity.[100] Pinckaers embraces Aquinas's prioritization of the procreative over the unitive meaning of marriage, though the two meanings are intrinsically linked. He critiques those who have attempted to displace this hierarchy and to prioritize the "mutual support" of the spouses as "an autonomous if not overriding end." This displacement threatens the very institution of marriage "because of the subjective, individual nature of the emotion of love."[101] He also highlights not just the procreative end of marriage but also the essential complement of that end, the education of children in which parents "collaborate in their complementarity tasks, in friendship and conjugal love" to instruct children in virtue.[102]

[97]Ibid., 158.

[98]Servais Pinckaers, *The Sources of Christian Ethics*, trans. Sr. Mary Thomas Noble, OP (Washington, DC: Catholic University of America Press), 453.

[99]Ibid., 439.

[100]Ibid., 441–42.

[101]Ibid., 445.

[102]Ibid., 446.

Although his focus on the virtues that should guide the marital relationship and his belief that we should instill those virtues in children through education are insightful and certainly correct, we note the following tension in Pinckaers's perspective on marriage. First, despite *Gaudium et Spes*'s and the 1983 *Code of Canon Law*'s elimination of the language of the hierarchy of the ends of marriage, he continues to use that language in his theology of marriage, directed toward parenthood and educating children in the virtues. Second, his claim that "the denial of the first end of marriage [procreation] leads almost necessarily to the failure of the second [unitive],"[103] seems to ignore the teaching of Pius XII that, for "serious reasons" of a "medical, eugenic, economic, or social kind,"[104] a couple can abstain from sexual intercourse and procreation for the duration of the marriage. Third, though highlighting an integrated, personalist view of marriage, biologically, psychologically, emotionally, spiritually, and relationally, and critiquing accounts that reduce sexuality to biological processes where "the predominant criterion for judging sexual behavior will then be health, which remains chiefly in the biological order,"[105] Pinckaers seems to overlook the Magisterium's own teaching in *Humanae Vitae*. Here, the only morally permitted use of "therapeutic means" (i.e., antiovulants) within the marital relationship is "to cure bodily diseases."[106] The predominant criterion for moral justification is biological, though it certainly has relational implications. However, in cases where the use of Natural Family Planning (NFP) to regulate fertility would cause excessive relational, emotional, and psychological stress within a marriage, and the use of antiovulants to regulate fertility could alleviate these stresses, it is morally forbidden.

Dynamic Interiority: The Interrelationship between Virtues and Acts. In marriage and all areas of applied ethics, Pinckaers proposes a "morality of dynamic interiority" to coordinate his virtue theory and action theory. He distinguishes three levels of the human act. The first level is "the material level of the external act;" the second is "the directly moral level of the interior act;" the third is the theological level relating us to God.[107] In every moral action, these three levels "converge and compenetrate each other, beginning from the dynamic interiority which conceives our acts and which is our very selves in our freedom received from God."[108] Although these three levels converge, "the interior act is paramount because it emanates

[103]Ibid.

[104]Pius XII, "Address to the Congress of the Italian Catholic Association of Midwives," *AAS* 43 (1951): 846.

[105]Pinckaers, *The Sources of Christian Ethics*, 441.

[106]*HV*, no. 15.

[107]Pinckaers, "Scripture and the Renewal of Moral Theology (1995)," *The Pinckaers Reader*, 62.

[108]Ibid.

directly from the will, from the person."[109] The interiority, "which is the realm of the virtues," is "the central focus of morality." This central focus "needs to be returned to the level of the interior act and seen from the viewpoint of the person who is acting."[110] Pinckaers's perspective is very much in line with *Veritatis Splendor*, which notes that in order to judge the morality of an act, it is essential "to place oneself *in the perspective of the acting person*."[111] The interior act takes precedence over the external act and emanates from virtue, the interior principle of action. From his dynamic interiority, Pinckaers posits the existence of universal, unchangeable norms and intrinsically evil acts, such as the universal norm prohibiting contraception as an intrinsically evil act that, by definition, is a violation of temperance and chastity and violates a virtuous disposition.[112]

We conclude our treatment of Pinckaers in his own words, which we fully endorse. A virtue-grounded ethic always remains incomplete. "Its real function surely is to open our minds and hearts to the mystery of the human person and God, so that our actions may participate in the 'unsearchable riches in Christ' in his mystery (Eph 3:8)."[113]

In these conservative definitions of human and sexual dignity, we are struck by the deductive methodology and the biological emphasis to arrive at them, an approach that reflects a strict prioritization of the sources of moral knowledge. Tradition, narrowly defined as magisterial teaching on absolute sexual norms, is defended as the primary ethical source and, in this sense, conservative methodologies serve as a form of ecclesial apologetics defending the Magisterium's absolute moral norms. Since the Magisterium does not, however, espouse or defend any specific ethical method, aside from a presently evolving natural-law method, conservative authors also draw from the Wesleyan Quadrilateral's four sources of ethical knowledge to formulate a method for defining human and sexual human dignity. NNLT draws from Aquinas's natural law, but nuances it by grounding the basic goods in practical reason to explain how specific rules for conduct are related to these goods. It also uses scripture to formulate "modes of responsibility," which specify the self-evident first principle of practical reason and allow NNLT to deduce absolute moral norms. It has a very limited consideration of experience in its method. Human experience that affirms the Magisterium's absolute norms is judged to be authentic human experience; human experience that does not affirm the Magisterium's absolute norms is judged to be inauthentic experience. Similarly, the biological or social sciences that

[109]Pinckaers, "The Role of Virtue in Moral Theology (1996)," *The Pinckaers Reader*, 291.
[110]Ibid., 292.
[111]*Veritatis Splendor*, no. 78, emphasis in original.
[112]See Pinckaers, "Revisionist Understandings of Actions in the Wake of Vatican II."
[113]Pinckaers, "The Role of Virtue in Moral Theology (1996)," 303.

affirm the Magisterium's absolute norms are judged to be good science; the sciences that do not affirm the Magisterium's absolute norms are judged to be bad science. Tradition is narrowly defined in terms of magisterial teaching. There is little or no role for the *sensus fidelium* or the authority of conscience in its method. As Grisez notes on the role of conscience in relation to non-infallible magisterial teaching, "For her members, the Catholic Church is the supreme moral authority under God. Catholics ought to conform their consciences to her teaching in every question, every detail, every respect. If they are faithful, they will."[114] Or again, "A Catholic conscience should conform absolutely to the Church's teaching."[115]

Rhonheimer draws from Aquinas, and focuses on a virtue approach. For NNLT, the basic good of marriage is grounded in a heterogenital, biological criterion where marital, reproductive-type sexual acts are "biologically *and thus* personally one." For Rhonheimer, the virtue of chastity and its requirement for heterosexual, noncontraceptive, reproductive-type sexual acts intrinsically links chastity to heterosexuality and biological openness to procreation. For John Paul II, there is only one theology of the body, heterosexually complementary bodies open to biological reproduction. For Pinckaers, his focus on virtue, experience as an essential source of moral knowledge, prioritization of dynamic interiority, and the internal act opens up the possibility for anthropological and normative developments. Unfortunately, his deference to magisterial teaching and commitment to unchangeable universal norms and intrinsically evil acts limit those developments. In conservative methods, the biological dimension of the definition of human and sexual dignity is emphasized in at least three ways.

First, conservative definitions of human and sexual dignity posit heterosexuality as ordered or natural and homosexuality as objectively disordered[116] or unnatural. Such a move is problematic metaphysically and scientifically. Metaphysically, Owen Sullivan judges, when conservative ethicists shift "the ground of moral debate from the inter-personal (e.g., human relationships) to the biological (e.g., objective disorder), it sounds like an admission of defeat. It's a materialistic argument which elevates the biological to the metaphysical."[117] Scientifically, it is a misrepresentation. Peer-reviewed scientific literature has documented same-sex sexuality in over three hundred species of vertebrates, including humans, as a natural component of the social system.[118] Based on such studies, James Alison

[114]Grisez, *The Way of the Lord Jesus. Volume One*, 566.

[115]Ibid., 666.

[116]*Persona Humana* (hereafter *PH*); *Catechism of the Catholic Church*, no. 2357.

[117]Owen Sullivan, "On Including Gays," *The Furrow* 61 (2010): 170.

[118]See Bruce Bagemihl, *Biological Exuberance: Animal Homosexuality and Natural Diversity* (New York: St. Martin's Press, 1999).

challenges the claim that a homosexual orientation is objectively disordered. "There is no longer any reputable scientific evidence of any sort: psychological, biological, genetic, medical, neurological—to back up the claim."[119] There is, in fact, substantial evidence to the contrary. Though men and women with a homosexual orientation make up a very small minority of the human population, some 2–5 percent, the homosexual orientation of this population is still an intrinsic dimension of human identity and dignity.[120]

Second, the scientific knowledge of homosexual orientation has implications for defining human and sexual dignity and assessing the ethics of homosexual acts. What is natural behavior for homosexuals and heterosexuals must be determined in terms of a person's sexual orientation and the meaning of the sexual act for that person in relationship. Just as it is unnatural for a heterosexual person to engage in homosexual acts, it is unnatural for a homosexual person to engage in heterosexual acts. These acts are judged unnatural, not because of a foundational biological, heterosexual criterion but because of an inadequate consideration of the sexual human person. There is no philosophical, theological, or scientific evidence to substantiate the claim that homosexual acts or nonreproductive heterosexual acts frustrate human and sexual dignity and are destructive of relationships. In fact, there is substantial scientific evidence to the contrary. Michael Hartwig notes "the overwhelming convergence of [scientific] evidence is that gay men and lesbians, as a group, display levels of health, family functioning and strength, personal development, mutuality, commitment, and, dare we say, love, similar to heterosexuals."[121] Earlier in this book we have already cited Lawrence Kurdek's data that points in the same direction.

Third, John Paul II's and Pinckaers's complementarity arguments, in which the biological, heterosexual differences are *sine qua non* for the personal characteristics that enable male and female to be "ontologically complementary," are not substantiated by biology. "Biology is no longer a prop," Christine Gudorf comments, "but a problem" for such arguments. "Whether we speak of sexual orientation, sexual identity, or sex differences," she continues, "biology and related sciences present us with com-

---

[119]James Alison, "The *Fulcrum of Discovery Or: How the 'Gay Thing' Is Good News for the Catholic Church," unpublished essay, 8.*

[120]See Richard C. Pillard and J. Michael Bailey, "A Biological Perspective on Sexual Orientation," *Clinical Sexuality* 18 (1995): 1–14; Lee Ellis and Linda Ebertz, *Sexual Orientation: Toward Biological Understanding* (Westport, CT: Praeger, 1997); Richard C. Friedman and Jennifer I. Downey, *Sexual Orientation and Psychoanalysis: Sexual Science and Clinical Practice* (New York: Columbia University Press, 2002). For a contrary perspective see Robert L. Spitzer, "Can Some Gay Men and Lesbians Change Their Sexual Orientation? 200 Participants Reporting a Change from Homosexual to Heterosexual Orientation," *Archives of Sexual Behavior* 32 (2003): 403–17.

[121]Michael J. Hartwig, "The Use of Sociological Studies to Confirm or Critique Roman Catholic Sexual Ethics," in *Applied Ethics in a World Church*, ed. Linda Hogan (Maryknoll, NY: Orbis Books, 2008), 257.

plex data that cannot be reduced simply to a dimorphic, complementary human sexuality."[122] This scientific data demonstrates that male–female sex differences may frustrate personal complementarity in a relationship rather than facilitate it, and experience shows that the social construction of these sex differences into gender differences further frustrates personal complementarity.[123] Conservative theologians have not gone far enough in incorporating contemporary biological or other scientific insights into their definitions of human and sexual dignity. Humans and their sexuality are influenced and shaped not only by biology but also by society, culture, religion, and experience.[124] Conservative definitions of human and sexual dignity generally tend to reduce the scientific contribution to actual or possible biological reproduction in reproductive-type sexual acts. This reductionist use of science and other sources of ethical knowledge that challenge absolute magisterial sexual norms fails to integrally and adequately consider the complexity of the sexual human person.

Progressive Ethicists and Human and Sexual Dignity

To define human and sexual dignity, conservative Catholic philosophers and theologians generally espouse a procreative model of marriage and prioritize the corporeal, biological dimension of the sexual person over the relational dimensions. Progressive Catholic philosophers and theologians do the opposite. They prioritize the relational dimensions over the corporeal, biological dimension and they offer a broader appreciation of biology when defining human and sexual dignity holistically.

Lisa Sowle Cahill: Family, Kinship, and Gender

Lisa Cahill brings to the discussion of human and sexual dignity a feminist perspective, "a commitment to equal personal respect and social power for women and men."[125] She asserts that these dimensions need to be complemented by a critical analysis of the "social ramifications of sex." Her method is grounded in Aristotle and Aquinas and is critically realist, experiential, inductive, and historically conscious. She uses social sciences to dialogue with other cultures to discern substantive universal goods associated with embodied personhood, including sex, gender, marriage, parenthood, and

---

[122]Christine Gudorf, "Gendered Identity Formation and Moral Theology," in *Applied Ethics in a World Church*, 114.

[123]For details, see Sandra Lipsitz Bem, *The Lenses of Gender: Transforming the Debate on Sexual Inequality* (New Haven, CT: Yale University Press, 1993).

[124]See Lawler and Salzman, "Human Experience and Catholic Moral Theology."

[125]Lisa Sowle Cahill, *Sex, Gender, and Christian Ethics*, New Studies in Christian Ethics (New York: Cambridge University Press, 1996), 1.

family.[126] While she is committed to the Catholic natural law tradition, she differs from the proponents of NNLT on the definition of the basic goods and their normative implications for human relationships.

Cahill posits goods that are both universal and particular. Goods are universal as "shared framing experiences and moral common ground,"[127] indicating "shared human being in the world."[128] Goods are particular, in that the " 'shared' is achieved not beyond or over against particularity but in and through it,"[129] and particularity is discerned through social analysis and intercultural dialectic.[130] While she shares with conservative theologians an emphasis on marriage and family as a universal good, Cahill provides an interpersonal-relational model of marriage that particularizes this universal good and eschews any emphasis on biologism and procreationism over relationship. She espouses an interpersonal-relational model and definition of human and sexual dignity but argues that it "should be placed in a deeper and more nuanced social context, with better attention both to the familial ramifications of sexual partnerships, and to differences and similarities in cross-cultural experiences of sex, gender, and family."[131] She highlights the importance of children as an aspect of the human good but emphasizes the need to see marriage and family as a complex interrelationship between relational, sexual, and social dimensions. In light of this totality and complexity, the absolute magisterial norm prohibiting artificial birth control needs to be refined and redefined. Equally feminist Christine Gudorf emphasizes pleasure and intimacy in her human and sexual anthropology.[132]

Margaret Farley: Just and Loving Sexual Acts

Margaret Farley emphasizes that the two sources of ethical knowledge, science and human experience, have contributed to our understanding of human sexuality by correcting past mistakes and by generating new insights that clarify sexual ethics and call into question long-taken-for-granted but unverifiable conclusions. Although the secular disciplines "give us a kind of 'access' to reality," they also require a sort of "exegesis" and interpretation to discern their relevance to a definition of human and sexual dignity and

---

[126]Ibid., 13.

[127]Ibid., 54.

[128]Ibid., 51.

[129]Ibid., 55.

[130]Martha Nussbaum, "Introduction," in *The Quality of Life*, ed. Martha Nussbaum and Amartya Sen (Oxford: Clarendon Press, 1993), 4. See Lisa Sowle Cahill, "Feminist Ethics, Differences, and Common Ground: A Catholic Perspective," in *Feminist Ethics and the Catholic Moral Tradition: Readings in Moral Theology No. 9*, ed. Charles E. Curran et al. (New York: Paulist Press, 1996), 195; Cahill, *Sex, Gender, and Christian Ethics*, 55–61.

[131]Cahill, *Sex, Gender, and Christian Ethics*, 10.

[132]Christine E. Gudorf, *Body, Sex, and Pleasure: Reconstructing Christian Sexual Ethics* (Cleveland, OH: Pilgrim Press, 1995).

sexual ethics.[133] This exegesis should be carried out through responsible and respectful dialogue that involves diverse voices honestly seeking to discern and formulate a credible definition of human and sexual dignity. Diversity must include gender, sex, sexual orientation, socioeconomic, ethnic, cultural, and historical dimensions. To explore diversity, Farley investigates the biological and social sciences.

First, the biological sciences indicate that there are chromosomal, hormonal, and anatomical differences among human beings classified as male and female. One should be aware, however, that both biological studies on human sexual differentiation and the use of those studies in constructing "sex-types" are subject to cultural interpretation and bias. Biological studies can be helpful for constructing a definition of human and sexual dignity, but one "should not expect more from them than they can deliver."[134] Farley's cautionary note reflects the position many scholars espouse, a nonreducible hierarchy in scientific disciplines. This nonreducible hierarchy begins with the hard sciences and moves upward to the soft sciences and the speculative sciences. On the one hand, the lower-level sciences place "constraints" on upper-level sciences; on the other hand, they allow for authentic "emergence" of upper-level laws, processes, and properties.[135] Many scholars locate theology at the top of the scientific hierarchy since it attempts to integrate the entirety of knowledge, but they also insist that it must be "maximally constrained" by the other scientific disciplines.[136]

Second, Farley uses the social sciences to explore cross-cultural and interreligious understandings of human anthropology and sexuality "in which sexuality gains its meaning in profoundly different ways of living and believing."[137] She cautions, however, against drawing overly strong conclusions from these investigations. The conclusion she does draw recognizes "the very plasticity of human sexuality, its susceptibility to different meanings and expressive forms."[138] Such sociological studies "belong to the map of human sexual meanings."[139] Though she recognizes the importance of biological, sociological, and anthropological insights, which alert theologians to the multifaceted historical, cultural, and religious understandings and expressions of human anthropology and sexuality, Farley rejects a reductionist, absolutist, "one-size-fits-all" definition. Instead, rely-

[133]Margaret Farley, *Just Love: A Framework for Christian Sexual Ethics* (New York: Continuum, 2008), 188–89.

[134]Ibid., 148.

[135]Russell and Wegter-McNelly, "Science," in *The Blackwell Companion to Modern Theology*, ed. Gareth Jones (Oxford: Blackwell., 2007), 516.

[136]Ibid.

[137]Farley, *Just Love*, 103.

[138]Ibid., 104.

[139]Ibid., 105.

ing on a combination of science and experience, she constructs a complex definition of human and sexual dignity and proposes *justice in love* as a principled approach to determine "when sexuality and its expressions are appropriate in human relationships."[140] She asserts that for sexual acts to facilitate human and sexual dignity, they must be just and loving, without any taint of violence or coercion. "Today we also know that the possibilities of mutuality exists for many forms of relationship—whether heterosexual or gay, whether with genital sex or the multiple other ways of embodying our desires and our loves."[141]

Todd Salzman and Michael Lawler: Holistic Complementarity and the Human Person Adequately Considered

In an effort to move a seemingly stalled Catholic sexual anthropology forward, we have recourse to both scientific and theological resources. We employ, as we do in this book, the four sources of the Wesleyan Quadrilateral, biological and social science, scripture, tradition, and human experience to do two things: first, to engage dialogically, critically, and historically–consciously both normative Catholic principles guiding sexual ethics and theological ethical analyses of those sources in order; and second, to construct a renewed definition of human and sexual dignity and to formulate a new foundational principle for sexual ethics, namely, holistic complementarity.[142] We appropriate to ourselves Pope John Paul II's judgment that dialogue "is rooted in the nature and dignity of the human person . . . an indispensable step along the path toward human self-realization."[143] Following the direction mapped out by that papal judgment, we enter into dialogue with both conservative and progressive theological positions on normative sexual ethics in order to articulate a renewed and critically realist Catholic definition of human and sexual dignity.

The biological sciences challenge the rigid magisterial male–female dimorphism of human sexuality and complementarity, and indicate the naturalness of heterosexual, homosexual, and bisexual orientations. Cross-cultural human experience shows the variety of sexual expressions that facilitate human and sexual dignity and the love of God, neighbor, and self.[144] The social sciences provide no data to support the claim that nonreproductive type sexual acts, heterosexual or homosexual, are destructive of human

[140]Ibid., 311.

[141]Ibid., 221.

[142]Salzman and Lawler, *The Sexual Person.*

[143]*UUS*, 28.

[144]Margaret Farley, "An Ethic for Same-Sex Relations," in *A Challenge to Love: Gay and Lesbian Catholics in the Church*, ed. Robert Nugent (New York: Crossroad, 1983), 99–100.

dignity.[145] Indeed, they supply a large volume of data to support the contrary claim.[146] Integrating scientific studies with scripture and tradition, we seek to renew the primarily procreationist Catholic definition of human and sexual dignity and replace it with a more integrally and adequately considered definition that prioritizes the personal-relational over the biological-procreative meaning of human sexuality. We develop a holistic complementarity that includes sexual orientation, personal, and biological complementarity, and the integration and manifestation of all three in just and loving sexual acts that promote human and sexual dignity and facilitate a person's ability to love God, neighbor, and self in a more personally profound and holy way.[147]

Joseph Selling: Meanings of Human Sexuality

In addition to his focus on historical studies tracing the "meanings" of human sexuality throughout Christian tradition,[148] Joseph Selling emphasizes the need to complement tradition with the other sources of ethical knowledge, experience, science, and scripture, to construct a personalist, holistic definition of human and sexual dignity. With respect to human experience, Selling notes that sexuality is not reducible to an exclusively physical-biological meaning. Rather, meaning "is the result of personal-social construction that is attributed to experience uniquely by human beings."[149] Discerning meaning is always a historical and contextual task. Selling has recourse to various scientific disciplines, which are essential complements in this process of discernment. He approvingly cites *Persona Humana's* statement on the findings of the sciences: "According to contemporary scientific research, the human person is so profoundly affected

[145]See, for example, USCCB, *Marriage: Love and Life in the Divine Plan* (Washington, DC: USCCB, 2009), 19.

[146]Lawrence A. Kurdek, "What Do We Know about Gay and Lesbian Couples?" *Current Directions in Psychological Science* 14 (2005): 251; Lawrence A. Kurdek, "Differences between Partners from Heterosexual, Gay, and Lesbian Cohabiting Couples," *Journal of Marriage and Family* 68 (May 2006): 509–28; Lawrence A. Kurdek, "Lesbian and Gay Couples," in *Lesbian, Gay and Bisexual Identities over the Lifespan*, ed. Anthony R. D'Augelli and Charlotte J. Patterson (New York: Oxford University Press, 1995), 243–61; Lawrence A. Kurdek, "Are Gay and Lesbian Cohabiting Couples *Really* Different from Heterosexual Married Couples?," *Journal of Marriage and Family* 66 (2004): 880–900. See also Ritch C. Savin-Williams and Kristin G. Esterberg, "Lesbian, Gay, and Bisexual Families," in *Handbook of Family Diversity*, ed. David H. Demo et al. (New York: Oxford University Press, 2000), 207–12.

[147]Salzman and Lawler, *The Sexual Person*, 124–61.

[148]See Joseph A. Selling, "The History of Conjugal Morality," in *Human Sexuality and Family Health Sciences, Leuven Monographs on Sexology*, ed. Alfons Vansteenwegen (Leuven, Belgium: Peeters, 1990): 58–76; Selling, "Magisterial Teaching on Marriage 1880–1968: Historical Constancy or Radical Development?," in *Historia: memoria futuri Mélanges Louis Vereecke, 70e anniversaire de naissance*, ed. Réal Tremblay and Dennis Billy (Rome: Ed. Academiae Alphonsianae, 1991), 351–402; Selling, "The Development of Catholic Tradition and Sexual Morality," in *Embracing Sexuality*, 149–62; Joseph A. Selling, "Magisterial Teaching on Marriage 1880–1968: Historical Constancy or Radical Development?," *Studia Moralia* 28 (1990): 439–90.

[149]Joseph A. Selling, "The 'Meanings' of Human Sexuality," *Louvain Studies* 23 (1998): 32.

by sexuality that it must be considered as one of the factors which give to each individual's life the principle traits that distinguish it . . . make that person a man or a woman, and thereby largely condition his or her progress towards maturity and insertion into society."[150]

Reviewing the findings of sexologists, psychiatrists,[151] and sociologists on the various meanings of human sexuality, Selling concludes that a holistic understanding of those meanings includes, among other dimensions, "not only intimacy ('unitive') and fertility ('procreative') but also pleasure, recreation (play), relief, affirmation, receptivity, self-acceptance, forgiveness, reconciliation, gratitude and, of course, respect." These meanings extend beyond the couple-in-relationship "to the social, institutional, political and religious meanings that can only be appreciated in those respective contexts."[152] While scripture does not give us a blueprint for a timeless meaning of human sexuality, it "always begins with a relational context and is only concerned with specific sexual behavior insofar as it has a bearing on the integrity of individual and social relationships."[153] Combined, the four sources of ethical knowledge point to relationality as "the primary characteristic of human sexuality" and, if relationality is the primary characteristic, and we accept that it is, then we should shift, Selling suggests, the focus of the discussion of appropriate sexual behavior from the virtue of temperance/chastity to the virtue of justice, which "respects persons and renders what is their due."

The progressive theological anthropologies we just explored have different nuances and priorities, but they share five things in common. First, they consider the primarily biological-procreative definition of sexual human dignity as reductionist. Second, they engage more comprehensively the sciences and human experience, especially as this is revealed through the social sciences, and seek both to facilitate dialogue between theology and science and to integrate scientific knowledge into a comprehensive theological definition of human and sexual dignity. This project is ongoing and requires care and humility in making normative assertions. Progressive theologians fully accept Pope John Paul II's invitation to theologians and scientists to search for truth through "critical openness and interchange" gradually growing and deepening "in its quality and scope."[154] This process of dialogue will require openness to exploring positions that may challenge

---

[150]*PH*, no. 1.

[151]See Jack Dominian, "Sexuality and Interpersonal Relationships," in Selling, *Embracing Sexuality*, 12–15.

[152]Selling, "The 'Meanings' of Human Sexuality," 35.

[153]Ibid., 36.

[154]John Paul II, "The Relationship of Science and Theology: A Letter to Jesuit Father George Coyne," *Origins* 18 (17 November 1988): 376.

traditional magisterial definitions of human and sexual dignity and the norms that are deduced from them. Third, dialogue will also require ongoing discernment of the four sources of ethical knowledge and their selection, interpretation, prioritization, and integration into the definition of human and sexual dignity. Fourth, progressive theologians manifest a degree of tentativeness toward the contributions of both the sciences and theology, though they tend to give greater weight to the sciences, experience, and tradition in respect of the authority of a well-informed conscience than do conservative theologians, who prioritize tradition-as-magisterial teaching as the primary source of ethical knowledge. Fifth, this tentativeness demands that all hypotheses about a comprehensive definition of human and sexual dignity be subjected to confirmation/disconfirmation by the sciences, experience, and the *sensus fidelium*.[155]

CONCLUSION

We argue that the Magisterium's definition of human and sexual dignity is inconsistent and problematic on at least two general counts. First, it applies only to married heterosexual couples and reproductive-type sexual acts. If the biological-procreative meaning of sexual intercourse can be intentionally avoided for a time, even for the duration of a marriage, how can it be that only reproductive-type sexual acts facilitate human and sexual dignity and nonreproductive-type sexual acts frustrate it? If the biological-procreative meaning of the sexual act is deemphasized, as it has been deemphasized in the contemporary Catholic tradition, it would seem that nonreproductive-type sexual acts could be considered conducive of human dignity and, therefore, ethical if those acts are unitive or are what we have called relational. Since women are known to be infertile for some 80 percent of their sexual lives, it makes no sense to speak of an intrinsic procreative meaning of each and every sexual act, unless procreative here is interpreted in a metaphorical sense to mean relationally life-giving, rather than in a *material* sense, meaning biologically life-giving. The act is procreative in a material sense only when actual reproduction is possible, and only then can the biological-procreative meaning of the act be strictly distinguished from its unitive meaning. That is why many theologians choose to discuss the unitive and procreative meanings, not of every sexual act but of marriage itself.[156]

---

[155]See, for example, Ted Peters, *Science and Theology: The New Consonance* (Boulder, CO: Westview Press, 1999), 18.

[156]Joseph A. Selling, "Magisterial Teaching on Marriage 1880–1986: Historical Constancy or Radical Development;" Bernard Häring, "The Inseparability of the Unitive-Procreative Functions of the Marital Act," in *Dialogue about Catholic Sexual Teaching* (New York: Paulist, 1993),163–64; Lisa Sowle Cahill,

The Magisterium's definition of human and sexual dignity is inconsistent and problematic on a second count in its treatment of nonheterosexual couples. Its definition of human and sexual dignity since Vatican II, with its growing emphasis on the unitive end of marriage or the sexual act, is applied only to heterosexual married couples and reproductive-type sexual acts. When it comes to nonreproductive-type sexual acts for both heterosexual and homosexual couples, the Magisterium reverts to a pre–Vatican II definition of human and sexual dignity, and a strict biological interpretation of the procreative end of marriage. It continues to assume implicitly, even though the Council rejected it, a hierarchy of the ends of marriage or meanings of the sexual act, the biological-procreative meaning being primary and the unitive-relational meaning secondary. This exclusive heterosexism places a biological, physical emphasis on its definition of human and sexual dignity rather than a personal, relational emphasis.

We believe and suggest that a consistent sexual anthropology and definition of human and sexual dignity, guided by the principles of holistic complementarity and just and loving sexual acts,[157] allow for ethical reproductive- and nonreproductive-type homosexual acts. *Holistic* complementarity unites people personally, affectively, spiritually, and bodily under the umbrella of a person's sexual orientation. Heterosexual complementarity is needed for possible reproduction, but it is not needed for the personal, affective, spiritual, and bodily connection between two people that the recent Catholic tradition acknowledges as an end of marriage equal to procreation.[158] Holistic complementarity includes orientation, biological, and personal complementarity, and the integration and manifestation of all three in mutually just and loving sexual acts that facilitate a person's ability to love self, neighbor, and God in a more profound and holy way. Though they cannot exhibit heterosexual complementarity, there is extensive empirical evidence that homosexual individuals can exhibit this holistic complementarity. Lawrence Kurdek who has done extensive and ongoing serious research on gay and lesbian couples and their relationships, as we have seen, compares their relationships favorably with those of married heterosexual couples. Gay and lesbian couples demonstrate greater conflict resolution skills, experience similar levels of relational satisfaction as heterosexual couples, and tend to have a more equitable and just distribution of household work.[159] *Gaudium et Spes* 's elimination of the hierarchy of the ends of marriage, its

---

"Sexuality: Personal, Communal, Responsible," in Selling, *Embracing Sexuality*, 165–72.

[157]For elucidation, see Salzman and Lawler, "Catholic Sexual Ethics: Complementarity and the Truly Human," 625–52.

[158]See *GS*, nos.48–50; *Code of Canon Law*, Can 1055, 1; Michael G. Lawler, *Marriage in the Catholic Church: Disputed Questions* (Collegeville, MN: Liturgical Press, 2002), 27–42.

[159]See note 120.

emphasis on the unitive end of marriage, and its shift to a more personalist approach to human sexuality, invite further theological reflection for their integration into a Catholic definition of human and sexual dignity and for deriving the normative implications of that definition. That reflection we continue in the next chapter.

5

Formulation and Justification of Principles and Norms

Seeking the Good

In this chapter, we explore the formulation and justification of principles and norms that facilitate attaining human dignity. We agree with Dietmar Mieth who asserts that the only absolute ethical norm is that "good is to be done and evil left undone"[1] and that every other ethical judgment requires an interpretive judgment.[2] We agree also with the International Theological Commission that "in the context of pluralism, which is ours, one is more and more aware that one cannot elaborate a morality based on the natural law without including a reflection on the interior dispositions or virtues that render the moralist capable of elaborating an adequate norm of action."[3] Formulating and justifying virtue and behavioral norms to facilitate attaining human dignity requires an epistemological justification for the normative claims we make and a specification of the content of principles and norms.

VIRTUE: ETHICS AND EPISTEMOLOGY

The call for renewal of theological ethics at the Second Vatican Council emphasized bringing "forth fruit in charity for the life of the world."[4] This

[1]See Thomas Aquinas, *Summa Theologiae,* I-II, 94, 2, for this first principle of practical reasoning (hereafter *ST*).

[2]Dietmar Mieth, *Moral und Erfahrung. Beitrage zur theologisch-ethischen Hermeneutik* (Freiburg, Germany: 1977), 34.

[3]International Theological Commission, *In Search of a Universal Ethic: A New Look at Natural Law* (May 20, 2009), n. 55, www.vatican.va/roman_curia/congregations/cfaith/cti_documents/rc_con_cfaith_doc_20090520_legge-naturale_en.html.

[4]*Optatum Totius*, no. 16, in *The Documents of Vatican II*, ed. Walter Abbott (New York: America Press, 1965).

emphasis on charity reflects earlier Catholic theological efforts to reform the manual method for doing moral theology.[5] Though the Council did not issue a specific call for a shift to virtue ethics from the legalistic and reductionist approach of the manuals, contemporary Catholic theological ethicists have been investigating and developing such a shift.

Virtue Ethics

Catholic normative method for the formulation and justification of norms initially focused on two methodological approaches: deontology and teleology. Deontology emphasizes rules, obligations, and duties; teleology emphasizes the consequences of actions and the maximizing of their good or value.[6] The Council's call for a focus on love and the contemporary renewed attention to virtue ethics have been the impetus for transforming Catholic ethical method from an ethics of law or consequences to a virtue ethics of being. Virtue ethics gives precedence, as we have several times noted, not to the actions of agents but to their personal character formed in their moral communities through the imitation of respected role models in those communities. We align with MacIntyre and the many other contemporary ethicists who advance virtue ethics as more promising to the ethical life than deontology or teleology.[7]

With the shift from deontology and teleology to virtue ethics comes also a fundamental methodological shift in what John Greco labels the "direction of analysis,"[8] which is a Copernican methodological shift. Traditional approaches to ethics understand the normative properties of an act in terms of its intrinsic meaning or consequences; the direction of analysis is from act to person. An act is said to be right or wrong based on law or consequences, and a person's character is morally evaluated as virtuous or vicious based on the acts chosen. A virtue approach to ethics understands the normative properties of acts in terms of the normative properties of persons. The direction of analysis is from person and personal character to acts. In other words, virtue theories make rightness follow from an action's "source in a virtue, rather than the other way around."[9] This methodological

---

[5]See Gerard Gilleman, *The Primacy of Charity in Moral Theology* (Westminster, MD: Newman, 1959).

[6]See Todd A. Salzman, *Deontology and Teleology: An Investigation of the Normative Debate in Roman Catholic Moral Theology* (Louvain, Belgium: Peeters, 1995).

[7]In addition to Foot and MacIntyre, whom most judge to be the preeminent contemporary virtue theorists, other important theorists in the field of virtue ethics will be introduced as our chapter unfolds.

[8]John Greco, "Virtue Epistemology," *Stanford Encyclopedia of Philosophy*, https://plato.stanford.edu/entries/epistemology-virtue/.

[9]Guy Axtell, *Knowledge, Belief, and Character: Readings in Virtue Epistemology* (Lanham, MD: Rowman & Littlefield, 2000), xiii.

shift prioritizes persons over acts, virtues over rules and consequences, and the subject over the object.

Some Catholic ethicists have returned to the virtue theories of Aristotle and Aquinas, and combined their visions of virtue with modern philosophical and theological developments and insights to methodologically construct a virtue ethic.[10] Aristotle, as we have seen, defined virtue as "a state of character concerned with choice, lying in a mean."[11] Aquinas defined it as a personal habit or disposition ordered to an act.[12] As character habits or dispositions, virtues explain not only why a person acts this way on this particular occasion but also why the person can be relied on to act this way always or, given human frailty, most of the time. Virtues also involve *phronesis* or practical wisdom, which is the ability to reason correctly about practical decisions. Without *phronesis*, Aristotle argues, no virtue is possible.[13] For Aquinas, the virtue that corresponds to *phronesis* is *prudentia* or prudence, which is, therefore, a cardinal virtue. Without prudence, he argues, no other virtue is possible.

Virtue Epistemology

Central to a theory of virtue is the notion that virtues are not only preconditions for human flourishing but also constituents of that flourishing. "A virtue is a character trait that human beings, given their physical and psychological nature, need to flourish (or to do and fare well)."[14] The person with the virtue of justice, for example, will *be* a just person who will, therefore, *act* justly. Ethical virtues are bases of excellent human being and doing, and so, too, "epistemic virtues are bases of excellent epistemic [being] and functioning."[15] The ethical virtues facilitate the attainment of human dignity; the epistemic or intellectual virtues facilitate the attainment of true knowledge to define human dignity and to formulate and justify

[10]See James F. Keenan, *Virtues for Ordinary Christians* (Lanham, MD: Sheed & Ward, 1996); James F. Keenan, "Proposing Cardinal Virtues," *Theological Studies* 56 (1995): 709–29; Jennifer A. Herdt, *Putting on Virtue: The Legacy of the Splendid Vices* (Chicago: University of Chicago Press, 2008); Paul J. Wadell, *Happiness and the Christian Moral Life: An Introduction to Christian Ethics,* 2nd ed. (Lanham, MD: Rowman & Littlefield, 2012); William C. Mattison III, *Introducing Moral Theology: True Happiness and the Virtues* (Grand Rapids: Brazos, 2008); Michael G. Lawler and Todd A. Salzman, "Virtue Ethics: Natural and Christian," *Theological Studies* 74 (2013): 432–73.

[11]Aristotle, *Nicomachean Ethics* 2.6.1106b, ed. Lesley Brown, trans. David Ross (New York: Oxford University, 2009), 29 (hereafter *NE*).

[12]*ST*, 1–2, q. 49, a. 1 and q. 49, a. 3.

[13]See Rosalind Hursthouse, *On Virtue Ethics* (Oxford: Oxford University Press, 2002), 12.

[14]Rosalind Hursthouse, "Applying Virtue Ethics," in *Virtues and Reason: Philippa Foot and Moral Theory*, ed. Rosalind Hursthouse et al. (Oxford: Clarendon, 1995), 68.

[15]Robert C. Roberts and W. Jay Wood, *Intellectual Virtues: An Essay in Regulative Epistemology* (Oxford: Oxford University Press, 2007), 7.

principles and norms that facilitate its attainment. "Moral responsibility for what we do," James Montmarquet notes, "is often dependent on epistemic responsibility for what we believe."[16] The shift toward virtue in ethical method has parallels with a shift toward virtue in epistemology and, combined with Lonergan's perspectivism, can ground a virtuous perspectivist epistemology. This epistemology, following the continuums of the virtue means, accounts for not only pluralism in ethical methods but also plural definitions of human dignity and the formulation and justification of plural norms that facilitate its attainment. To explain virtuous perspectivism, we define virtue epistemology and its methodological shift, the types and interrelationships of epistemic virtues, virtue epistemology's parallels with Lonergan's perspectivist epistemology, and illustrate the application of virtue ethics and virtue epistemology by considering the nature and types of norms to guide human character and action.

Virtue epistemology is a relatively new movement in philosophy, developing over the last thirty years, and it includes diverse schools and methods. They all adhere, however, to four basic commitments. First, virtue epistemology is a normative discipline. Second, rational persons are the foundation of epistemic value and the focus of epistemic evaluation.[17] Third, Greco's "shift in the direction of analysis" evident in virtue ethics is applied also to virtue epistemology, and this shift distinguishes it from traditional epistemological methods. "Non-virtue theories try to analyze virtuous character in terms of justified belief, defining the former in terms of dispositions to achieve the latter." Greco proposes a directional reversal, "defining justified belief in terms of virtuous character. Virtuous character is then defined in terms of successful and stable dispositions to form belief."[18] Justified beliefs "are those that issue from responsible inquiries of virtuous inquirers. It is a mistake to put it the other way round: epistemic virtues are those habits and dispositions that lead us to have justified beliefs."[19] Fourth, the intellectual virtues are prioritized in the search for justified belief and knowledge.

Epistemic Virtues

An epistemic or intellectual virtue is "an innate ability or acquired habit that allows one to reliably achieve some intellectual good, such as truth."[20] Epistemic virtues include both faculty virtues, like imagination, perception,

---

[16]James A. Montmarquet, *Epistemic Virtue and Doxastic Responsibility* (Lanham, MD: Rowman & Littlefield, 1993), vii.

[17]John Greco, *Virtue Epistemology: Contemporary Readings* (Boston: MIT Press, 2012).

[18]John Greco, "Agent Reliabilism," *Philosophical Perspectives* 13 (1999): 290.

[19]Christopher Hookway, "Cognitive Virtues and Epistemic Evaluations," *International Journal of Philosophical Studies* 2 (1994): 225.

[20]Greco, "Virtue Epistemology."

memory, intuition, introspection, and character virtues, like reliability, responsibility, conscientiousness, carefulness, and open-mindedness. Faculty virtues are indispensable to account for knowledge from the past. Character virtues are indispensable to account for the ongoing intellectual achievements of understanding and wisdom that presuppose past knowledge and build on and transcend it. The development, exercise, and prioritization of the intellectual virtues in the theological ethicist impact the marshaling of evidence to justify a theological anthropology that defines human dignity and formulates and justifies principles and norms that facilitate its attainment.

Virtue epistemologists in general agree on the directional shift in epistemology and the centrality of intellectual virtues in the process of attaining knowledge. They disagree on the interrelationship between virtue epistemology and virtue ethics, on whether and how the epistemic *ought* relates to the ethical *ought*. Lorraine Code agrees with Greco's and Ernest Sosa's directional shift in epistemology that emphasizes the cognitive activities of a subject in community guided by the social practices of investigation. She criticizes Sosa, however, for not integrating the insights from ethical virtue theory with virtue epistemology. Specifically, Code believes that epistemology should emphasize virtues that relate to human agency in the process of attaining and justifying knowledge. To that end, she proposes *responsibilism* as a virtue-epistemological theory that posits the agent's responsibility as the primary intellectual virtue. Responsibilism emphasizes both the knower as active agent and the knower's choice as essential elements in the pursuit and justification of knowledge. All other intellectual virtues emanate from this central virtue.[21]

James Montmarquet agrees with Code that ethical virtue theory and virtue epistemology should be more closely aligned. Code focuses on *responsibilism* as the foundational intellectual virtue for epistemic claims, and Montmarquet focuses on *conscientiousness*, which he defines as an appropriate desire for truth.[22] He specifies conscientiousness in three categories of epistemic virtues. The virtue of *intellectual impartiality* includes openness to another's ideas, willingness to learn from another, suspension of personal bias toward another's ideas, and recognition of one's own fallibility. The virtue of *intellectual sobriety* disposes the inquirer, "out of sheer love of truth, discovery, and the excitement of new and unfamiliar ideas, to embrace what is not really warranted, even relative to the limits of his own evidence." The virtue of *intellectual courage* includes "the willingness to conceive and examine alternatives to popularly held beliefs, perseverance in the face of

[21]See Lorraine Code, *Epistemic Responsibility* (Hanover, NH: University Press of New England Press, 1987).

[22]Montmarquet, *Epistemic Virtue and Doxastic Responsibility*, 23.

opposition from others (until one is convinced one is mistaken), and the determination required to see such a project through to completion."[23] The different virtues of responsibilism and conscientiousness account for different selection, interpretation, prioritization, and integration (SIPI) of the four sources of ethical knowledge to define human dignity and to formulate and justify norms for its attainment. They also emphasize both the need to justify one's definition of human dignity and normative claims in dialogue with others, and to have the courage to revise, if necessary, one's perspective based on this process of justification.

Reliabilism vs. Responsibilism

An emphasis on the responsibilism and conscientiousness of the knower agent is necessary in virtue epistemology but, we suggest, it is not sufficient. One can be very responsible and conscientious in one's intellectual activity and still be incorrect in one's knowledge and understanding. While all virtue epistemologists accept the change in the direction of analysis from act to person, defining justified belief and knowledge in reference to their source in personal virtues, they disagree on how to define virtuous character. For Greco, who is in the reliabilist school, virtuous character is "defined in terms of successful and stable dispositions to form belief" and a consequential focus on "reliable success in producing true belief."[24] For Hookway, who is in the responsibilist school, a virtuous character decentralizes "questions of the epistemic status of beliefs in favor of questions of agency and inquiry."[25] The reliabilist school focuses on getting knowledge right; the responsibilist school focuses on the knower's motivation for seeking justified knowledge.

The reliabilist/responsibilist debate, we suggest, ought not to be construed as an either/or but as a both/and debate. Guy Axtell argues that there is a shared assumption in virtue epistemology of a "dual component" account of the justification of true knowledge that reflects a complementarity between reliabilism and responsibilism. Such an account integrates "constraints on the agent's faculty reliability," his/her imagination, perception, and memory, "with constraints on the agent's responsibility in gathering and processing evidence."[26] Linda Zagzebski's "dual component" account of the justification of true knowledge balances the *motivation* of the knower with *success* in achieving true knowledge. The intellectual virtues have "a characteristic motivation to produce a certain desired end and reliable success in bringing

[23]Ibid.

[24]Guy Axtell et al., *Knowledge, Belief, and Character* (Lanham, MD: Rowman & Littlefield, 2000), xiv.

[25]Ibid., xiii–xiv.

[26]Ibid., 188.

about that end."[27] In Sosa's virtue perspectivism a proposition is known by a knower "only if *both* he is rationally justified in believing it *and* he is in a position to know . . . whether it is true."[28] Greco's "mixed theory" account of justification is that "an adequate account of knowledge ought to contain both a responsibility condition and a reliability condition. Moreover, a virtue account can explain how the two are tied together. In cases of knowledge, objective reliability is grounded in epistemically responsible action."[29] A dual-component virtue epistemology, which we espouse, seeks an integration and balance between reliabilist and responsibilist accounts of justified belief and knowledge.

Virtuous Perspective

The emphasis in virtue ethics on the agent rather than on the agent's actions is replicated in virtue epistemology's emphasis on the knower rather than on the knower's separate faculties of intellect and will. This emphasis on the knower and the knower's virtues, the directional shift in analysis, and the complementarity proposed by Zagzebski, Greco, and us between the subjective motivation of the knower and his/her success in achieving true knowledge, we suggest, all closely parallel perspectivism. According to Lonergan, human knowing is not simply "taking a look" at reality. It is endlessly discursive; it cycles and recycles through various levels of cognitive operations until knowledge and partial truth are reached in the judgment, deliberated on, and a decision is made for action according to the truth arrived at in the judgment. It begins with attention and cycles on through perception, imagination (sometimes as memory), insight, conceptualization, deliberation, and weighing of evidence, and culminates in the judgment of truth.[30] It is only in the judgment of truth, as we have emphasized throughout, that genuine human knowledge and partial truth are achieved.

Perception is critical in the process of coming to know. Remember that perception is, according to Lonergan, a function of a subject's relationship to an object, the subject's active patterning of the object in the phenomenal world. The phenomenal object does not simply impress itself upon rational subjects, as it impresses itself upon nonrational animals; nor do rational subjects simply construct or project it. Rather, the appearances of the

---

[27]Linda Zagzebski, *Virtues of the Mind: An Inquiry into the Nature of Virtue and the Ethical Foundations of Knowledge* (Cambridge: Cambridge University Press, 1996), 134.

[28]Ernest Sosa, *Knowledge in Perspective: Selected Essays in Epistemology* (Cambridge: Cambridge University Press, 1991), 28, emphasis in original.

[29]Greco, "Virtue Epistemology."

[30]Bernard J. F. Lonergan, *Insight: A Study of Human Understanding* (London: Longmans, 1957), 273–74.

phenomenal world are shaped by the subjects' attention, interests, loves, immediate and ultimate goals, emotional interactions, and in general *the character lens* through which they view the object. According to virtue epistemology, that character lens is shaped by both the intellectual and ethical virtues. The phenomenal world that persons encounter and attend to is not a world of naked sense data that is "already out there now real,"[31] but a world shaped by their interpretations called perceptions. What we "see" is a function of who we are, and who we are, according to virtue epistemology, is fashioned by the intellectual and ethical virtues we adopt and prioritize. Both virtue epistemology and perspectivism emphasize that this adoption and prioritization is influenced, in turn, by social context and historical narrative.

Who we are as knowing subjects is discerned by responding to two factors for knowing. First, knowers are selective, given their past socialization, personal experience, data offered to them, and the intellectual and ethical virtues they prioritize and excel in. Second, knowers are individually different, and, given all the variables just enumerated, we can expect them to make different selections of data and exercise different intellectual and ethical virtues. In her virtue epistemology, Code articulates similar factors for knowing. Traditional epistemology underestimates the impact of the social and contextual dimensions of the knowing subject because it begins with the object, not the subject. Beginning with the subject, as virtue ethicists do, requires that we give greater attention to those dimensions that shape the subject and his/her knowledge. Drawing on MacIntyre, Code argues that we understand the knowing subject and his/her virtues through lived narrative,[32] which is the context for prioritizing and excelling in virtue. Integrating a virtuous perspective into ethical method recognizes the essential engagement of the theological ethicist and his/her perspective in the discipline.

Klaus Demmer argues that theological ethics "inevitably contains a biographical element that reflects the personality of theologians and their particular life story."[33] This life story is especially evident in the habits of virtues, ethical and intellectual, that shape the perception of the theological ethicist and his/her SIPI of the sources of ethical knowledge. Rooting epistemology in the knower's character and virtues, revealed through his/her lived narrative, highlights the complexity of formulating and applying criteria for epistemic evaluation. All knowledge claims are made in a particular historical and cultural context, all of which helps fashion the

[31]Ibid., 251; see also Bernard J. F. Lonergan, *Method in Theology* (Toronto: University of Toronto Press, 2003), 263.

[32]Lorraine Code, *Epistemic Responsibility* , 222.

[33]Klaus Demmer, *Shaping the Moral Life: An Approach to Moral Theology*, ed. James F. Keenan (Washington, DC: Georgetown University Press, 2000), 1.

knower's lived narrative and knowledge claims. In nonvirtue epistemologies, the historical and cultural dimensions of knowledge and their impact on the knower's lived narrative are largely ignored. Virtue epistemology and perspectivism acknowledge these variables and attempt to integrate them fully into epistemological theory. Their integration marks a fundamental transition from classicism, where knowledge is a static, permanent achievement, to historical consciousness, where knowledge is a dynamic, ongoing process. The International Theological Commission's document on natural law affirms the insights of virtue epistemology and virtue ethics, and draws out their logical implications for formulating norms. There are "anthropological constants"[34] in human persons that allow them to spontaneously grasp fundamental values, and virtuous dispositions, especially prudence, facilitate an awareness of these values and sensitize knowing subjects to their relevance for the attainment of human dignity.

CONSERVATIVE AND PROGRESSIVE PERSPECTIVES ON VIRTUE EPISTEMOLOGY, PRINCIPLES, AND NORMS

Conservative and progressive virtuous perspectives adhere to different epistemologies that result in fundamentally different perspectives on the formulation and justification of principles and norms and their role with respect to the knowing and acting subject. Both recognize reliabilism and responsibilism in virtue epistemology. They differ, however, on their prioritizations of reliabilism and responsibilism, on the epistemological criteria for determining reliabilism and responsibilism, on the virtues directing the assessment of those criteria, and on their prioritizations of the knowing subject and the known object.

Conservative and Progressive Virtuous Perspectives on Reliabilism and Responsibilism

A conservative virtuous perspective (CVP) prioritizes reliabilism over responsibilism. Knowledge and understanding of moral norms are reliable if they agree with what is taught by the Magisterium. The Magisterium's claims about the truth of sexual moral norms, for instance, are reliable for CVP and are its point of departure for justifying those norms. Tradition, narrowly defined as magisterial teaching, is the primary source of ethical knowledge. A CVP in general agrees with the knowledge claims of the Magisterium although, as we saw in the previous chapter, it constructs unique

[34]International Theological Commission, *In Search of a Universal Ethic*, 61.

anthropologies, like the theology of the body, and a unique methodology to justify those claims. Responsibilism for a CVP is guided by strict magisterial parameters. CVP prioritizes the virtue of *obsequium*, which it translates as submission, to magisterial teaching as the epistemological criteria for the SIPI of the sources of ethical knowledge for the formulation and justification of moral principles and norms.

A progressive virtuous perspective (PVP) emphasizes the complementarity of reliabilism and responsibilism proposed by Greco, Zagzebski, and us between a knower's motivation and his/her success in achieving true knowledge. We believe this complementarity reflects the vocation of the Catholic ethicist. Reliabilism cautions that it is not for theologians alone to formulate the ethical doctrine and practice of their church; that task is for the whole People-of-God-in-Communion. The task of the theologian in the People of God is a different and critical one. In the words of the Congregation for the Doctrine of the Faith's International Theological Commission, it is the task of "interpreting the documents of the past and present Magisterium, of putting them in the context of the whole of revealed truth, and of finding a better understanding of them by the use of hermeneutics."[35] Interpretation, contextualization, and discovery of a better understanding all require both responsibilism and reliabilism. The theologian "is charged with developing the tradition beyond its current state so that it can meet new questions, needs, and circumstances."[36] It is that difficult theological task of "maintaining the balance between 'immobilism' and 'eccentricity'"[37] that progressive Catholic ethicists seek to fulfill.

The epistemological criteria for determining reliabilism and responsibilism are grounded in the virtuous perspective and conscience of the ethicist. We will have much more to say about conscience in the next chapter, but we note here that the authority of conscience in ethical judgment is also the authority of conscience in epistemological judgment. A progressive virtuous perspective embraces the tradition's and, more recently Pope Francis's, emphasis on the authority of conscience. As Francis notes in *Amoris Laetitia*, the church has been called to form the consciences of the faithful, not to replace them.[38] In the formation of their theological consciences, ethicists must seek reliable truth responsibly. They must avoid vincible ignorance and realize that invincible ignorance is always a possibility in the pursuit of knowledge. Theologians can be, and have been, wrong in their knowledge

---

[35]International Theological Commission, *Theses on the Relationship between the Ecclesiastical Magisterium and Theology* (Washington, DC: USCC, 1977), 6.

[36]Johann Sebastian Drey, *Brief Introduction to the Study of Theology with Reference to the Scientific Standpoint of the Catholic System* (Notre Dame, IN: University of Notre Dame Press, 1944), xxv.

[37]Ibid., xxvi.

[38]*Amoris Laetitia*, no. 37 (hereafter *AL*).

claims, and so, too, has the ecclesial Magisterium. We believe unshakably that the church is guided by the Holy Spirit, but this guidance extends to the whole church, who cannot err in faith and morals.[39] The discernment of ethical truth is a process that takes time and, since neither theologians, the faithful, nor the Magisterium have a monopoly on truth, it also demands Pope John Paul II's "dialogue of charity," to which we have referred several times, because we believe it is a crucial tool to move Catholic ethics forward beyond its present, apparently intractable impasse.[40]

A progressive virtuous perspective does not prioritize *obsequium* as submission or obedience to Catholic magisterial teaching, which, it judges, may limit ethicists' consciences and damage their task of developing the tradition. It does, however, prioritize *obsequium* as respect,[41] as one of the many virtues that should guide Catholics in general in discerning ethical knowledge. There is a presumption of truth in favor of magisterial teaching, but through the complementarity of reliabilism, responsibilism, intellectual and ethical virtues, CVP ethicists critically analyze magisterial teaching by incorporating a broader sense of tradition allied to the other three sources of ethical knowledge. Where there is tension between tradition narrowly defined as magisterial teaching and tradition more broadly defined to include *sensus fidelium* and the other three sources of ethical knowledge, then there must be a respectful and open-minded dialogue of charity about ethics in general, sexual ethics in particular, and all that is involved in the life of Christian discipleship.

A Copernican-Style Methodological Shift: Conservative and Progressive Perspectives

The most striking epistemological difference between conservative and progressive Catholic ethicists, we believe, is that the former have not fully embraced the methodological shift in the direction of analysis from the object to the subject. This shift, Greco argues, is essential for virtue ethics;[42] it totally alters the lens for the SIPI of the Wesleyan Quadrilateral's four sources of ethical knowledge. To define the morality of an act, a conservative methodological approach, such as that evident in John Paul II's *Veritatis Splendor*, focuses on the act rather than on the virtuous person doing the act

[39]*Lumen Gentium*, no. 12.

[40]*Ut Unum Sint*, nos. 17, 51, 60. See *Gaudium et Spes*, no. 92 (hereafter *GS*).

[41]See James A. Coriden, et al., eds., *The Code of Canon Law: A Text and Commentary* (New York: Paulist Press, 1985), c. 752, which also translates *obsequium* as *respect* in the official translation. Cf., Francis A. Sullivan, *Magisterium: Teaching Authority in the Catholic Church* (Dublin, Ireland: Gill and Macmillan, 1985), 159–64.

[42]See John Greco, "Virtue Epistemology."

with all his/her contextual circumstances. It focuses on the act of stealing a pair of jeans from a store rather than on the person stealing the jeans; it focuses on the act of sexual intercourse rather than on the persons engaging in the act. Romanus Cessario, a conservative Catholic ethicist, asserts that the focus of Aquinas's ethics in the *Summa Theologiae* was on the virtuous and acting person rather on his/her act, and that something similar to virtue ethics has always been present in Catholic theological ethics following Aquinas.[43] That assertion is true, but it is also true, we judge, that Aquinas's focus on the virtuous person was largely lost in the tradition of the manuals' focus on moral acts rather than on virtuous persons that controlled Catholic ethics up to the Second Vatican Council. It was retrieved, we further judge, only in the 1990s, after the revision of Catholic theological ethics was well under way in the wake of the Council.[44]

In the wake of the Council's call for the renewal of theological ethics, ethicists critically analyzed the manuals that had shaped theological ethics from the sixteenth century to the Second Vatican Council in the twentieth, and reacted against both the manuals' focus on acts rather than on persons in their context and their declaration that certain acts were intrinsically evil *ex objecto*. The object in this approach was defined in a purely material sense; it was simply the physical act of telling a falsehood or of sexual intercourse. Focusing only on the act would mean that every act of telling a falsehood would be declared intrinsically evil even though, on occasion, doing so could be morally justified, as in telling a falsehood in response to a German soldier's question about the presence of Anne Frank in your attic. Given what he is likely to do, and in fact did, with the truth, the soldier has no right either to ask for or to be given true information about Anne's whereabouts. In this case, the value of saving an innocent human life from an unjust aggressor far outweighs the disvalue of telling a falsehood about her presence in the attic, and the act of telling a falsehood is morally right. To counteract manualist and magisterial absolutism, progressive ethicists point beyond a mere act to what Selling calls the total "moral event,"[45] which always includes the subject's conscience, virtues, motive, end, intention, circumstances and choice. The manualist legacy of prioritizing the object and the act, of lying or of practicing artificial contraception, for instance, continues today and is evident in magisterial teaching on sexual and biomedical ethics and in the scholarship of conservative Catholic ethicists.

[43]Romanus Cessario, "The Meaning of Virtue in the Christian Moral Life: Its Significance for Human Life Issues," *The Thomist* 53 (1989): 173–96.

[44]See Joseph Selling, *Reframing Catholic Theological Ethics* (Oxford: Oxford University Press, 2016), 153–55.

[45]See ibid., 166–67, 170.

Veritatis Splendor *and the Primacy of the Ethical Object*

Pope John Paul II's 1993 encyclical *Veritatis Splendor* is fundamentally concerned with exploring and defining criteria for the ethical evaluation of human acts or what ensures the "*ordering of human acts to God? Is it* the *intention* of the acting subject, the *circumstances*—and in particular the consequences—of his action, or the *object* itself of his act?" John Paul responds that the answer to this question is "what is traditionally called the problem of the sources of morality,"[46] object, intention or end, and circumstances. The object is the external act; the end is the subject's intention for choosing the act; and the circumstances are those variables that impact, but do not change, the morality of the act, such as how, where, and when the act was chosen.[47] If the circumstances are serious enough to impact the morality of the act, such as unjustified stealing from a church rather than a convenience store, making the act one of theft and sacrilege, rather than just theft, they are incorporated into a description of the object. The object is primary in the ethical evaluation of the act; this primacy is especially evident in "intrinsically evil acts," acts that can never be morally justified by intention or circumstances since the object can never be ordered toward the good. John Paul explains: "The primary and decisive element for moral judgment is the object of the human act, which establishes whether it is *capable of being ordered to the good and to the ultimate end, which is God*."[48] It notes again that "if the object of the concrete action is not in harmony with the true good of the person, the choice of that action makes our will and ourselves morally evil."[49] The encyclical also condemns ethical theories that deny the existence of intrinsically evil acts, theories that it calls *teleologism*.

Initially, *Veritatis Splendor* casts teleological theories in a somewhat positive light, commenting that Catholic ethical theologians who follow a teleological ethical theory distance themselves from utilitarianism and pragmatism, and "rightly recognize the need to find ever more consistent rational arguments in order to justify the requirements and to provide a foundation for the norms of the moral life. This kind of investigation is legitimate and necessary, since the moral order, as established by natural law, is in principle accessible to human reason."[50] In teleological attempts to work out a rationalist morality, the encyclical asserts, "there exist *false solutions, linked in particular to an inadequate understanding of the object of the moral action*."[51]

[46] *Veritatis Splendor*, no. 74 (hereafter *VS*).
[47] Ibid.
[48] *VS*, no.79.
[49] *VS*, no. 72.
[50] *VS*, no. 74.
[51] *VS*, no. 75. See also Pope John Paul II, *Reconciliatio et Paenitentia*, in *Acta Apostolicae Sedis* 77

John Paul rejects ethical theories that hold "that it is impossible to qualify as morally evil according to its species—its 'object'—the deliberate choice of certain kinds of behavior or specific acts, apart from a consideration of the intention for which the choice is made or the totality of the foreseeable consequences of that act for all persons concerned."[52] Quite simply, the object or act alone defines the ethical choice of the acting subject; neither intention nor circumstances can change the ethics of such a choice. That last claim runs counter to the Catholic tradition and the teaching of the *Catechism of the Catholic Church* about the diminishing or even nullifying effect of circumstances on the sinfulness of an act to which we have referred several times. Even though, for instance, there is documented and undeniable evidence of the correlation between poverty, child homelessness, and lack of access to artificial birth control in the Philippines, the use of artificial birth control within a marital relationship to regulate fertility is judged to be intrinsically evil on the basis of the object or act alone.

Progressive virtue ethicists judge that external acts or objects *in se* have no ethical meaning without the intention of the acting subject and his/her circumstances. They acquire ethical meaning through the subject's intention and may also be morally modified by circumstances. The Magisterium's absolute proscriptive norms against artificial contraception, homosexual acts, and reproductive technologies reveal the failure to account for the perspective of the *actual* acting subjects and *assume* the subjects' intention in the object *a priori*. Intention, however, cannot be determined without knowing the perspective of the acting subject. *Veritatis Splendor* implies that progressive ethicists, including those theological ethicists whom we have described as having a progressive virtuous perspective,[53] maintain that a good intention can justify intrinsically evil acts such as artificial contraception.[54] Those ethicists are mistaken, it asserts, because they have misconstrued the traditional understanding of the object, end, and circumstances, giving *intention* instead of *object or act* the preeminent position.

(1985): 185–275, at 221, n. 17, where he makes a similar point regarding the object of the act: "some sins are *intrinsically* grave and mortal by reason of their matter. That is, there exist acts which, *per se* and in themselves, independently of circumstances, are always seriously wrong by reason of their object."

[52] *VS*, no. 79, emphasis in original.

[53] Many Catholic ethicists who defended a so-called proportionalist method have evolved to adopt a progressive virtuous perspective. Selling, *Reframing Catholic Theological Ethics*, 153, notes that in Peter Knauer's articles, which were the impetus for proportionalism, one can also find the impetus for what we call a progressive virtuous perspective, though this focus on virtue in Knauer's articles was overlooked.

[54] See *VS*, no. 75.

The Ethical Primacy of the Object

Though conservative virtue ethicists prioritize the object over the subject, they have at least two ways of conceptualizing the object in relation to the subject. The first way is found in William Mattison III's textbook on virtue and theological ethics and betrays a lack of the turn to the subject in his articulation of acts in relation to virtue. Although he emphasizes the importance of intention and virtue as foundational for judging good acts, he states that the object, "what is actually done,"[55] is more important than either intention or virtue. He offers an example taken from Aristotle and Aquinas.[56] A ship's captain encounters a storm that endangers cargo, ship, and crew. To save the ship from sinking, he orders the crew to throw the cargo overboard to lighten and save the ship and the crew. Mattison uses this scenario to describe the *fontes moralitatis*, object, end, and circumstances. Naming the object is tricky, he admits, but it must be named "in the most specific way possible, without reference to long-term goals."[57] The object in the case in question is "throwing the cargo overboard. This names the specific action that is done in a meaningful way. . . . The *intention* is the goal or purpose we have in mind for doing an action. . . . *Circumstances* are features of the situation which, although secondary, help determine the morality of the act."[58] He later asserts that a "virtue is named for the sort of activity which is being done well" and identifies the activity as the object.[59]

According to Mattison, "throwing cargo overboard" is a definition of an object or act done in a meaningful way. We cannot know, however, if this is being done well or badly unless we *first* know intention: *Why* is this being done? Is the intention to prevent the ship from sinking and to save the lives of the crew, or is it to dispose of illegal contraband to avoid arrest when the ship reaches port? The captain's intention is essential to the definition of the moral object in this case and to the judgment of whether "throwing cargo overboard" is a morally good act to save the ship and crew or a morally bad act to avoid arrest. In general, the acting subject's intention must be known before we can morally assess an object or act. The circumstance that there is a storm may or may not be relevant in this case to determine the morality of the act. If the intention is to avoid arrest, then the circumstance that there is a storm and throwing the cargo overboard saves the ship and crew is merely fortuitous. It does not change the badness of the total moral event.

A second conceptualization of the object comes from Martin Rhonheimer

[55]Mattison, *Introducing Moral Theology*, 49.

[56]See *NE*, III.1 1110a; *ST*, I-II, 6, 6.

[57]Mattison, *Introducing Moral Theology*, 49.

[58]Ibid.

[59]Ibid., 65.

who, arguing against proportionalists, critiques a conceptualization of the object similar to the one Mattison offers. In his critique, Rhonheimer presents Josef Fuchs's description of theft in terms of the *fontes moralitatis*: action ("taking money from another"), circumstance ("who is very poor"), and intention ("to be able to give pleasure to a friend"), and notes that "taking money from another" is not a good description of the act or object.[60] Rhonheimer offers a better description of the theft: "Appropriating money, taking it from its legitimate owner, against his will."[61] If we were to follow Rhonheimer, a better description of Mattison's object would be: "Throwing cargo overboard *to save the ship and the crew from death*." The intention is part of the description of the object, what Rhonheimer calls the "basic intentional content, that is, the object."[62] The subject first selects an end and then chooses the appropriate act or object for realizing that end, not vice versa. The act of taking money from another or throwing cargo overboard is *morally* meaningless *in se* until we know the intention for which it is chosen and the circumstances under which it is chosen. It may be an act that facilitates or frustrates human dignity, but until we know the intention and the circumstances we cannot judge its morality.

Though not using the language of virtue epistemology, in his recent book, Joseph Selling presents a model that illustrates well the Copernican-style shift in how we analyze and evaluate what he calls a "moral event," a complete and unified account of the acting subject choosing a "circumstantiated action" or behavior.[63] As we have seen, traditional and conservative Catholic theological ethics prioritizes the object over the subject in the moral evaluation of an act; a virtuous perspective prioritizes the subject over the object in the moral evaluation of an event.

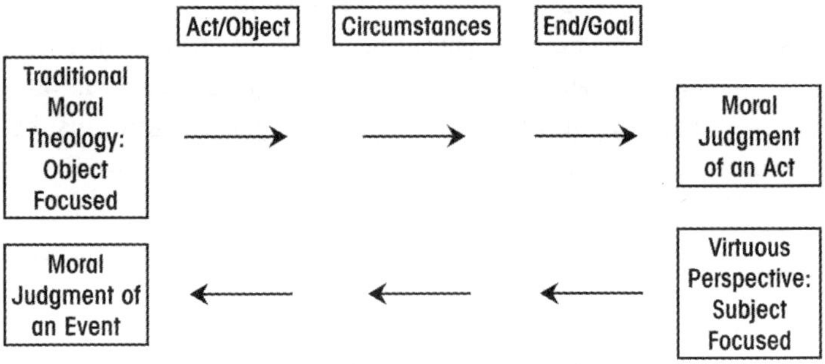

[60] Martin Rhonheimer, "Intentional Actions and the Meaning of the Object: A Reply to Richard McCormick," *The Thomist* 59 (1995): 289.

[61] Ibid.

[62] Ibid., 302.

[63] Selling, *Reframing Catholic Theological Ethics*, 166–67, at 170. See also "The Fundamental Polarity of Moral Discourse," in *Method and Catholic Moral Theology: The Ongoing Reconstruction*, ed. Todd A. Salzman (Omaha, NE: Creighton University Press, 1999), 22–45.

Conservative theological ethics prioritizes the object in the ethical judgment of an act. The direction of analysis is from the object or act, considering the relevant circumstances, the agent's intention, to the moral judgment of the act. In a virtuous perspective, the direction of analysis is the opposite, from the agent's intention or end, considering the relevant circumstances, to the act or object, to the moral judgment of the act. The Magisterium recognizes the turn to the subject. Even though it prioritizes the object as "the primary and decisive element for moral judgment" of a human act, the object is "the proximate *end* of a deliberate decision."[64] The proximate end is determined from the perspective of the acting subject. Rhonheimer approvingly cites *Veritatis Splendor*: "In order to be able to grasp the object of an act which specifies that act morally, it is therefore necessary to place oneself *in the perspective of the acting person*."[65] We fully agree with Rhonheimer even though he accuses teleological approaches to ethics of failing to consider this perspective. This accusation is remarkable, for it is precisely "the perspective of the acting subject,"[66] he argues, that can, for instance, distinguish the use of artificial contraception as an act to realize the end of responsible parenthood from an act to realize the end of a contralife will.

Considering the acting subject's perspective prioritizes the subject over the object and fundamentally challenges the Magisterium's and conservative claims to absolute proscriptive norms that assume, without searching them out, the perspective and intention of the subject in those norms. Absolute norms prohibiting artificial contraception, masturbation, artificial reproductive technologies, and homosexual acts assume the subject's perspective, *regardless of his/her actual perspective*. If the subject's actual intention coincides with the intentional content indicated in the absolute norm, a contralife will in the case of artificial contraception, for instance, then the act is morally bad. The subject's perspective and intention, however, may or may not coincide with the norm's intention. Without knowing the subject's perspective and his/her actual intention, we cannot know if a specific act of artificial contraception, masturbation, artificial reproductive technologies, or homosexual activity is a violation of the norm. Such absolute norms prioritize the object over the subject and the subject's intention, and essentially reduce the object to an intentional act detached from the acting subject. Detached from the perspective of the acting subject, however, no human or moral acts exist.

For progressive ethicists, the ethical evaluation of an event always begins

---

[64] *VS*, no. 78.

[65] Martin Rhonheimer, "'Intrinsically Evil Acts' and the Moral Viewpoint: Clarifying a Central Teaching of *Veritatis Splendor*," *The Thomist* 58 (1994): 282, citing *VS*, no. 78. Emphasis in original.

[66] Ibid.

with the subject "seeking an end." That is, in the moral realm, the subject first has an intention or an end and then seeks the appropriate act or object to attain that end. The end is willed first by the subject mind but is executed last by him/her.[67] The will and intellect, in combination, intend an end and choose the means to attain that end. In reality, the direction of a moral event is in the opposite direction from that presented by conservative theological ethicists. The Magisterium's and conservative ethicists' attempt to name the perspective and intention of the acting subject in absolute norms merely intentionalizes the object but does not seek an answer to the question of whether the intentionalized object coincides with the perspective and intention of the acting subject. It assumes that it does and condemns such acts absolutely. Whether the perspective and intention of the subject coincides with the absolute norm, however, has to be determined empirically and on a case-by-case basis. There is not a full turn to the subject in those who embrace a CVP; there is only an addition of an assumed intention to the object *in abstracto*.

A progressive virtuous perspective begins with the acting subject, an approach that reflects the teleological perspectives of Aristotle and Aquinas. Human beings always act toward ends, be that end human flourishing, friendship with God, or the facilitation of human dignity. Moral acts are ways to realize an end, and the end suggests the appropriate act for its realization. Virtue, remember, is a continuum mean between two extremes and, in the continuum between the two extremes, there are a variety of appropriate acts to reach the intended end, all of them dependent on the subject's virtuous perspective and intention.

Selling presents a model for "seeking the end" that is representative of progressive virtue ethicists and exemplifies the turn to the subject in virtue epistemology and virtue ethics. It begins with "a basic life orientation," a fundamental perspective or stance,[68] which coincides well with MacIntyre's first question of virtue ethics, "Who am I?" A person's fundamental stance indicates "habitual tendencies," virtues or vices, which guide the person and his/her intentions. A positive fundamental stance is a person's basic orientation embracing God, neighbor, and self; a negative fundamental stance is a person's basic orientation rejecting God, neighbor, and self.[69] Since all human beings sin, the fundamental stance in relation to those

[67]See *ST*, I-II, q. 1, a. 1, ad 1.

[68]We intentionally use the phrase "fundamental stance," rather than "fundamental option." Fundamental stance indicates the basic orientation of a person. Fundamental option indicates a choice that either affirms or rejects one's fundamental stance. See Richard M. Gula, *Reason Informed by Faith: Foundations of Catholic Morality* (New York: Paulist Press, 1989), 78–81.

[69]Grabowski also explores the importance of fundamental option in developing virtue ethics. See Grabowski, *Sex and Virtue*, 91–92.

habitual tendencies is not an either/or, either virtue or vice, but often a combination of both. Hence, MacIntyre's second question, "Who do I want to become?," provides a direction for either pursuing virtue or overcoming vice, reinforcing a positive fundamental stance, or pursuing vice and suppressing virtue, a negative fundamental stance. Since Christians seek to become united with God via friendship with Christ, they focus also on how to act from a fundamental Christian perspective or stance when seeking an end and choosing a good act to realize that end.

A person's fundamental perspective or stance "provides a direction toward which a person 'moves,'" what Selling labels motivation.[70] There is an important distinction, not always followed in the literature, between motivation and intention. Richard McCormick highlights this distinction in his critique of *Veritatis Splendor* and its defenders. Intention is what the subject wants to accomplish in and through an act; motivation is a "further aimed-at good."[71] Philosopher Russell Hittinger accuses progressive ethicists of "shifting intentions to and fro,"[72] and Pope John Paul II maintains that there are intrinsically evil acts that "no intention can ever legitimate."[73] For progressive ethicists, if the act description includes a morally bad intention and the relevant circumstances, such as murder, then the act is defined as morally bad and can never be justified. It is the question of intention and the inclusion of the subject's actual intention in the object that is at the root of the debate between conservative and progressive ethicists. If the subject's intention is included in the act description, stealing money to buy a gun to murder a gay man, then an act can certainly be declared intrinsically evil and no further "intention" (Hittinger) or "motive" (McCormick) could justify it.[74] Conservative and progressive ethicists agree on the definition of the object *if* the object includes the intention of the acting subject that specifies it morally.

The act descriptions of conservative scholars such as Mattison and Rhonheimer, however, either do not include the subject's intention in the description of the object ("throwing cargo overboard"), or assume in the object of the act an intention that does not necessarily correspond to the acting subject's intention. In his definition of theft, Rhonheimer notes that an "intentional description of an act called 'theft' . . . has its moral form *independently from whether the acting person has this or another*

[70]Selling, *Reframing Catholic Theological Ethics*, 167.

[71]Richard A. McCormick, "Some Early Reactions to *Veritatis Splendor*," in *John Paul II and Moral Theology: Readings in Moral Theology No. 10*, ed. Charles Curran and Richard McCormick (New York: Paulist Press, 1998), 20.

[72]Russell Hittinger, "The Pope and the Theorists," *Crisis* 11 (December 1993): 34.

[73]McCormick, "Some Early Reactions," 18.

[74]Ibid.

'purpose'."[75] No, we respond, it does not. It has its moral form from the perspective and intention of the acting person, which both Rhonheimer and *Veritatis Splendor* theoretically assert. Mattison's view, we judge, is a reductionist view of the object; Rhonheimer's and the Magisterium's is a presumptive view of the subject's intention. For Selling, motivation helps to identify "specific goals or states of affairs that reflect the kind of life to which one aspires"[76] and defines the end. This begins to answer MacIntyre's third question of virtue ethics, "how do I get there?"

NORMATIVE ETHICS AND VIRTUE ETHICS

Selling's model illustrates well the epistemological shift from object to subject in the process of evaluating a moral event from a virtuous perspective. James Keenan illustrates the shift by contrasting a normative approach to ethics with a virtue approach to ethics.[77] Ethics in general, and Catholic ethics in particular, has been primarily concerned with normative ethics, that is, with formulating norms or laws for what one can and cannot do morally. Even formal norms dealing with virtue, be just, be chaste, be respectful, were formulated on the basis of the prescription or proscription of acts identified with particular virtues. Being just proscribes stealing; being chaste proscribes adultery; being respectful prescribes honoring your parents. Herbert McCabe notes that for Aquinas, and we add for progressive virtue ethicists like us, norms and laws arise from virtues.[78] For conservative ethicists, virtues become the "handmaiden" of norms and laws and the acts they prescribe or proscribe;[79] for them, a predescribed act defines a virtue or vice. For progressive ethicists, a virtue or vice indicates a continuum of acts between virtue and excess and the subject's choosing of the most appropriate act within that continuum in light of his/her intention and morally relevant circumstances.

The preoccupation with normative ethics has limited appreciation of virtue and its role and function in the formulation and justification of principles and norms. In fact, one of the main criticisms against virtue ethics is that it does not give adequate direction for what acts a person can or cannot perform. This criticism, we believe, is evidence of an underly-

---

[75]Rhonheimer, "Intentional Actions," 289, emphasis added.

[76]Selling, *Reframing Catholic Theological Ethics*, 167.

[77]James F. Keenan, "Seven Reasons for Doing Virtue Ethics Today," in *Virtue and the Moral Life: Philosophical and Theological Perspectives*, ed. William Werpehowski and Kathryn Getek Soltis (Lanham, MD: Lexington Books, 2014), 3–18.

[78]Herbert McCabe, "Manuals and Rule Books," *Considering Veritatis Splendor*, ed. John Wilkins (Cleveland, OH: Pilgrim Press, 1994), 67–68.

[79]See James F. Keenan, *A History of Catholic Moral Theology in the Twentieth Century: From Confessing Sins to Liberating Consciences* (New York: Continuum, 2010), 129.

ing legalism that normative ethics has fostered and that creates a sense of dependence on being told clearly, even absolutely, what acts one can or cannot perform. Kohlberg and other developmental psychologists have had much to say about this and, indeed, in some ways, it is a "safer" approach to the moral life. With legalism, ethical responsibility entails following the norm; with virtue, it entails a personal choice to do the right thing on this occasion, toward this right person, and for this right intention. Normative ethics, especially deontological ethics, can tend to offer a letter-of-the-law approach to ethics; virtue ethics tends to provide a "spirit of the law" approach, though not without guidelines. The necessity for such guidelines led William Frankena to observe that "Virtues without principles are blind; principles without virtues are impotent."[80]

Two important questions for virtue ethics and a virtuous perspective are the following. First, can virtue ethics aid in the formulation and justification of principles and norms? Second, if so, how does it do so and impact the SIPI of the Wesleyan Quadrilateral's four sources of ethical knowledge in the process? In answer to the first question, Keenan maintains that principles (rules, norms, or laws) and virtues complement one another. Virtues require principles to specify actions that facilitate attaining the virtue. Principles, however, require virtues, especially the virtue of prudence, to navigate complex situations where there are conflicting principles or contextual ambiguities that do not allow for an unambiguous application of the principle or require a virtue, such as fortitude, to follow the principle.[81] Recognizing the complementarity between virtues and principles, Keenan asks which comes first, the virtue or the principle.[82] Can virtue ethics aid in the formulation and justification of principles, norms, and laws, or do we deduce principles, norms, and laws from other approaches to ethics and then rely upon virtue to apply them in a given context?

Historically, Catholic ethics has tended to focus on normative ethics, on general principles, specific norms, and specific laws. It has either forgotten or assumed the individual and communal virtuous perspectives that define the good and formulate and justify principles and norms that facilitate or frustrate its attainment. This focus on impersonal normative ethics is, in large part, what sparked a return to virtue ethics. Normative ethics defines right or wrong acts and attempts to codify those acts (deontology) or their consequences (teleology) in principles, norms, and, laws. If we forget, however, the virtuous perspective at the root of the formulation and justification of principles, norms, and laws in the first place, they themselves,

[80]William Frankena, *Ethics*, 2nd ed. (Englewood Cliffs, NJ: Prentice Hall, 1973), 65.
[81]Keenan, "Seven Reasons for Doing Virtue Ethics Today," 8–9.
[82]Ibid., 8.

rather than the virtuous perspective that was at the root of their formulation and justification, become sacrosanct. In magisterial ethics, for instance, the sacrosanct nature of the norms themselves, the claim to their absoluteness, and the virtues of submission and obedience to them, have obstructed a demonstrated need for the evolving historically conscious virtuous perspective guided by induction, ethnographic studies, lived narrative, and imagination grounded in human experience that continue to seek answers to the complex ethical questions facing human beings.[83] In a way, the Magisterium's failure to espouse a particular ethical method is an indication of its option for the sacrosanct nature of the norms themselves over and above the method for arriving at them, either through normative or virtue ethics.

Normative ethics and virtue ethics complement one another, but virtue ethics, we suggest, precedes normative ethics. It is only after we ask and respond to the first two questions of virtue ethics, who are we and who do we want to become, that we answer the third question: how do we get there? It is the getting there of normative ethics that specifies the virtuous perspective in the form of principles and norms. As that virtuous perspective evolves and changes, as it has evolved and changed in history, so too do principles and norms evolve and change.

There is a type of norm, labeled a synthetic norm[84] or tautology,[85] that combines an act norm and a virtue norm, "do not kill unjustly," for example. These norms include an act norm, "do not kill," and a virtue norm prescribing a virtue, "be just," or proscribing a vice, "don't be unjust." They also often imply morally relevant circumstances. Examples of such norms are "do not murder," "do not commit adultery," "do not lie." Such absolute norms are not entirely helpful for at least two reasons. First, it is not always clear what constitutes murder, adultery, or a lie. Was the case at St. Joseph's Hospital in Phoenix, Arizona, where an eleven-week old fetus was aborted to save the life of the mother, and where both mother and fetus would have died if nothing was done, a direct abortion and therefore a violation of the norm "do not murder," or was it an indirect abortion, morally acceptable and not a violation of the norm "do not murder," as the Ethics Committee at St. Joseph's hospital and the majority of Catholic ethicists judged?[86] When Mrs. Bergmeier in a Soviet Gulag has sex with a prison guard in order to get pregnant and be returned to Germany to care

[83]*GS*, no. 44.

[84]Gula, *Reason Informed by Faith*, 288–89.

[85]Bruno Schüller, "What Ethical Principles Are Universally Valid?," *Theology Digest* 19 (1974): 23–28.

[86]See Jerry Filteau, "No Direct Abortion at Phoenix Hospital, Theologian Says," *National Catholic Reporter* (December 23, 2010), www.ncronline.org/news/no-direct-abortion-phoenix-hospital-theologian-says; Kevin O'Rourke, "What Happened in Phoenix," *America* (June 21, 2010), americamagazine.org/issue/741/100/what-happened-phoenix.

for her ailing husband and family, is she committing adultery or an act of charitable self-sacrifice?[87] When a German citizen speaks an untruth to an SS soldier inquiring whether or not he is harboring Jews, is he violating the synthetic norm "do not tell a lie" or speaking a morally justified falsehood? The answer to the question whether a subject is choosing an act that violates a synthetic norm cannot be determined in the abstract. It can only be determined in the concrete circumstances of an individual subject in light of the virtue or vice guiding the subject.

In summary, a virtuous perspective indicates who we are and who we want to become. Virtue norms indicate how we are to get there by indicating an end that the subject seeks to attain. Behavioral norms indicate how we get there by selecting an appropriate act to attain the end. Synthetic norms indicate virtues that should be pursued and vices that should be avoided, and the acts that will generally fulfill or violate any given virtue. Such norms could be considered to fulfill the paradigmatic acts that we discussed in Chapter 4. However, we reassert what we asserted there: "If an act embodies a virtue, it is an authentic expression of that virtue; if an act violates a virtue, it is an inauthentic expression of that virtue." Determining whether an act is an authentic or inauthentic expression of a virtue requires a comprehensive evaluation of the complex moral event. Ethics fulfills its crucial function when it determines when a judgment fulfills or frustrates a norm, or facilitates or frustrates human dignity. As noted earlier, a principle of Thomas Aquinas recently cited by Pope Francis is apropos. "I earnestly ask that we always recall a teaching of Saint Thomas Aquinas and learn to incorporate it in our pastoral discernment: 'Although there is necessity in the general principles, the more we descend to matters of detail, the more frequently we encounter defects. . . . The principle will be found to fail, according as we descend further into detail'."[88] The devil, as the popular saying goes, is always in the details, and only an informed conscience, which we will discuss in detail in the next chapter, can make a truly ethical judgment about any human action.

IMPLICATIONS OF A VIRTUOUS PERSPECTIVE FOR THE FORMULATION AND JUSTIFICATION OF NORMS

The turn toward the subject in virtue epistemology has implications for the definition of the object, the interrelationship between virtue ethics and

[87]See James F. Keenan, "Proposing Cardinal Virtues," *Theological Studies* 56 (1995): 709–10.
[88]*AL*, no. 304.

normative ethics, and the different types of norms appropriate to virtue ethics and normative ethics. In this final section, we propose some guidelines from a virtuous perspective for the theological ethicist, the SIPI of the sources of ethical knowledge, and the formulation and justification of virtue norms and behavioral norms. We illustrate the different methodological approaches to the SIPI of the sources with an example.

Virtuous Perspective and Catholic Ethicists

We embrace the International Theological Commission's statement on the importance of "the interior dispositions or virtues that render the moralist capable of elaborating an adequate norm of action,"[89] Klaus Demmer's assertion that there is an autobiographical component in the work of the ethicist,[90] and Enda McDonagh's allusion to the ethicist's personal quest for moral truth.[91] For the ethicist, virtue begins at home. It includes epistemic virtues already discussed, both intellectual virtues (like imagination, perception, memory, intuition, introspection) and character virtues (like reliability, responsibility, conscientiousness, carefulness, and open-mindedness), which shape ethicists' perspectives and relational interactions in the process of fulfilling their vocation. To serve both the human and church communities, epistemic virtues invite ethicists to be diligent in their scholarship and committed to ongoing and ever-developing knowledge, understanding, and dialogue. As knowledge becomes more specialized, technical, and prolific, epistemic virtues invite interdisciplinary relationships between ethicists and scholars in other disciplines. Only in this way will they gain insight into the complexity of those disciplines, how they can impact ethics and facilitate greater understanding of human dignity, and how they can be incorporated into ethical discourse to facilitate the definition and attainment of human dignity.

In addition to epistemic virtues, there are other virtues that Catholic ethicists should cultivate. These virtues include, of course, the theological virtues of faith, hope, and love; the cardinal virtues of prudence, justice, temperance, and fortitude; and others such as compassion, empathy, mercy, patience, and solidarity. Pope Francis's call for Christian ministers to smell like the sheep is, we believe, one example of an affirmation of the impor-

---

[89]International Theological Commission, *In Search of a Universal Ethic: A New Look at Natural Law* (May 20, 2009), n. 55, www.vatican.va/roman_curia/congregations/cfaith/cti_documents/rc_con_cfaith_doc_20090520_legge-naturale_en.html.

[90]Klaus Demmer, *Shaping the Moral Life: An Approach to Moral Theology*, ed. James F. Keenan (Washington, DC: Georgetown University Press, 2000), 1.

[91]Enda McDonagh, *Doing the Truth: The Quest for Moral Theology* (Notre Dame: University of Notre Dame Press, 1979), 12–13.

tance of ethnographic studies in developing virtue by sharing the lived experience of people, especially those who often have no voice, the poor, the marginalized, the mentally ill, the disabled, and members of the LGBT community. The explicit goal of this experiential sharing is, first, to deepen the ethicist's imitation of Christ and to enable, second, this Christian perspective to inform and form ethical discourse on the definition of human dignity and the norms that facilitate its attainment.

Virtue epistemology and virtue ethics can provide insight into addressing the differences between conservative and progressive virtue ethicists. First, virtue epistemology's turn toward the subject empowers Catholic ethicists to pursue a dual-component virtue epistemology by seeking an integration between reliabilist and responsibilist accounts of knowledge to discern ethical knowledge and to formulate and justify principles and norms. Catholic ethicists must seek a balance between intellectual virtues that draw from the wisdom and knowledge from the past and character virtues that sustain ongoing cognitive developments. Second, this dual component must ensure freedom, exercised responsibly, to pursue knowledge and address both old ethical questions with fresh perspectives and new ethical questions that inevitably arise. The church should not fear such pursuits but encourage and promote them as a commitment to define and to realize the good in ever-changing historical, cultural, and contextual circumstances. The ethical history of the church has been marred by suspicion, judgment, and even persecution of theologians committed to serving the church. Virtue epistemologists must embrace the virtue of love and presume good faith in all Catholic ethicists in their attempt to live their imitation of Christ through their scholarship. Pope Francis supports this vision of the theologian's vocation.[92] If the church has questions regarding a particular theologian's scholarship, virtue should guide due process in discerning differences and seeking a just and fair resolution to those differences.

Differences between conservative and progressive theological ethicists can be an opportunity for individual and communal growth and development, if they are addressed in a patient dialogue of charity. Such dialogue requires the virtues of justice and civility,[93] humility, patience, and fidelity to the process of dialogue. Perhaps that is where virtue could have the greatest impact initially in toning down the vitriol between different virtuous perspectives and emphasizing what is shared in common rather than what divides. Such dialogue could serve the ongoing discernment of ethical truths

[92]See Carol Glatz, "Pope Francis: Engaging with People's Real Lives Does Not 'Bastardize' Theology," *America* (September 28, 2017), https://www.americamagazine.org/faith/2017/09/28/pope-francis-engaging-peoples-real-lives-does-not-bastardize-theology.

[93]*Dignitatis Humanae*, no. 7 (hereafter *DH*).

that can better serve people on their journey of discipleship and foster communities of discipleship. Truth, the Second Vatican Council rightly taught, "cannot impose itself except by virtue of its own truth, as it makes its way into the mind at once quietly and with power."[94]

The Selection, Interpretation, Prioritization, and Integration (SIPI) of the Sources of Ethical Knowledge and the Formulation and Justification of Norms

In approaching the SIPI of the sources of ethical knowledge, we begin by restating the position we formulated in *The Sexual Person*.

> Though there is a presumption of truth in favor of magisterial teaching, that teaching is to be critically reflected upon in light of theologically sound scriptural exegesis, the reasonable input of the sciences in areas where it has competence, and the cultural, historical, and relational experiences of the faithful, not necessarily in that order. When there is a conflict between these sources, a process of research, dialogue, and discernment must be undertaken to determine right understanding of divine law. This is a complex and involved process, which takes time, patience, and a commitment to dialogue.[95]

We continue to defend this formulation, but we expand on it in light of the progressive virtuous perspective we have developed in this book.

We invite all Catholic ethicists to reflect on those dimensions of virtue we have highlighted throughout this book, to nuance and expand them, and to explore their interrelationship to draw out their anthropological and normative implications. Those dimensions of virtue include the following: an appreciation for neuroscience and the bicameral brain and its impact on virtuous perspectives; a dynamic understanding of virtue individually and communally; the influence on virtue of gender in its patriarchal and egalitarian-feminist paradigms; a holistic appreciation for human development and how virtue impacts all dimensions of the human person adequately considered; the impact of culture on virtue; the importance for ethics of ethnographic studies that engage the complexity of experiential human reality and prevent the incarnation of the gospel message in a one-size-fits-all ethics that has turned the gospel of love, compassion, and mercy into what Pope Francis calls "dead stones to be hurled at others;"[96] the nature of vir-

---

[94]*DH*, no. 1.

[95]Salzman and Lawler, *The Sexual Person*, 214–15.

[96]*AL*, no.49.

tues in relation to the acts traditionally called the "object;" the importance of inductive reasoning when seeking an end and choosing the appropriate behavior to reach that end; deontological and teleological approaches to virtue that appreciate the role and function of rules and consequences in both virtue ethics and human behavior. These dimensions shape the understanding of virtue and indicate responses to the first two questions of virtue ethics: who are we and who do we want to become? They provide a framework to construct a virtuous perspective to define human dignity. In light of the definition of human dignity virtues indicate, through the formulation and justification of norms, a response to the third question: how do we get there?

To avoid unnecessary and divisive methodological debates, care must be taken to distinguish between virtue ethics and normative ethics and their respective norms. For virtue ethics and virtue norms, discerning the interrelationship between the virtues is an ongoing challenge that requires scholarly attention. We have outlined a Christian virtue ethic in Chapter 2. The gospel imperative to "go and do likewise" shapes the Christian virtuous perspective that defines the end sought and controls everything ethical that Christians are called to do to reach that end. The followers of Jesus are invited to imitate him, to *become* and *be* like him, and because they *are* like him to *do* like him. Virtue, we have argued, is learned by imitation, Christian virtue is learned by the imitation of Christ. We are thoroughly persuaded that in Christian virtue ethics the Christian narrative, as it is revealed in scripture and tradition, is the point of departure for shaping a virtuous perspective. When we make the shift from focusing on the object to focusing on the subject, scripture and tradition are to be complemented with human experience, and the secular sciences that help to explain persons and their virtues in their historical, cultural, relational contexts. It is this complexity that allows for the broad parameters of a virtuous perspective and the maintenance of a balance between the universal and particular in the mean of virtue. Both virtue ethics and normative ethics indicate how to reach the end we are seeking. The norms, however, are distinct.

The behavioral norms of virtue ethics are not absolute norms that indicate the *specific* moral act to attain the end. Virtue ethics indicates, rather, an *appropriate* act for reaching the desired end, selected from the continuum that lies between virtuous excess and defect. The behavioral norms of virtue ethics function as guidelines that, depending on the subject's perspective and context, will facilitate attaining the desired end. The virtue norms "be just" and "be compassionate" tell an agent to be just and to be compassionate, but they do not tell him/her the specific just or compassionate action in this contextual situation. The specific action has to be carefully discerned from a SIPI of the four ethical sources. That SIPI of the sources will depend on an agent's perspective, the end he/she seeks, and an appropriate action for attaining the end. An example of two recent perspectives on communion for the divorced and remarried will illustrate conservative and progressive virtuous perspectives, the ends sought, and the appropriate behavior for attaining the end. It will also illustrate the different SIPI of the sources to reach behavioral norms that guide conservative and progressive approaches.

Communion for the Divorced and Remarried

To illustrate different virtuous perspectives, ends sought, and the SIPI of the sources of ethical knowledge to formulate an appropriate behavioral norm for attaining a desired end, we consider a hotly debated Catholic ethical issue that generated heated discussion in the Synods on the Family in 1980, 2014, and 2015. The issue is whether Catholics who are divorced and remarried without annulment can be permitted to receive communion. We present Catholic conservative and progressive positions on this issue to illustrate the differences between the two perspectives on the SIPI of the sources of ethical knowledge. The end sought by both conservative and progressive ethicists in this situation is that the divorced and remarried without annulment be included in the Catholic community in a way that is appropriate for their current marital status. What divides them are the virtues that guide them in defining what it means to be included in the Catholic community, in a way that is appropriate for their current marital and ethical status, and how they formulate and justify norms to indicate the appropriate inclusion.

Prioritizing the virtue of submission as obedience to ecclesial authority, conservative ethicists begin with tradition narrowly restricted to magisterial teaching. They advance the Congregation for the Doctrine of the Faith's teaching about divorce and remarriage without annulment, prioritizing its claim that this teaching is mandated by "fidelity to the words of Jesus Christ" in Mark 10:11–12. The implication they advance is that, since the teaching is based on fidelity to the gospel words of Jesus, as interpreted by the Magisterium, Catholic doctrine about divorce and remarriage is irreformable and must be obeyed. That argument would be true, progressive ethicists respond, if the teaching of Jesus cited from Mark was the only teaching in the New Testament on divorce and remarriage; but it is not.

Turning to scripture as a source of ethical knowledge, progressive ethicists note that the New Testament has five reports of words of Jesus about divorce and remarriage (Mk 10:11–12; Mt 5:32, 19:9; Lk 16:18; 1 Cor 7:10–11). What is noteworthy about these five reports, they point out, is that they are not all in agreement, and they are not all derived from Jesus. Paul reports a prohibition by Jesus of divorce and remarriage (1 Cor 7:10–11) but immediately nuances it in the situation of his own churches (7:12–16). That nuance, permitting divorce and remarriage, passed into the law of the Roman Catholic Church as the Pauline Privilege. Matthew also nuances Jesus's word with his own genuine Jewish exception (5:32; 19:9) to Jesus's received words, though we agree that the meaning of that exception "is not self-evident to modern interpreters."[97] Jewish Matthew's formulation in 19:6 is enlightening: "What therefore God has joined together, *let not man put asunder*." That "*let not* man put asunder," progressives argue, is a far cry from the church's "man *cannot* put asunder."

These divergent accounts, progressive ethicists continue, exist because divergent Christian communities had divergent concerns about marriage and divorce that needed resolution and divergent perspectives on how to resolve them. The nuancing of the words of Jesus on the basis of contextual need, begun by Paul and the early church, was continued in the sixteenth-century church by Popes Paul III (1537), Pius V (1561), and Gregory XIII (1585), and their nuances permitting divorce and remarriage passed into Catholic history under the misleading heading of the Petrine Privilege.[98] This constant nuancing of the words of Jesus in the church makes any argument based exclusively on the Markan words of Jesus at best narrow and partial, and at worst dishonest. Because divergent instructions on divorce and remarriage, deriving not only from Jesus but also from Paul and Matthew and the sixteenth-century church, are part of the received tradition in the Catholic Church, any effort to allow one instruction to override all the others as *the* word of God falsifies God's word and should be discontinued.

Canon 8, progressive ethicists continue, of the much-venerated Council of Nicea (325), which firmly established the essential doctrine of the Catholic faith in its Creed, also established a doctrine on divorce and remarriage contrary to the words of Jesus, which it must have known.

> As regards those who define themselves as the "Pure" and who want to join the Catholic and Apostolic Church, the holy and great Council decrees that they may remain among the clergy once hands have been imposed upon them. But beforehand they will have to promise in writing to comply with the teachings of the Catholic and Apostolic Church and to make them the rule of their conduct. That is to say, they will have to communicate both with *those who married a second time* (*digamoi*) and with those who failed under persecution but whose time

[97]Raymond F. Collins, *Divorce in the New Testament* (Collegeville, MN: Liturgical Press, 1992), 205.

[98]See Michael G. Lawler, *Marriage and Sacrament: A Theology of Christian Marriage* (Collegeville, MN: Liturgical Press, 1993), 92–93.

> has been established and whose moment of reconciliation has arrived. They will, therefore, be bound to follow the teaching of the Catholic and Apostolic Church completely.[99]

According to this canon, the pure, those who belonged to the rigorous sect called Novatians,[100] had to promise in writing to accept the teaching of the Catholic Church before they could be reconciled with it. Specifically, they had to accept its teaching concerning those who had been married twice (*digamoi*) and had to agree to live in communion with the twice-married after they had completed a period of penance and had been reconciled to the Catholic Church.

According to the Council, what the Novatians considered the "sin" of remarriage can be forgiven, and reconciliation with the church can be achieved after suitable penance. Acutely relevant is the fact that neither the church before Nicea nor the Council itself required the repudiation of the new spouse as a prerequisite for forgiveness and reconciliation. This was in keeping with the proscriptions of Deuteronomy 24:1–4, which was taken to be binding in the church before Nicea and which forbade a husband to take back his first wife after she had married another.[101] The eastern Father of the Church, Basil, reports the treatment of a man who had abandoned his wife and remarried; who had "done penance with tears"; and who, after seven years, had been accepted back "among the faithful."[102] The man's second marriage is accepted, and neither the repudiation of his second wife nor his taking back of the first is demanded as a prerequisite for full communion. Basil's teaching, we explain, is the foundation for the ongoing practice of the Orthodox Church known as *oikonomia*.

The Synod on the Family in 1980 presented to Pope John Paul II a request that the Orthodox practice of *oikonomia* be studied for any light it might shed on an approach to Roman Catholics who are divorced and remarried without annulment. Many of those second marriages, the Synod noted, have become so stable, and the families nurtured in them so experientially Christian, that they cannot be abandoned without serious spiritual, personal, and economic harm. It is surely past time, progressives argue, for the church to respond to that synodal request and to consider whether its understanding of the mercy, compassion, and love of Jesus permits or

---

[99]J. D. Mansi, ed., *Sacrorum Conciliorum Nova et Amplissima Collectio* (Paris: Welter, 1903–1927), II, 672, emphasis added.

[100]See Charles J. Hefele, *History of the Christian Councils* (Edinburgh, Scotland: Clark, 1883), I, 410.

[101]See, for instance, Origen, *Comm. in Matt. XIV*, 20, *Patrologia Graeca* 13, 1237; Cyril of Alexandria, *The Adoration and Worship of God in Spirit and Truth*, VIII, *Patrologia Graeca* 68, 584; Jerome, *Epist. ad Amandum*, 4, *Patrologia Latina* 22, 563.

[102]Basil, *Patrologia Graeca* 32, 804–5.

precludes an *oikonomia* approach to its members in second marriages without annulment. The feeling of the 1980 Synod was that it did not preclude such an approach. It is time for the church, progressive ethicists argue, to abandon its predominantly letter-of-the-law approach to the divorced and remarried; to respond with the gospel virtues of love, mercy, and compassion to the Synod's request and the demonstrated suffering of thousands of its members in stable second marriages; and to find an *oikonomia* approach that permits Catholics remarried without annulment to receive communion.

Conservative ethicists object that fidelity to the words of Jesus is not the only reason the Roman Catholic Church holds marriage to be indissoluble. There is also the law of the church that prescribes that "the essential properties of *marriage* are unity and indissolubility" (Canon 1056, emphasis added). The church would be violating its own law if it recognized the validity of second marriages after divorce without annulment. If the church truly believed that indissolubility was an essential property of marriage, and that by the will of God "from the beginning" (Mk 10:6; Mt 19:4), progressive ethicists respond, then it would treat all marriages as indissoluble. It does not and never has. It accepts the marriages of the nonbaptized as valid when they have been performed according to the laws that govern them and yet, utilizing the Pauline Privilege, it regularly dissolves them "in favor of the faith of the party who received baptism" (Canon 1143). It has further extended the Pauline Privilege in history to embrace the method of dissolving valid marriages established, without any gospel precedent, by sixteenth-century popes and, therefore, named the Petrine Privilege.[103] In Christian marriages, it teaches that indissolubility acquires "a distinctive firmness by reason of the sacrament" (Canon 1056), and yet valid sacramental marriages that have not been consummated are dissolved "by the Roman Pontiff for a just reason, at the request of both parties or of either party" (Canon 1142). Long-standing church practice with respect to the dissolution of valid marriages demonstrates anything but a belief that an essential property of all marriages is indissolubility. The actual teaching of the Western Catholic Church is that only the marriage "which is ratified [as sacrament] *and* consummated cannot be dissolved by any human power other than death" (Canon 1141). The two conditions that make a marriage absolutely indissoluble in the eyes of the Catholic Church, that it be simultaneously sacramental *and* consummated, are not conditions ever mentioned or even insinuated by Jesus. They are both the result of historical church nuancing long after Jesus, despite the patently historically false teaching of the *Catechism* that "the marriage bond has been established by

---

[103]See Michael G. Lawler, *Marriage and Sacrament: A Theology of Christian Marriage* (Collegeville, MN: Liturgical Press, 1993), 92–94.

God himself in such a way that a marriage concluded *and consummated* between baptized persons can never be dissolved."[104] That the marriage bond becomes indissoluble, even in a sacramental marriage, only when the marriage is sexually consummated is, as historians well know, not God's law but a law added by the Italian canonist Gratian and the Roman Church in the twelfth century.[105]

In his letter announcing the Jubilee Year in 2016, Pope Francis writes that "the Church's very credibility is seen in how she shows merciful and compassionate love." This virtuous perspective and the shift in focus from law and obedience to the virtues of love, mercy, and compassion are evident again in his apostolic exhortation, *Amoris Laetitia*. His footnote 351, strangely not placed in the text itself, offers the possibility that couples could be admitted to communion in certain circumstances. In keeping with his general theme of love, mercy, and compassion, he points out that the Eucharist "is not a prize for the perfect but a powerful medicine and nourishment for the weak."[106] He stops short of a blanket permission for the admission to communion of the divorced and remarried without annulment, but he leaves admission open in carefully discerned pastoral cases. He does not automatically open the door to a change in *doctrinal* teaching, but he lets us know where the *pastoral* key to the door is. It is under the mat of a virtuous perspective that includes gospel love, mercy, and compassion, and that guides the SIPI of the sources of ethical knowledge that allow for plural perspectives, guided by an internal-forum discernment, and the decision of an informed conscience. It is to conscience and choosing the good that we now direct our attention.

[104]*Catechism of the Catholic Church*, no. 1640, emphasis added.

[105]For a full analysis of the theology involved in the issue of divorce and remarriage without annulment, see Michael G. Lawler and Todd A. Salzman, "Catholic Doctrine on Divorce and Remarriage: A Practical Theological Examination," *Theological Studies* 78 (2017): 326–47.

[106]*AL*, footnote 351.

6

Conscience and Virtuous Perspective

Choosing the Good

In this chapter, we focus on choosing the good and the practical moral judgment called conscience, and argue for the authority of individual conscience in general and for the authority of the theological ethicist's conscience in particular. The Catholic ethicist, in communion with the People-of-God-in-Communion, seeks to develop a methodology and anthropology, and to formulate and justify moral principles and norms that facilitate the attainment of human dignity.

CONSCIENCE

In the thirteenth century, Thomas Aquinas, who developed and shaped the Catholic theological tradition more than any other theologian, established the inviolability of conscience in memorable words. "Anyone upon whom the ecclesiastical authorities, in ignorance of the true facts, impose a demand that offends against his clear conscience, should perish in excommunication rather than violate his conscience."[1] For any person in search of truth, no clearer statement on the inviolability of personal conscience could be found. Aquinas goes further and insists that even the dictate of a mistaken conscience must be followed and that to act against such a dictate is immoral. In this context, he offers an argument that has often been repeated: "To believe in Christ is good in itself and necessary for salvation; all this does not win the will unless it be recommended by reason."[2]

Seven hundred years later the Second Vatican Council's *Gaudium et Spes* issued a clarion cry with respect to conscience.

[1]Thomas Aquinas, *In IV Sent.*, dist. 38, q. 2, art. 4.

[2]Thomas Aquinas, *Summa Theologiae*, I-II, 19, 5 (hereafter *ST*).

> Man has in his heart a law inscribed by God. To obey it is the very dignity of man; according to it he will be judged. Conscience is the most secret core and sanctuary of man. There he is alone with God whose voice echoes in his depth. In a wonderful manner conscience reveals that law which is fulfilled by love of God and neighbor. In fidelity to conscience, Christians are joined with the rest of men in search for truth, and for the genuine solution to so many moral problems which arise both in the life of individuals and from social relationships.[3]

Dignitatis Humanae, the Council's Decree on Religious Freedom, went further to assert the inviolability of conscience.

> In all his activity a man is bound to follow his conscience faithfully, in order that he may come to God, for whom he was created. It follows that he is not to be forced to act in a manner contrary to his conscience. Nor, on the other hand, is he to be restrained from acting in accordance with his conscience, especially in matters religious. For, of its very nature, the exercise of religion consists before all else in those internal, voluntary, and free acts whereby man sets the course of his life directly toward God. No merely human power can either command or prohibit acts of this kind.[4]

In the 1960s, these were seldom-heard words in Catholic magisterial circles, but the undoubted reality is that they are ideas deeply rooted in the Catholic moral tradition and, indeed, are constitutive of it.

From Aquinas, we learn that conscience is related to reason, and its understanding is situated in Aquinas's anthropology. Closely following Aristotle, he considers the human person to be a being endowed with a body and a rational soul that vivifies it as human. Reason distinguishes humans from all other animals, and the rational soul has two powers, intellect and will, intimately related and involved in the process of knowledge. All knowledge begins with experience[5] and proceeds through understanding to judgment and decision, which is then actualized in action. Conscience is the act of practical judgment that something is right or wrong, good or bad, to be done or not done. It acts in two ways. "In one, we are directed through the disposition of knowledge to do or not to do something. In the other, the actualization is tested, after it has taken place, by the disposition

---

[3] *Gaudium et Spes*, no. 16 (hereafter *GS*).

[4] *Dignitatis Humanae*, no. 3 (hereafter *DH*).

[5] See *ST*, I, 79, 2. For an excellent summary, see Kenneth L. Schmitz, "St. Thomas and the Appeal to Experience," *Proceedings of the Catholic Theological Society of America*, 47 (1992): 1–20.

of knowledge, for whether it be right or not right."[6] In other words, conscience illumines us to do or not to do something and, when something has been done, "conscience is said to accuse or worry us if what has occurred is found to be out of accord with the knowledge by which it was tested, and to defend or excuse us if what has occurred is found to have turned out in accordance with the piece of knowledge."[7] Conscience, Robert Smith asserts, is "the act of practical judgment on a particular moral issue . . . that commands us to do this or not to do that."[8]

Following James Halstead's dissertation on conscience,[9] Smith makes a distinction between what he calls a, "man-in-relationship-to-law" model of conscience and a "restless-heart-toward-God" model.[10] He offers as exemplars of these two models, Germain Grisez and Bernard Häring, respectively. Grisez holds that the only way to form one's conscience is to *conform* it to the teaching of the church.[11] Ultimately, though Grisez waxes enthusiastically about human freedom; conscience is about obedience to church teaching. Pope John Paul II follows this same approach in his *Familiaris Consortio*, which is wholly rooted in both the truth of sexuality and marriage *as taught by the church* and the obligation of the laity to make that truth their own and to obey it. Almost nowhere in the document does the church's teaching on the inviolable primacy of individual conscience, even in sexual matters, appear. Häring is diametrically opposed to that perspective. In the context of his overall approach to theological ethics, conscience, "man's innermost yearning toward 'wholeness' which manifests itself in openness to neighbor and community in a common searching for goodness and truth,"[12] must be free and inviolable, and "the Church must affirm the freedom of conscience *itself*."[13] Church doctrine is at the service of women and men in their conscience who search for goodness, truth, and Christian wholeness. "It staggers the imagination," Häring writes, "to think that an earthly authority or an ecclesiastical Magisterium could take away from man his own decision of conscience."[14]

---

[6]Aquinas, *Disputed Questions*, 131.

[7]Ibid.

[8]Robert J. Smith, *Conscience and Catholicism: The Nature and Function of Conscience in Contemporary Roman Catholic Theology* (Lanham, MD: University Press of America, 1998), 12.

[9]James Halstead, *Conscience, the American Bishops and the Renewal of Moral Theology: The Notion of Conscience in the Pastoral Letters of the American Bishops* (University of Louvain, Doctoral Dissertation, 1986).

[10]Smith, *Conscience and Catholicism*, 65.

[11]Germain Grisez, *The Way of the Lord Jesus. Vol. 1, Christian Moral Principles* (Chicago: Franciscan Herald Press, 1983), 567.

[12]Bernard Häring, *A Theology of Protest* (New York: Farrar, Strauss, and Giroux, 1970), 65.

[13]Häring, *Free and Faithful in Christ: Moral Theology for Priests and Laity,* Vol. 1 (New York: Seabury, 1978), emphasis in original.

[14]Häring, *The Christian Existentialist: The Philosophy and Theology of Self-Fulfillment in Modern*

There is an important corollary that flows from the foregoing. One lone theological voice, whether it be that of Aquinas, Grisez, Häring, or Pope John Paul II speaking noninfallibly, does not make a tradition. If a sincere and good conscience is inviolable, then the sincere and good consciences of theologians, like Grisez and Häring, are inviolable. Both perspectives must acknowledge this Catholic conscience tradition, cease their mutual condemnations, and open themselves to honest dialogue in the search to expand and deepen their understandings of moral goodness and truth. Pope Francis is profoundly pertinent here:

> Differing currents of thought in philosophy, theology, and pastoral practice, if open to being reconciled by the Spirit in respect and love, can enable the Church to grow, since all of them help to express more clearly the immense riches of God's word. For those who long for a monolithic body of doctrine guarded by all and leaving no room for nuance, this might appear as undesirable and leading to confusion, But, in fact, such variety serves to bring out and develop different facets of the inexhaustible riches of the Gospel.[15]

Conscience comes at the end of a thoroughly rational process, which is a cognitional process of experience, understanding, judgment, and decision. This process includes acts of both powers of the soul, that is, intellect and will. It also includes a natural, innate grasp of moral principles that Aquinas calls *synderesis*.[16] He never makes these principles clear anywhere, but Jean Porter argues, and we agree, that these first principles of practical reason are self-evident and that Aquinas's "general theory of goodness requires him to hold that the first principle of practical reasoning is self-evident to all."[17] To make a decision of conscience on an ethical question involves a reliable grasp of these first principles of practical judgment, a responsible gathering of as much evidence as possible, a weighing and understanding of the evidence and its moral implications, and finally a conscientious and honest judgment that this action is to be done and that action is not. A moral action is one that comes as the outcome of such a process. It is commonplace theologically to insist that, in order to be right and moral, conscience must be informed, and that formation is precisely the process from gathering informational evidence to judgment we have just outlined.

Since conscience is a practical judgment that comes at the end of a de-

---

Society (New York University Press, 1968), 63.

15 *Evangelii Gaudium*, no. 40.

16 *ST*, I, 79, 13.

17 Jean Porter, *The Recovery of Virtue: The Relevance of Aquinas for Christian Ethics* (Louisville KY: Westminster/John Knox, 1990), 85–86.

liberative process about the relationship of means to ends, it necessarily involves the virtue of prudence, the virtue by which "right reason is applied to action."[18] Aquinas locates prudence in the intellect[19] together with *synderesis* and *conscientia. Synderesis* provides the first principles of practical reason; prudence discerns those principles, applies them to particular situations, and enables conscience to make the practical judgment that this is the right thing to do on this occasion, toward this person, and with this good intention.[20] Prudence, therefore, needs to know "both the general moral principles of reason and the individual situation in which a human action takes place."[21] A central element of virtue, Aristotle insists, is that it is the result of deliberation and judgment that are always about means, never about ends. It is the task of prudence to monitor the process of deliberation and judgment to ensure that this is the right occasion, the right person, and the right good intention for compassion toward and aid of the poor, for example. As prudence controls the right exercise of compassion toward the poor, so also does it control and integrate the exercise of all other moral virtues. It is, as we explained in Chapter 2, a *cardinal* virtue around which all other virtues pivot, integrating both agents and their actions.[22] Because prudence controls the judgments that precede the exercise of all other virtues, and must precede them if those virtues are to be moral, Aquinas holds that "no moral virtue can be possessed without prudence, since it is proper to moral virtue to make a right choice."[23]

Unfortunately, given human weakness, all judgments, even the most prudential practical judgments of conscience, can be in error. That raises the question of the possibly erroneous conscience noted above, and so we need to introduce some important distinctions. Ethicists note that there are two poles in every moral judgment. It is always a free, rational human *subject* who makes a judgment, and so one pole of the judgment is a subjective pole. But every subject makes a judgment about some objective reality, poverty or homosexual activity, for instance, and so there is always also an objective pole. The subject arrives at his/her judgment either by following the rational process outlined above or by negligently shortchanging that process. In the first case, the subject arrives at a right moral understanding and conscience judgment about the object; in the second case, the subject arrives at a wrong or erroneous understanding and conscience judgment about the object. The subject follows the practical judgment of conscience

[18] *ST*, II-II, 47, 5.
[19] *ST*, II-II, 47, 1.
[20] See *ST*, II-II, 47, 6.
[21] See *ST*, II-II, 47, 3.
[22] See *ST*, I-II, 61, 2 and 3.
[23] *ST*, I-II, 65, 1.

by the practical decision to do or not to do something about the object, to give or not to give alms to the poor, for instance. If that decision flows from a right understanding and judgment about the object, then conscience is also said to be good; if it flows from an erroneous understanding and judgment, then conscience is also said to be erroneous.

If the rational error of understanding and judgment can be ascribed to some moral fault on the part of the subject, taking "little trouble to find out what is true and good,"[24] for instance, or negligent failure to be sufficiently attentive to the necessary experience, to gather the necessary evidence, to engage in the necessary deliberation, to take the necessary advice, then the wrong understanding and the practical judgment of conscience flowing from it are both deemed to be culpable and cannot be morally followed. If the error cannot be ascribed to some moral fault on the part of the subject, then both the understanding and the practical judgment of conscience flowing from it are deemed to be nonculpable and not only can but must be followed, even contrary to ecclesiastical authority, as we saw Aquinas argue above. Subjects are bound not only *to conscience* but also *for* conscience, that is, they must do all in their power to ensure that conscience is good; any negligence in the search for objective goodness is immoral. There is one final distinction to be added here. The ethics of an action is largely controlled by the subject's intention. A good intention, giving alms to the poor *because* the poor need help and to help them is the right thing to do, results in a moral action. A bad intention, giving alms to the poor *because* I want to be seen and to be praised by men (Mt 6:2, 5) will result in an immoral action. The object or act, giving alms to the poor, is always a right act; the subject's intention determines whether or not it is also a moral or immoral act.

A decision of good conscience is clearly a complex process. It is also a private, *individual* process; but it is far from an *individualistic* process. The Latin word *con-scientia* literally means knowledge together, perhaps better rendered as to know together. It suggests what human experience universally demonstrates, that being freed from the confining prison of one's individual self into the challenging company of others is a surer way to come to right knowledge of ethical truth and right moral judgment, of what one ought to do or not to do. This community basis of the search for truth, conscience, and moral action builds a sure safeguard against both an isolating egoism and a personal relativism that negates all universal truth. The community foundation of consciences has been part of the Christian tradition since Paul, who clearly believed in the inviolability and primacy of conscience (1 Cor 10:25–27; 2 Cor 1:12; 4:2; 1Ti 1:5) and who wrote to his Corinthian Christians that the "stronger" members of the community

---

[24]*GS*, no. 16.

in conscience should be sensitive to and careful of the "weaker" members whose consciences might easily be "defiled" by the stronger conscience's most conscientious actions (1 Cor 8:7–13). Häring calls this community dimension of conscience "the reciprocity of consciences."[25]

At this point a final and sometimes-pressing question arises. Among the many communities to which Catholics belong is the Catholic Church, but when we try to make that statement theologically clearer by asking what is specifically meant by "church" it actually becomes less clear, for there are several distinct meanings of church in contemporary Catholic theology.[26] For our purpose here, we isolate only two major ones. Between the two Vatican Councils, from 1870 to 1964, the dominant understanding was of church as a hierarchical institution. In 1964, with the publication of the Second Vatican Council's Constitution on the Church, *Lumen Gentium*, a new model, or more accurately a *renewed* model, became available, an understanding of church as a People-of-God-in-Communion.[27] Yves Congar, arguably the greatest ecclesiologist of the twentieth century, demonstrates that the communion model of church "prevailed during the first thousand years of Christianity and the hierarchical model dominated in the West between the eleventh-century reformation and Vatican II."[28]

These two models continue to be available to anyone who asks about church teaching and conscience, and they fuel disagreements on the answer to the final question of this section. That question is how are Catholics to behave in conscience when their understanding of a noninfallible magisterial teaching differs from that proposed by the Magisterium, as is now the case for the majority of Catholic faithful, for instance, on the issues of divorce and remarriage, contraception, and homosexual behavior?[29] Congar points out that historically when the church is conceived as a hierarchical institution, obedience to church authority is called for; when it is conceived as a communion, dialogue and consensus are called for.[30] These two ecclesiological perspectives coincide well with our discussion of conservative and progressive virtuous perspectives. Conservative ethicists, like Germain Grisez, Martin Rhonheimer, and Pope John Paul II, who conceive church as a hierarchical institution, continue to prioritize the virtue of obedience to tradition narrowly defined as magisterial teaching as a source of knowledge for

---

[25]Bernard Häring, *Free and Faithful in Christ. Moral Theology for Clergy and Laity* (New York: Crossroad, 1981), 2:25.

[26]See Avery Dulles, *Models of the Church* (New York: Doubleday, 1974).

[27]*Lumen Gentium*, nos. 9–17.

[28]Yves Congar, "Reception as an Ecclesiological Reality," in *Election and Consensus in the Church*, ed. Giuseppe Alberigo and Anton Weiler, *Concilium 77* (New York: Herder and Herder, 1972), 62.

[29]For detail on these differences, see Univision Communications, *Global Survey of Roman Catholics* (New York: February 2014).

[30]Congar, "Reception as an Ecclesiological Reality," 62.

reaching ethical truth. Progressive theologians, like Yves Congar, Bernard Häring, and us, who conceive church as a People-of-God-in-Communion, prioritize the virtues of prudence and personal responsibility in dialogue to discern communal consensus on ethical truth. Having respectfully and seriously considered magisterial teaching and deliberated the theological evidence supporting it, we argue, the individual is inviolably free in conscience to make his/her own personal choice about what to believe or not to believe, about what to do or not to do.

Having made a practical judgment and decision of conscience, the church teaches, as we explained at the opening of this section, no Catholic is "to be forced to act in a manner contrary to his conscience. Nor . . . is he to be restrained from acting in accordance with his conscience, especially in matters religious"[31] and, we might add, moral. Theologian Joseph Ratzinger, long before he became Pope Benedict XVI, points out that "not everything that exists in the Church must for that reason be also a legitimate tradition. . . . There is a distorting as well as legitimate tradition." The long adherence of the church to teachings on the taking of interest on loans, slavery, and religious freedom are well-known examples of distorting traditions that it now rejects. Ratzinger concludes to what is obvious: "consequently tradition must not be considered only affirmatively but also critically."[32] The *Catechism of the Catholic Church* repeats the teaching of the Second Vatican Council and places both the Council's and the church's teaching beyond doubt: men and women have "the right to act in conscience and in freedom so as personally to make moral decisions."[33] A well-informed, and therefore well formed, conscience is undoubtedly the Catholic way to choosing the true and the good.

GAUDIUM ET SPES, HUMAN EXPERIENCE, AND ETHICAL METHOD

Gaudium et Spes has two parts. Part One (nos. 1–45) deals with the situation of women and men in the world and the message the church has for them and for the contemporary world in which they live. Part Two (nos. 47–93) deals with "some problems of special urgency," specifically marriage and family, culture, economic, social, and political life, and the bonds between nations, particularly peace. Paragraph 46 stands as a transition between the two parts. It states,

[31] *DH*, no. 3.

[32] Joseph Ratzinger, "The Transmission of Divine Revelation," in *Commentary on the Documents of Vatican II*," vol 3, ed. Herbert Vorgrimler (New York: Herder, 1969), 185.

[33] *Catechism of the Catholic Church*, no. 1782.

> This council has set forth the dignity of the human person and the work which men have been destined to undertake throughout the world both as individuals and as members of society. There are a number of particularly urgent needs characterizing the present age, needs which go to the roots of the human race. To a consideration of these *in the light of the Gospel and of human experience*, the Council would now direct the attention of all.[34]

Joseph Selling writes that this paragraph "stands as a milestone in the evolution of Roman Catholic moral theology,"[35] because it initiates a monumental methodological shift in Catholic ethical method. That shift roots Catholic ethics in both the gospel *and* human experience. Traditional Catholic theological ethics, as we explained in Chapter 1, was and continues to be rooted in natural law, the "participation of the eternal law in the rational creature,"[36] and humans know this natural law through right reason. Prior to the Second Vatican Council, the emphasis on the knowledge of natural law and its contents in sexual ethics was through reason's reflection on *biological* animal nature. Both reason and *human* nature were often defined narrowly in terms of the biological order. Norms were then formulated that facilitated attaining this biological definition of human nature. *Gaudium et Spes* expanded this narrow, biological approach and focused more broadly on the human person, inaugurating a methodological revolution in how to discern truth in the Catholic tradition, though it is more correct to say that the Council's approach is more a return to Aquinas's understanding of right reason rather than a revolution.

It is significant that paragraph 46 of *Gaudium et Spes* includes "human experience" as an essential source of ethical knowledge. Human experience both reflects Aquinas's right reason more adequately and embraces the totality of right-hemisphere inclinations to know and understand the whole of a reality in the process of discerning truth.[37] This whole includes a comprehensive understanding of reality including the attention, understanding, judgment, and decision that go to make up a comprehensive understanding of the dignity of the human person spiritually, relationally, psychologically, emotionally, physically, and intellectually.[38] Since these understandings are always finite, since humans are notoriously finite knowers, there will

---

[34]*GS*, no.46.

[35] Joseph Selling, "*Gaudium et Spes*: A Manifesto for Contemporary Moral Theology," in Leo Kenis and Matthew Lamberigts, eds., *Vatican II and Its Legacy* (Leuven: Peters, 2003), 151.

[36]*ST, I–II, q. 91, a. 2.*

[37]Richard M. Gula, *Reason Informed by Faith: Foundations of Catholic Morality* (Mahwah, NJ: Paulist Press, 1989), 224.

[38]Selling, "*Gaudium et Spes*," 151.

always be partial perspectives on and definitions of the whole of a reality. A well-formed conscience gives these partial definitions ethical authority, and *Gaudium et Spes* provides methodological components to guide in their ongoing comprehension. Human experience, then, in light of the gospel and a holistically understood human nature, allows us to judge certain actions as right or wrong. We offer here just one example among many in which human experience changed ecclesial norms, the example of slavery. Only in 1890 did Pope Leo XIII, after two hundred years of negative human experience of, resistance to, and revolution against slavery, reject the ecclesial norm judging slavery to be moral.

Contemporary progressive ethicists acknowledge experience as a central source of ethical truth.[39] Both conservative and progressive ethicists, however, are challenged to discern which human experience may lead to the formulation, perhaps the transformation, of moral principles and norms and which human experience is to be judged by those principles and norms. The former is authentic human experience that leads to human flourishing; the latter is inauthentic human experience that does not lead to human flourishing. We consider three types of experience as a concrete way of separating authentic and inauthentic experience.

One type of experience that provides a basis of reflection for the construction of an ethical method is cultural experience.[40] "Thanks to the experience of past ages, the progress of the sciences, and the treasures hidden in the various forms of human culture," *Gaudium et Spes* teaches, "the nature of man himself is more clearly revealed and new roads to truth are opened." It adds that "from the beginning of [the church's] history, she has learned to express the message of Christ with the help of the ideas and terminology of various peoples," [41] that is, with the help of cultural experience. It is undoubtedly true that the church is called on occasion to be countercultural, to confront cultural theories and actions that do not lead to human flourishing, the rabid individualism rampant in every capitalist culture, for example, and the too-easy availability of abortion for purely selfish reasons. It is also undoubtedly and equally true that reflection on cultural experience can lead to insight into ethical truth and facilitate the communication of that truth within a culture and from one culture to another. The pastoral letters of the bishops of the United States on the economy and nuclear war are examples of the dialectic between culture and the development of moral norms. These letters draw on the traditional Catholic principles of justice to formulate

[39] For example, see John Giles Milhaven, "Objective Moral Evaluation of Consequences," *Theological Studies* 32 (1971): 421–30.

[40] See Todd A. Salzman, *What Are They Saying About Catholic Ethical Method?* (New York: Paulist Press, 1989), 48–79.

[41] *GS*, no. 44.

culturally specific norms, but the understanding of justice they evince is transformed in light of the cultural experiences to which they respond.

Another type of experience is scientific experience and the expansion of scientific knowledge, where new discoveries challenge traditional moral norms based on inaccurate or incomplete scientific knowledge and raise new ethical questions that require new answers. Some answers will be drawn from traditional moral principles but in a new, nuanced way that will lead to the formulation of new norms and criteria. A current and widely debated question is what is and what is not an ethical use of medical technologies to begin, sustain, restore, or end life. The successful mapping of the human genome is making possible genetic engineering. Is it ethical to use such engineering to eliminate, for instance, Huntington's disease? What about beginning-of-life decisions in the case of a fetus with an incurable defect or end-of-life decisions in the case of a person in a persistent vegetative state? What about health insurance for those who can and cannot afford it? What about the Catholic principle of the common good in such cases? Ethical reflection on, and responses to, these questions may generate new moral insight and lead to new moral norms.

A third type of experience is the experience of the socioeconomic oppression of the poor in Latin America that led to what was called liberation theology and further led to a variety of feminist theologies that grew out of reflection on the universal experience of gender oppression.[42] "Feminist ethics," Lisa Sowle Cahill asserts, "begins with the particular, with practice, with experience, with the situation—but out of the particular (not over against it) feminists recognize what furthers or damages 'full humanity' for women and men."[43] The experience of women, past and present, challenges the moral norms that oppress them by challenging, for instance, the very definition of authentic personhood. Any norm that proscribes women, the impossibility of their ordination to the priesthood, for instance, is a norm that requires, at the very least, serious reconsideration.

All three of these categories of experience require criteria for determining what is and what is not authentic experience leading to human flourishing and fulfillment. All theologians, aware of theological history, agree that adjustment or reversal of moral norms is possible, but they disagree about the criteria for such adjustment. Conservative theologians, following a line we have seen clearly demarcated by Pope Pius X, hold that the Magisterium

---

[42]See, for instance, Charles E. Curran et al., *Readings in Moral Theology No. 9: Feminist Ethics and the Catholic Moral Tradition* (New York: Paulist Press, 1996).

[43]Lisa Sowle Cahill, "Feminist Ethics, Differences, and Common Ground: A Catholic Perspective," in *Feminist Ethics in the Catholic Moral Tradition*, ed. Charles Curran et al. (Mahwah: Paulist Press, 1996), 185. See also Lisa Sowle Cahill's *Sex, Gender, and Christian Ethics* (Cambridge: Cambridge University Press, 1996) for her emphasis on experience in developing a credible sexual ethic.

is the only authority to judge such development and adjustment.[44] No matter how rational the argument grounded in experience, scripture, tradition, and science to reverse a gender-oppressive norm, the ordination of women to the priesthood, for example, conservative theologians conform to magisterial teaching.[45] Progressive theologians, on the other hand, while acknowledging, respecting, and appreciating the role of the Magisterium to speak on theological questions, do not acknowledge it as the ultimate determinant of ethical truth regardless of contrary discernment of the sources of ethical knowledge. Catholic history abundantly justifies such caution.[46]

It is now time to clarify again what we mean by experience. The experience we speak of, with Neil Brown, intends the "capacity to encounter the surrounding world consciously, to observe it, to be affected by it, and to learn from it."[47] It is of the essence of such experience that it is never a pure, unadulterated encounter with the world. It is always interpreted, construed, socially constructed by both individuals and communities in specific socio-historical contexts. It is, therefore, also dialectical, differently construed, perhaps, by "me," by "you," by "us," and by "them," by conservative and progressive theologians, for instance. For human experience as we have defined it, the dialectic is necessarily a "dialectic of reason *and* experience" and never a dialectic controlled by either reason or experience alone. It is a dialectic that results not in an absolutist moral code but in "various revisable rules."[48] In a church that is the People-of-God-in-Communion,[49] the resolution of different construals of experience to arrive at ethical truth requires an open, respectful, charitable, and prayerful dialogue, such as that we have several times seen lauded by Pope John Paul II.[50] Charitable dialogue must occur in the People of God, some of whom are laïty, some of whom are theologians, and some of whom are bishops including the Bishop of Rome,[51] all of whom acquire knowledge through practice or action,[52] that is,

---

[44]See Grisez, *Christian Moral Principles*, 10–11.

[45]See Germain Grisez, *The Way of the Lord Jesus. Volume Two: Living a Christian Life* (Quincy, IL: Franciscan Herald Press, 1993), 387–89.

[46]John T. Noonan, *A Church That Can and Cannot Change: The Development of Catholic Moral Teaching* (Notre Dame, IN: Notre Dame University Press, 2005).

[47]Neil Brown, "Experience and Development in Catholic Moral Theology," *Pacifica* 14 (2001): 300.

[48]Edward Collins Vacek, "Catholic 'Natural Law' and Reproductive Ethics," *Journal of Medicine and Philosophy* 17 (1992): 342–43.

[49]For the explanation of church as communion, see J. M. R. Tillard, *Church of Churches: The Ecclesiology of Church as Communion* (Collegeville, MN: Liturgical Press, 1992); Michael G. Lawler and Thomas J. Shanahan, *Church: A Spirited Communion* (Collegeville, MN: Liturgical Press, 1995).

[50]*Ut Unum Sint*, nos. 28–39. See Todd A. Salzman and Michael G. Lawler, "Theologians and the Magisterium: A Proposal for a Complementarity of Charisms through Dialogue," *Horizons* 36 (2009): 7–31.

[51]We shall use this tripartite division of believers throughout for purposes that will become apparent as we proceed.

[52]Richard Bernstein, *Beyond Objectivism and Relativism* (Philadelphia: University of Pennsylvania

through experience. Lisa Sowle Cahill states well the relationship between human experience and moral norms. "The essential point to emphasize for an ethics which begins with, and remains respectful of, differences in experience, while not giving up the possibility of normative ethics, is that the 'shared' is not achieved beyond or over against [experience], but rather in and through it."[53] The challenge for both conservative and progressive theologians is to discern carefully what constitutes authentic experience that may transform or revise norms and what constitutes inauthentic experience that must be judged by established norms.

Cultural Differences

Experiences are different in different cultures and histories, and contemporary believers must be aware of the differences between the culture of biblical times and our time. Those differences require that biblical texts be first exegeted in their context and then interpreted in our contemporary context. Pope Pius XII, as we saw in Chapter 3, already laid the foundation for the methodological integration of scripture into ethical method by endorsing the historical–critical method for interpretation. The Second Vatican Council's *Dei Verbum* reaffirmed that method, prescribing that scriptural texts must be read in the "literary forms" of the writers' "time and culture."[54] The Pontifical Biblical Commission added that the proper understanding of biblical texts "not only admits the use of [the historical–critical] method but actually requires it."[55] The Catholic method for correctly reading the Bible, as we explained earlier, is clear: first, an in-depth exegesis of the texts in their cultural context and, then, an interpretation that sets them into a contemporary cultural context. We illustrate this approach by a consideration of the biblical texts dealing with homosexuality.

The Congregation for the Doctrine of the Faith (CDF) turns to the Bible in its discussion of the "problem of homosexuality," and rhetorically asserts that "there is . . . a clear consistency within the sacred Scriptures for judging the moral issue of homosexual behavior. The Church's doctrine regarding this issue is thus based, not only on isolated phrases taken out of context, from which could be developed uncertain theological arguments, but rather on the solid foundation of a constant biblical testimony."[56] In the light of

Press, 1985), 74.

[53]Cahill, *Sex, Gender, and Christian Ethics*, 55.

[54]*Dei Verbum*, no. 12 (hereafter *DV*); and Pius XII, *Divino afflante spiritu*, *Acta Apostolicae Sedis* 35 (1943): 297–325 (hereafter *AAS*).

[55]Pontifical Biblical Commission, "Interpretation of the Bible in the Church," *Origins* 24 (January 6, 1994): 500.

[56]*Letter to the Bishops of the Catholic Church on the Pastoral Care of Homosexual Persons*, 5, *AAS* 79 (1987): 545.

contemporary Catholic biblical scholarship, it is impossible to agree that the texts on which this Catholic tradition of the ethics of homosexual acts is based are "unambiguous" and provide "solid foundation." When read as the Magisterium requires that they be read, that is, in the "literary forms" of the writer's "time and culture,"[57] the texts that are advanced as a solid and unambiguous foundation of the Catholic teaching on homosexual acts are far from solid and unambiguous. Three questions are central to this issue. First, does the Bible say anything about homosexuality as we understand it today? Second, if it does say something, what does it say and, most importantly, what does it mean? Third, can the Bible speak to and enlighten the confusion that characterizes contemporary Christian dialogue about homosexuality?

The first question is a question of definition. What do we mean today by the words *homosexuality* and *homosexual*? The answer to that question is embedded in what the sciences and the Magisterium of the Catholic Church now take for granted, namely, the distinction between homosexual *orientation* and homosexual *behavior*.[58] In contemporary scientific and theological literature, the noun *homosexuality* and the adjective *homosexual* are used to refer first to a person's *psychosexual condition* and only secondarily to refer to a person's sexual behavior. Sexual orientation, in general, is defined as "the sustained erotic attraction to members of one's own gender, the opposite gender, or both—homosexual, heterosexual, or bisexual respectively."[59] Homosexual orientation is "a *condition* characterized by an emotional and psycho-sexual propensity towards others of the same sex,"[60] and a homosexual is "a person who feels a most urgent sexual desire which *in the main* is directed towards gratification with the same sex."[61]

Neither the Bible nor Christian teaching rooted in it prior to the twentieth century ever considered the homosexual condition as it is understood today; they took for granted that everyone was *heterosexual*. To look for any mention in the biblical texts of what today is called "homosexual orientation" is simply anachronism. One might as well search the Bible for advice on what car or what computer to buy. The biblical passages most frequently

[57]*DV*, no. 12. See also Pius XII, *Divino Afflante Spiritu*.

[58]See Pim Pronk, *Against Nature? Types of Moral Argumentation Regarding Homosexuality* (Grand Rapids: Eerdmans, 1993); Richard C. Pillard and J. Michael Bailey, "A Biological Perspective on Sexual Orientation," *Clinical Sexuality* 18 (1995): 1–14; Lee Ellis and Linda Ebertz, *Sexual Orientation: Toward Biological Understanding* (Westport, CT: Praeger, 1997); Richard C. Friedman and Jennifer I. Downey, *Sexual Orientation and Psychoanalysis: Sexual Science and Clinical Practice* (New York: Columbia University Press, 2002).

[59]Pillard and Bailey, "A Biological Perspective on Sexual Orientation," 1.

[60]D. Sherwin Bailey, *Homosexuality and the Western Christian Tradition* (New York: Longman's, 1955), x, emphasis added.

[61]Donald W. Cory, *The Homosexual in America* (New York: Julian Press, 1951), 8, emphasis in original.

cited as condemning *homosexuality* actually condemn homosexual *behaviors*, and they condemn those behaviors specifically as a *perversion* of the heterosexual condition they assume to be the natural condition of every human person. In its modern meaning, homosexuality is not a perversion of the heterosexual condition because homosexuals, by natural orientation, do not share that condition. Homosexuality is, rather, an *inversion* of the heterosexual condition that psychosexual homosexuals, by no choice of their own, do not naturally share, and they cannot be held morally accountable for something they did not freely choose.[62]

The context in which both Testaments are presumed to condemn homosexual acts is a false assumption, shaped by the sociohistorical conditions of the times in which they were written, that all human beings naturally share the heterosexual condition and that, therefore, any homosexual behavior is a perversion of "nature" and unethical. Since that biblical assumption is now scientifically shown to be incorrect, the Bible has little to contribute to the discussion of homosexuality as we understand it today. That conclusion will become clearer when we consider our second question: what does the Bible say about homosexual behavior and what does it mean when it says that?[63] We might add here with Edward Vacek what is obvious, namely, that the Bible contains many questionable moral teachings, on sex during menstruation, stoning adulterers, women's roles, slavery, and a host of others, all of which have been rejected by modern Catholic theological ethicists.[64]

The single most influential biblical passage leading to the condemnation of homosexual behavior acts is probably the *interpretation* given to the biblical story of Sodom. Our historical and contextual exegesis will show that the homosexual interpretation of the Sodom story is not accurate and is not supported by a reading of the passage in the literary form of its socio-historical context. The biblical story is not as straightforward as it appears to the biblically untrained reader. The context of the story and its meaning begins, not with Lot and the men of Sodom in chapter 19, but with the story of Abraham's hospitality to "three men," in chapter 18. Three "men" pass by Abraham's tent on their way to Sodom, and Abraham offers the

---

[62]See *Persona Humana*, no. 10; United States Conference of Catholic Bishops, "Always Our Children: A Pastoral Message to Parents of Homosexual Children and Suggestions for Pastoral Ministers," www.usccb.org/issues-and-action/human-life-and-dignity/homosexuality/always-our-children.cfm.

[63]Our argument in what follows is in full agreement with Gareth Moore: "there are no good arguments, from either Scripture or natural law, against what have come to be known as homosexual relationships. The arguments put forward to show that such relationships are immoral are bad. Either their premises are false or the argument by means of which the conclusion is drawn from them itself contains errors." See Gareth Moore, *A Question of Truth: Christianity and Homosexuality* (London: Continuum, 2003), x. See also Robin Scroggs, *The New Testament and Homosexuality* (Philadelphia: Fortress Press, 1983).

[64]See Edward Vacek, "A Christian Homosexuality," *Commonweal* (December 5, 1980): 681–84.

strangers the hospitality required by the Levitical law: "When a stranger sojourns with you in your land, you shall not do him wrong . . . you shall love him as yourself" (Lv 20:33234). Abraham invites the strangers to his tent and offers them refreshment and food (Gn 18:4–2). He has his wife, Sarah, bake cakes for them, he kills a calf "tender and good" for them, and he serves them himself. Abraham's goodness is established by his hospitable reception of the three strangers, and so, too, will his nephew Lot's goodness be established in the sequel.

"Two angels came to Sodom in the evening and Lot was sitting in the gate of Sodom" (Gn 19:1). Lot offered the two angels the required hospitality, bringing them to his house and feeding them, but before they retired for the night the men of Sodom surrounded the house and called for Lot to bring the two men out "that we may know them (*yadha*)" (Gn 19:5). Now *yadha* is the ordinary Hebrew word for the English word *know*, as it is translated in the Revised Standard Version, but it is also used on occasion to mean specifically sexual intercourse. We interpret it here to refer to sexual intercourse for two reasons. First, if all the men of Sodom wanted to do was to meet and know the strangers, learn their identity, what they were about, why would Lot beg them "do not act so wickedly" (Gn 19:7); second, the same word *yadha* is used in a clearly sexual sense when Lot offers his two daughters to the crowd: "Behold I have two daughters who have not known man (*yadha*), let me bring them out to you . . . only do nothing to these men *for they have come under the shelter of my roof*" (Gn 19:8, emphasis added). Ignoring the ethics of Lot's willingness to offer up his two daughters to the crowd, which further highlights the importance of reading the text in its historical–cultural context, we believe there is clear insinuation of homosexual intent against the two strangers at Sodom, which does not mean that the sin of the men of Sodom was the sin of homosexual behavior.

The clearer sin in both the Hebrew text and context is the sin of inhospitality. That Lot is concerned about that hospitality is made evident in the phrase we have underscored above, "do nothing to these men for they have come under the shelter of my roof," that is, under the shelter of my hospitality, which embraces protecting them against the wrongful designs of the crowd. The men of Sodom are as bound by the law of hospitality as is Lot, but they demonstrate their sinfulness by not living up to the law. If *yadha* is to be understood in its sexual connotation, and we believe it is, then the men of Sodom demonstrate the extent of their inhospitality by seeking violent homosexual rape of the strangers. If any actions are condemned in the text, it is the crimes of inhospitality and wrongful *homosexual* rape carried out by perverted *heterosexual* men. If the act of male homosexual rape perpetrated by perverted heterosexuals is condemned in this text, that is a long way from a clear and unambiguous condemnation of the loving, just, and faithful homosexual acts of contemporary persons of homosexual orientation.

The interpretation of the text we propose is supported by the fact that in the rest of the Old Testament, where Sodom is regularly mentioned, not once is its crime said to be homosexual behavior. Ezekiel describes it as refusal to aid the poor (Ez 16:49), and Isaiah writes in the same vein (Is 1:17). The Book of Wisdom explicitly charges both the men of Sodom and the Egyptians with inhospitality: "Others [the men of Sodom] had refused to receive strangers when they came to them, but these [the Egyptians] made slaves of guests who were their benefactors" (Ws 19:14). For Christians, a prime argument in support of our interpretation that the sin of Sodom is inhospitality is Jesus's mention of Sodom in the same breath as the inhospitality accorded his disciples (Lk 10:10–12).[65] Jewish Jesus also makes hospitality or inhospitality a major cause of salvation or damnation in the great judgment scene in Matthew 25:34–36.

If the Sodom story is ultimately about inhospitable acts, no such reservation can be made about the prescriptions of the Holiness Code in Leviticus. "You shall not lie with a male as with a woman; it is an abomination" (Lv18:22). What the Holiness Code says could not be clearer, male homosexual behavior is an *abomination*. It is important to realize it is *male* acts that are prohibited in these texts; lesbian acts are not part of the prohibition. The word *you* in "you shall not lie" can be misleading. In English *you* applies indiscriminately to both males and females; in Hebrew the word that is used is used only of males. It is male homosexual acts that Leviticus says are an abomination, and that restriction yields some insight into both the sociohistorical context in which Leviticus says what it says and what it might mean when it says it.

The first thing to be noted about the Hebrew context is what we have already noted: all men and women are assumed to be naturally heterosexual and, therefore, homosexual acts are acts of *perversion* of nature. The second thing to be noted is bad biology. The ancient Hebrew, Greek, and Roman understanding was that the male gave "seed" that contained the whole of life; the female simply provided the "ground" or the "field" in which the "seed" would grow into a fully fledged human.[66] To spill that seed anywhere it could not develop properly, on the ground or in a male body, for instance, was regarded as tantamount to murder, and murder was always held as an abomination. Those guilty of murder suffered the same penalty as our present

[65]Compare Mt 10:14–15.

[66]For Greek society, see Paige duBois, *Sowing the Body: Psychoanalysis and Ancient Representations of Women* (Chicago: University of Chicago Press, 1988), 39–85. For Jewish society, see Sirach 26:19; *Mishna*, Ketuboth, 1, 6. For Muslim society, see Carol Delaney, *The Seed and the Soil: Gender and Cosmology in Turkish Village Society* (Berkeley: University of California Press, 1991).

text prescribes for male homosexual acts, namely, death (Lv18:22). Since they waste no life, probably also because women in that highly patriarchal society simply do not count, female homosexual acts are not considered worthy of consideration in the Holiness Code or anywhere else in the Old Testament. The fact that it is only male homosexual acts that are declared an abomination introduces another contextual consideration, that of male honor and the actions appropriate to it.

There is a more personal and social meaning embedded in the Holiness Code. Extended family was and is "the primary economic, religious, educational, and social network"[67] in Mediterranean society. Family was also the locus of honor, carried exclusively by males, particularly the patriarch who headed families and, for all intents and purposes, owned the females in it, whether they were wives or daughters or slaves. For a male to "lie with" another male, that is, to act passively like a female, compromised male honor, not only that of the male being penetrated but also that of every male in the family or clan. The passivity of a male, who was expected to be active in all things, including the sexual, was always a dishonorable abomination. In such a sociohistorical context, male homosexual acts are, indeed, an abomination, not because they are homosexual acts but because they are passive and dishonorable acts that threatened the patriarchal gender arrangement of the culture.[68]

But what of a different social context: a context in which not every human being is assumed to be by "nature" heterosexual and some are known to be by "nature" homosexual; a context in which honor is not the dominant concern; a context in which male and female are understood to contribute equally to the procreation of new life? In such a context, male homosexual acts need not be judged as dishonorable and, therefore, immoral. Just and loving homosexual acts, flowing from an innate homosexual orientation, cannot be regarded as a perversion of a universal heterosexual condition and, therefore, cannot be judged *ipso facto* unethical; and the spilling of male semen or seed would no longer be regarded as the spilling of life, murder, and an abomination. In short, when the interpreter considers what the Bible says about male homosexual acts and the sociohistorical context in which it says it, it is difficult to consider the Bible as saying anything more instructive in the present sociohistorical context than what it says

[67]Bruce J. Malina and Richard L. Rohrbaugh, *Social Science Commentary on the Synoptic Gospels* (Minneapolis: Fortress Press, 1992), 202. See also Carolyn Osiek and David L. Balch, *Families in the New Testament World: Households and House Churches* (Louisville, KY: Westminster/John Knox Press, 1997).

[68]The same system of honor and shame existed among the Greeks. Though it was acceptable for a boy to behave passively sexually, it was not acceptable for an adult male. See Michel Foucault, *The History of Sexuality, Vol. 2: The Use of Pleasure* (New York: Pantheon, 1985), 187–225.

about *kosher* laws (Lv11). As understood today, male homosexual acts may or may not be immoral, but current judgment of their morality cannot be based on what the Old Testament says about them in the context of its own time and place.

What, however, about the New Testament and homosexual acts? We exegete what is considered the centerpiece of what the New Testament says, namely, Chapter One of Saint Paul's letter to the Romans. It is important again to note the context that is a Pauline attack, not on homosexual acts but on degenerate Gentile society and the idolatrous acts it practices. After introductory greetings, Paul launches into standard Jewish accusations about Gentile idolatry. "What can be known about God is plain to them [Gentiles] because God has shown it to them" (Rom 1:19). But, however plain the existence of the true God of Israel might be and however much Gentiles ought to have known God from the things God made, they did not acknowledge God, they "did not honor God as God or give thanks to God." Rather, "they *exchanged* the glory of the immortal God for images resembling a mortal human being or birds or four-footed animals or reptiles" (Rom 1:21–23). What is radically wrong with Gentiles, Paul charges, is that they do not worship the true God, they are idolaters, and he immediately moves on to describe the behavior of such idolaters. *Because* they are idolaters, in some divine punishment, "God *gave them up* in the lusts of their heart to impurity, to the dishonoring of their bodies. . . . God *gave them up* to dishonorable passions. . . . God *gave them up* to a base mind and to improper conduct."[69] The dishonorable passions and homosexual acts performed again by perverted *heterosexuals* are God's punishment on Gentiles for their idolatry. It is Gentile *idolatry* that is directly at stake in the Pauline text, and the perverted, and therefore dishonorable, homosexual acts of male heterosexuals to which it is presumed to lead, not the homosexual acts of those who by "nature" share a homosexual orientation and the just and loving acts in which it might issue.[70] It is noteworthy, as William Countryman points out,[71] that Paul nowhere in this text uses the language of *sin*; Gentiles have been given up only to *uncleanness*.[72]

[69]Rom 1:24–28, emphasis added.

[70]See Dale B. Martin, "Heterosexism and the Interpretation of Romans 1:18–31," *Biblical Interpretation* 3 (1995): 332–55. For a contrary reading, see Richard B. Hays, *The Moral Vision of the New Testament: Community, Cross, New Creation: A Contemporary Introduction to the New Testament* (San Francisco: Harper, 1996), especially chap. 16.

[71]William Countryman, *Dirt, Greed, and Sex: Sexual Ethics in the New Testament and Their Implications for Today* (London: SCM Press, 1989), 100–17.

[72]The two remaining texts cited by the CDF as solid foundation for the church's teaching on the immorality of homosexual acts, 1 Corinthians 6:9–10 and 1 Timothy 1:10, present a serious difficulty of translation. Space restrictions prevent us from dealing with them here. Those who wish to see our exegesis of them can consult our book, *The Sexual Person: Toward a Renewed Catholic Anthropology* (Washington, DC: Georgetown University Press, 2008), 222–23.

This leads us to our third question and its answer: can the Bible speak to the confusion that characterizes contemporary Christianity with respect to homosexuality? An easy answer is provided by the semantic fact that there is not even a word for homosexuality in either ancient Hebrew or Greek. Because of the difficulty of translating meanings diachronically or across different eras, the Christian traditions are moving away from a *biblical rules* approach to moral judgments and are exploring a more profound interrelationship between rules, values, and virtues. This shift is evident in Pope Francis's *Amoris Laetitia*, where the focus is on virtue, not on rules and laws. Historically, Eugene Rodgers notes, this movement can already be found in Aquinas's *Commentary on Romans*, which demonstrates a keen awareness of the interrelationship between scripture, anthropology, experience, natural law, and virtue, which has implications for interpreting scripture on homosexuality and "*requires* theologians to keep the matter open."[73] Lisa Cahill puts the matter succinctly: "Realizing the impossibility of transposing rules from biblical times to our own, interpreters look for larger themes, values or ideals which can inform ethical reflection without determining specific practices in advance."[74] Victor Furnish articulates the broad theme we can abstract from both the Old and New Testaments on homosexual behavior. "Paul, in common with the tradition by which he was influenced and in accord with the wisdom of his day, saw the wickedness of homosexual practice to adhere in its lust and its *perversion of the natural [heterosexual] order*."[75] Judgments against uncontrolled and violent lust and a perversion of the natural order cannot automatically be applied to just and loving homosexual acts in persons whose natural sexual orientation is to persons of the same sex. Richard Sparks's judgment is also ours: "on scriptural evidence alone we are left short of a clear and clean condemnation of what might be called committed or covenantal homosexual acts."[76] The foregoing leads us to conclude this section with a renewed Catholic principle: In the formation of conscience and in the definition of human dignity and the formulation and justification of norms to facilitate its attainment, the Bible is to be read in its own context and not in the context of contemporary, largely untrained, readers.

---

[73]Eugene F. Rogers Jr., "Aquinas on Natural Law and the Virtues in Biblical Context," *Journal of Religious Ethics* 27 (1999): 52.

[74]Lisa Sowle Cahill, "Is Catholic Ethics Biblical?," *Warren Lecture Series in Catholic Studies, No. 20* (Tulsa, OK: University of Tulsa, 1992), 5–6.

[75]Victor Paul Furnish, *The Moral Teaching of Paul: Selected Issues* (Louisville, KY: Abingdon, 1985), 78, emphasis added.

[76]Richard Sparks, *Contemporary Christian Morality* (New York: Crossroad, 1996), 81.

The Sciences

The contemporary experience of the sciences is also to be factored into any contemporary ethical method. To illustrate how such scientific experience can be a fact, we consider here the experience of artificial reproductive technologies (ARTs) as elucidated by contemporary fertility science and the Magisterium. The CDF has issued two *Instructions* that reject ARTs as immoral. In 1987, it issued the *Instruction Donum Vitae* and, in 2008, the *Instruction Dignitas Personae*, an update "which addresses some recent questions in the light of the criteria expressed in the Instruction *Donum Vitae* and which also examines some issues that were treated earlier, but are in need of additional clarification."[77] The CDF notes that, although ARTs are to be rejected as immoral, they are not to be rejected on the ground that they are artificial for, as such, "they bear witness to the possibilities of the art of medicine."[78] Rather, they "must be given a moral evaluation in reference to the dignity of the human person,"[79] and on this basis "all techniques of heterologous artificial fertilization . . . as well as those techniques of homologous artificial fertilization . . . which substitute for the conjugal act, are to be excluded."[80]

There is no doubt why the two CDF *Instructions* proscribe both heterologous and homologous artificial fertilization: they are immoral *because they violate human dignity*; always the dignity of the parents; and on occasion the dignity of an embryo presumed to be human, when it is treated inhumanly, frozen, for instance, or aborted, or used for research. We consider now the two types of ARTs the *Instructions* name. First, *heterologous* artificial fertilization, "techniques used to obtain a human conception artificially by the use of gametes coming from at least one donor other than the spouses who are joined in marriage." Second, *homologous* artificial fertilization, "the technique used to obtain a human conception using the gametes of the two spouses joined in marriage."[81] It is to be noted from the outset that the *Instructions'* judgment on the ethics of ARTs is arrived at differently in the case of heterologous and in the case of homologous artificial fertilizations.

Donum Vitae begins its treatment of heterologous artificial fertilization by answering the question "Why must human procreation take place in marriage?" Its answer and its reference to *Gaudium et Spes* reflect a personalist

[77]CDF, Instruction *Dignitas Personae* on Certain Bioethical Questions (2008) (hereafter *Dignitas Personae*).

[78]CDF, *Donum Vitae*: Instruction on Respect for Human life in Its Origin and on the Dignity of Procreation (1987) (hereafter *Donum Vitae*); *Dignitas Personae*, 12.

[79]*Donum Vitae*, Introduction, 3. See also *Dignitas Personae*, 1.

[80]*Dignitas Personae*, 12.

[81]Ibid., endnotes 22 and 23; *Donum Vitae*, II.

interpretation of natural law. Procreation "must be the fruit and the sign of the mutual self-giving of the spouses, of their love and of their fidelity."[82] The emphasis is not on the biological act of sexual intercourse that features so centrally in magisterial statements about sexual ethics but on the marital *relationship* between the spouses, its mutual love, self-giving, and fidelity. The *Instruction* grounds its ethical assessment of heterologous artificial fertilization in a personalist interpretation of natural law. Procreation must take place in marriage because of the relational implications for the spouses with one another, "mutual self-giving" and with the child who is "the living image of their love," the "permanent sign of their conjugal union."[83] The focus of the *Instruction*'s treatment of heterologous artificial fertilization is on the personal and relational dimensions of the spouses, their union, and their relationship with the child. In light of these relational criteria, *Donum Vitae* asks the question "Does Heterologous Artificial Fertilization conform to the Dignity of the Couple and to the Truth of Marriage?" It answers the question by setting forth several ways in which heterologous artificial fertilization violates numerous relationships.

First, it violates the marital relationship. "Respect for the unity of marriage and for conjugal fidelity demands that the child be conceived in marriage; the bond existing between husband and wife accords the spouses, in an objective and inalienable manner, the exclusive right to become father and mother solely through each other."[84] Second, the introduction of a third party into fertilization through the use of donor gametes "constitutes a violation of the reciprocal commitment of the spouses and a grave lack in regard to that essential property of marriage which is its unity." Third, heterologous artificial fertilization "violates the rights of the child; it deprives him of his filial relationship with his parental origins and can hinder the maturing of his personal identity." Fourth, it threatens the vocation to parenthood since "it offends the common vocation of the spouses who are called to fatherhood and motherhood . . . it brings about and manifests a rupture between genetic parenthood, gestational parenthood, and responsibility for upbringing." The violation of all of these relationships leads "to a negative moral judgment concerning heterologous artificial fertilization."[85]

If *Donum Vitae* were consistent in its ethical reasoning, it would evaluate the ethics of homologous artificial fertilization employing the same personalist, relational principle. It does not. When it addresses homologous artificial fertilization, it shifts emphasis to a different foundational principle,

---

[82]*Donum Vitae*, II, A, 1.

[83]Ibid.

[84]Ibid.

[85]*Donum Vitae*, A, 2.

the traditional Catholic focus on the sexual act. Its treatment opens with the question "What connection is required from the moral point of view between procreation and the conjugal act?"[86] The shift in the question from "Dignity of the Couple and the Truth of Marriage" to "Procreation and the Conjugal *Act*" reflects a methodological shift from the subjects to the object, from the primacy of a personal-relational principle to the primacy of an act-biological principle. Following *Humanae Vitae*, the foundational principle for *Donum Vitae*'s ethical analysis of homologous artificial fertilization is the inseparability principle: "The Church's teaching on marriage and human procreation affirms the inseparable connection, willed by God and unable to be broken by man on his own initiative, between the two meanings of the conjugal act: the unitive meaning and the procreative meaning. Indeed, by its intimate structure, the conjugal act, while most closely uniting husband and wife, capacitates them for the generation of new lives, according to laws inscribed in the very being of man and of woman."[87] Three questions emerge regarding the *Instruction*'s introduction of this principle. First, why does it make this methodological shift from a focus on relationships when morally evaluating heterologous artificial fertilization to a focus on the inseparability principle when morally evaluating homologous fertilization? Second, what are the weaknesses of the inseparability principle with regard to homologous artificial fertilization? Third, what would be the ethical implications for homologous fertilization if the *Instruction* was methodologically consistent?

First, while the arguments against heterologous artificial fertilization appear reasonable to us, given the relational complications of nonspousal gametes and their potential impact on marital and familial relationships, the relationship of the parents with the child, the donor's relationship with both the parents and the child, and the social implications with regard to the nature of the family, the same relational complications do not arise in homologous fertilization. When the gametes belong to the parents, and a surrogate is not used to carry the embryo, the relational complications do not exist. All that can be claimed in the case of homologous artificial fertilization is that the physical act of sexual intercourse is not *immediately* responsible for procreation. This point, however, while it gives us insight into the *procedure* facilitating reproduction, gives us no insight into the moral *meaning* of that procedure. Moral meaning is discerned not through any fact of reality, in this case the fact of the use of scientific technology to assist reproduction, but in the *meaning* of that fact for individual consciences and marital relationships. If the same personalist principle is applied to

[86] *Donum Vitae*, II, B, 4.
[87] *Donum Vitae*, II, B, 4, a.

homologous artificial fertilization as is applied to heterologous, one could come to a different conclusion about its ethics.

Second, by introducing the inseparability principle in its discussion of homologous artificial fertilization, the *Instruction* clearly recognizes a shift in the foundational moral principle in analyzing and morally evaluating heterologous and homologous artificial fertilizations. *Donum Vitae*'s condemnation of homologous artificial fertilization is founded on a single principle, the inseparability principle. Richard McCormick notes that the *Instruction*'s claim of strict dependence is a "remarkable statement" since previous magisterial documents indicated that the prohibition of homologous artificial fertilization is "not strictly dependent on the analyses given or available to support it."[88] It follows from the *Instruction*'s strict dependence on a particular principle to justify its argument against homologous artificial fertilization that the argument is only as strong as the principle; if the principle is weak, so, too, is any ethical conclusion drawn from it.

We believe the "inseparability principle" used to prohibit homologous artificial fertilization is a weak principle on several counts. First, there is no intrinsic procreative meaning to each and every sexual act unless one interprets procreative in a metaphorical or *formal* sense, meaning *relationally* life-giving, as opposed to a biological or *material* sense, meaning *biologically* life-giving. Sexual acts in a known infertile relationship cannot have any intrinsic material procreative meaning, though they do contain a formal procreative meaning. In these cases, however, as well as in cases where the couple avoids procreation for serious reasons, the formal procreative meaning has merely been elided into the unitive meaning, since there seems to be nothing unique about the procreative meaning in a formal sense that would not apply to the unitive meaning of the sexual act. The act is procreative in a material sense only when biological reproduction is possible, and only then can the procreative meaning of the act be strictly distinguished from its unitive meaning. That is why many theologians choose to discuss the unitive and procreative meanings of, not every sexual act, but of the overall marital relationship.[89] That is why Rhonheimer argues that marital acts extend beyond sexual acts to include abstinence, and such

[88]Richard A. McCormick, *The Critical Calling: Reflections on Moral Dilemmas Since Vatican II* (Washington, DC: Georgetown University Press, 1989), 347. We are indebted to McCormick's critique of the "inseparability principle" (347–49).

[89]See, for example, ibid., 346–47; Joseph A. Selling, "The Development of Catholic Tradition and Sexual Morality," in *Embracing Sexuality: Authority and Experience in the Catholic Church*, ed. Joseph A. Selling (Burlington, VT: Ashgate, 2001), 149–62; Joseph A. Selling, "Magisterial Teaching on Marriage 1880–1986: Historical Constancy or Radical Development?," in *Dialogue about Catholic Sexual Teaching: Readings in Moral Theology No. 8*, ed. Charles Curran and Richard McCormick (New York: Paulist Press, 1993), 93–97; Lisa Sowle Cahill, "Sexuality: Personal, Communal, Responsible," in Selling, *Embracing Sexuality*,165–72.

marital acts are *both* procreative of the relationship and unitive.[90] We agree that marital acts extend beyond sexual acts, and we argue that the acts of the spouses in homologous artificial fertilization are certainly marital acts and that they are both procreative and unitive as traditionally defined and, therefore, according to traditional Catholic marital ethics, thoroughly moral. The distinction between procreation formally understood and procreation materially understood seems to open up the moral possibility of homologous artificial fertilization that is not the result of sexual intercourse as traditionally defined.

Second, the inseparability principle contains a "germ of truth" in what Richard McCormick calls an "aesthetic or ecological (bodily integrity) concern," by which he means that all artificial interventions into the sexual relationship, whether they are to prevent or procure reproduction, are a kind of "second best."[91] To deprive a procedure of its "proper function," however, does not make the artificial procedure *ipso facto* morally wrong in every situation, unless, McCormick legitimately insists, we "elevate an aesthetic-ecological concern into an absolute moral imperative."[92] The "aesthetic-ecological concern" is a product of the biologism that controlled the Catholic natural law tradition for centuries, grounded in both a flawed biology and a flawed theology of marriage. In that tradition up until the Second Vatican Council, the *primary end* of marriage was always said to be procreation. Our modern understanding of biology and human sexuality, however, teaches us that procreation is not even possible in the vast majority of marital acts. It is logical, therefore, to argue that not only are the formal-unitive and material-procreative meanings of the sexual act separable, and often in fact naturally separated, but also that the formal-unitive meaning that is always in play is the primary end of marriage and the material-procreative meaning the secondary end.

Third, while *Donum Vitae* correctly notes that "the one conceived must be the fruit of the parents' love," it has not explained how the one conceived in homologous artificial fertilization is not the fruit of the parents' love. It is not enough simply to state that homologous artificial fertilization separates the unitive and procreative meanings of the sexual act and to conclude, therefore, that the child conceived in homologous fertilization is not the fruit of the parents' love, for that conclusion is a *non sequitur.* Elsewhere, *Donum Vitae* gives insight into why it believes that the child conceived via homologous artificial fertilization is not the fruit of the parent's love. "The one conceived

[90]Martin Rhonheimer, "Contraception, Sexual Behavior, and Natural Law: Philosophical Foundation of the Norm of '*Humanae Vitae*'," *Linacre Quarterly* 56, no. 2 (1989): 41–42.

[91]McCormick, *Critical Calling*, 348.

[92]Ibid.

. . . cannot be desired or conceived as the product of an intervention of medical or biological techniques; that would be equivalent to reducing him to an object of scientific technology."[93] To substitute the marital act of the spouses with a technological act, the *Instruction* suggests, is to objectify the embryo and treat him/her as a product. Grisez affirms this position, noting that to choose IVF is "to will the baby's initial status as a product."[94]

As parents, we protest any "product" language and point out that it is a foreign language for couples mutually committed to procreating a child. Our personal experience of couples who have conceived through homologous artificial fertilization, and also of several couples who have failed to conceive despite several expensive attempts, appears to show that the circumstantial frustration and desperation of infertile couples and all the inconvenience they are willing to undergo, social, emotional, physical, and certainly economic, is a powerful sign of their mutual love, their desire to keep spousal love and fertility together, and their desire to offer to one another a child, "the supreme gift of marriage."[95] It is incredibly and uncharitably dismissive of and insulting to their shared pain to interpret their seeking a child through ART as seeking *only* some product. We suggest that it is more ethical and certainly more Christian to hope that their passionate desire to procreate a child together might be fulfilled through the help of advanced medical techniques. The experience of mutual love and joy of spouses as they hold their baby procreated by ART is more than enough to dispel any thought of a "product." Those who speak of the baby as a "product" must never, we assume, have had such an experience. There is no intrinsic moral meaning to ART, and there is no intrinsic moral intention in couples who might be driven in desperation to choose ART. The meaning of ART and the intention for choosing it are determined, not by its presumed object but by the actual intention of two spouses within the context of their marital relationships. Meaning and intention are determined by the couple's perspective, their motives, desires, dreams, and reasons for choosing ART. To posit an intrinsic objective meaning to ART apart from the actual intention of the spouses who choose it is tantamount to a focus on the object and lacks virtue ethics' turn to the subject. It also reflects an ignorance of the experiential, relational, emotional, and marital struggles of an infertile couple who have chosen to use ART as a last desperate medical, but no less marital, effort to enable their marital relationship to give life to a new human being, their very own child.[96]

---

[93]*Donum Vitae*, II, B, 4, c.

[94]Germain Grisez, *The Way of the Lord Jesus, Vol. 2: Living a Christian Life*, 267; *The Way of the Lord Jesus, Vol. 3: Difficult Moral Questions* (Quincy, IL: Franciscan Herald Press, 1997), 240–41.

[95]*GS*, no. 50.

[96]To date, IVF has contributed to some five million births. See Joseph Norquist, "IVF: What Are

Fourth, *Donum Vitae* itself claims that "homologous IVF and ET fertilization is not marked by all that ethical negativity found in extra-conjugal procreation; the family and marriage continue to constitute the setting for the birth and upbringing of the children."[97] The relational complications involved in heterologous artificial fertilization make it more ethically objectionable, the *Instruction* asserts, than the violation of the inseparability principle in homologous artificial fertilization. By its own admission, then, the inseparability principle on the basis of which *Donum Vitae* condemns homologous artificial fertilization does not carry the same ethical weight as the relational principle condemning heterologous fertilization. It is relational considerations, we argue, that both condemn heterologous artificial fertilization as unethical and make homologous artificial fertilization ethical in a marriage. Since there may be no sexual intercourse in homologous fertilization, however, why would the *Instruction* base its moral condemnation of homologous artificial fertilization on the act of intercourse and the inseparability principle? It must do so because the relational considerations that prohibit heterologous artificial fertilization do not warrant an absolute prohibition of homologous fertilization. We find *Donum Vitae*'s argument less than ethically compelling.

Based on the foregoing analysis, we can now answer our third question concerning the ethical implications for homologous fertilization if the *Instruction* was methodologically consistent and draw, what we believe, is a safe, logical, and thoroughly ethical conclusion about the ethics of this procedure. If the premise, we already noted, is weak, then any conclusion drawn from that premise will also be weak. We believe the inseparability principle cannot bear the weight of *Donum Vitae*'s conclusions absolutely prohibiting homologous artificial fertilization. Given the desperation of an infertile couple to crown their marriage with a child and their intention, grounded in mutual justice, love, respect, and responsibility to have their marital relationship "crowned"[98] intramaritally by a child who is in every sense *their* child, we believe the use of homologous artificial fertilization can be ethical and facilitate both the unitive and procreative meanings of *marriage* and the bonded union of the spouses. Lisa Sowle Cahill has advanced the same conclusion. Many Catholics, she notes, "perceive a difference larger than the Vatican allows between therapies used in marriage, even if they do temporarily circumvent sexual intercourse, and methods which bring donors into the marital procreative venture." She believes, and

Test Tube Babies," *Medical News Today* (January 26, 2016). It is ludicrous to suggest that desperate spouses spent so much time, psychological stress, and expense merely to have a technological product.

[97] *Donum Vitae*, II, B, 5.

[98] *GS*, no. 48.

we agree, that "donor methods are more morally objectionable because they do not appreciate the unity as *relationship* of sexual expression, committed partnership, and parenthood."[99]

In the foregoing we considered the ethics of homologous artificial fertilization *in se*. We did that to distinguish and separate homologous artificial fertilization and its ethics from factors related, but external, to it, specifically embryo destruction, cryopreservation, and stem cell harvesting. The standard contemporary IVF procedure is to harvest a number of ova, to fertilize them, to allow the zygote to develop to the embryonic stage, to transfer into the woman's uterus more embryos than are needed for a single conception, and to freeze the rest for cryopreservation and, perhaps, future uterine transfer or medical research. The first ethical question here is the destruction, willed or foreseen as inevitable, of embryos that are not implanted in the maternal uterus. Both *Donum Vitae* and *Dignitas Personae* insist that "the fruit of human generation, from the first moment of its existence, that is to say from the moment the zygote [the cell produced when the nuclei of the male and female gametes have fused] has formed, demands the unconditional respect that is ethically due to the human being in his bodily and spiritual totality"[100] or, in Janssens's phrase used throughout this book, the human being "integrally and adequately considered." When *human* life begins is much debated in the scientific community, and *Dignitas Personae* acknowledges this debate.[101] It insists, however, that the zygote must be held to be human from the moment of conception and so also, therefore, is the embryo that is formed from it. Any destruction of an embryo is therefore the direct killing of an innocent human being and unethical.

A second ethical question is the cryopreservation or freezing of embryos. The process of *in vitro* fertilization usually "involves a single intervention in which multiple oocytes are taken, followed by cryopreservation of a considerable number of the embryos conceived *in vitro*."[102] This procedure is followed as the least invasive way to ensure the availability of embryos for future attempts at implantation if a first, second, or third attempt should fail. *Donum Vitae* declares that cryopreservation "constitutes an *offence* against the respect due to human beings by exposing them to grave risks of death or harm to their physical integrity and depriving them, at least temporarily, of maternal shelter and gestation."[103] *Dignitas Personae* de-

[99]Lisa Sowle Cahill, *Women and Sexuality* (New York: Paulist Press, 1992), 75, emphasis in original. See also Thomas Anthony Shannon and Lisa Sowle Cahill, *Religion and Artificial Reproduction : An Inquiry into the Vatican "Instruction on Respect for Human Life in its Origin and on the Dignity of Human Reproduction"* (New York: Crossroad, 1988), 103–32.

[100]*Donum Vitae*, I, 1; *Dignitas Personae*, 1.

[101]*Donum Vitae*, I, 1.

[102]*Donum Vitae*, 18.

[103]*Donum Vitae*, I, 6.

clares more strongly that it is "a *situation of injustice which in fact cannot be resolved*."[104] The latter judgment that cryopreservation is "a *situation of injustice*" is a more damning moral judgment than the former claim that it "constitutes an *offence* against the *respect* due to human beings." It leads to the reaffirmation of John Paul II's appeal to the conscience of the scientific community that "the production of human embryos be halted, taking into account that there seems to be no ethically licit solution regarding the human destiny of thousands and thousands of 'frozen' embryos which are and remain the subjects of essential rights and should therefore be protected by law as human persons."[105] We are convinced that homologous artificial fertilization *in se* can be absolutely and conscientiously ethical with the harvesting of ova and implantation in the wife of a reasonable number of fertilized ova. We are equally convinced that the cryopreservation of human embryos can knowingly damage and even kill them, as can their later unfreezing and use in research. Directly killing an innocent human being is outlawed by every moral law in the world. More importantly, we add, it is outlawed by the law of God that illuminates the life that Christians are called to live as the concretization of their belief in, covenant with, and commitment to God-in-Christ.

A third ethical question related to, but external to, homologous artificial fertilization is the harvesting of stem cells, undifferentiated cells that can multiply themselves and still maintain their undifferentiated state. When transplanted into damaged human tissue, stem cells promote cell growth and regeneration of damaged tissue, an obviously powerful tool for regenerative medicine. The ethical question about stem cells is about their origin, from where are they harvested. *Dignitas Personae* prescribes unequivocally that "methods which do not cause serious harm to the subject from whom the stem cells are taken are to be considered licit. This is generally the case when tissues are taken from: a) an adult organism (amniotic fluid, bone marrow, for instance); b) the blood of the umbilical cord at the time of birth; c) fetuses who have died of natural causes." It proscribes as unethical the harvesting of stem cells from a living human embryo because "it invariably causes the death of the embryo and is consequently gravely illicit."[106] The reasoning is clear: unconditional respect is ethically due to the human being integrally and adequately considered and, since the harvesting of stem cells from a living embryo denies that respect, it is, therefore, unethical.

[104]*Dignitas Personae*, 19.

[105]Pope John Paul II, "Address to the Participants in the Symposium on '*Evangelium Vitae* and Law,'" *AAS* 88 (1996): 943–44.

[106]*Dignitas Personae*, 32.

CONCLUSION

We conclude this chapter by reemphasizing what is its major focus. The ultimate authority of every moral action is a subject's free, informed, practical judgment of conscience. This is true, not only for the moral decisions exemplified in this chapter but for all moral decisions. Our hope is that in this book we have helped the Catholic Church forward in its discernment of ethical truth by providing a methodological road map, grounded in a virtuous perspective that changes the primary focus in Catholic theological ethics from a law-based, act-centered ethics of doing to a virtue-based, person-centered ethics of being.

Index